The War of 1898

"SAVE ME FROM MY FRIENDS!"

The War of 1898

1898

The United States
and Cuba in History
and Historiography

Louis A. Pérez Jr.

The University of North Carolina Press *Chapel Hill & London*

© 1998

The University of North Carolina Press

All rights reserved

Designed by Richard Hendel

Set in Monotype Garamond and Meta types

by Keystone Typesetting, Inc.

Manufactured in the United States of America

The paper in this book meets the guidelines for

permanence and durability of the Committee on

Production Guidelines for Book Longevity of the

Council on Library Resources.

Library of Congress

Cataloging-in-Publication Data

Pérez, Louis A., 1943–

The war of 1898 : the United States and Cuba in

history and historiography / by Louis A. Pérez.

   p. cm.

Includes bibliographical references (p.   ) and index.

ISBN-13: 978-0-8078-2437-5 (cloth : alk. paper)

ISBN-10: 0-8078-2437-2 (cloth : alk. paper). —

ISBN-13: 978-0-8078-4742-8 (pbk. : alk. paper)

ISBN-10: 0-8078-4742-9 (pbk. : alk. paper)

   1. Spanish-American War, 1898—Historiography.

I. Title.

E715.P45   1998

973.8'9'072—dc21   98-2615

                CIP

10   09   08   07   8   7   6   5

FRONTISPIECE

"Save Me from My Friends!" Cartoon appearing in
Puck, September 7, 1898. "Taking Cuba from Spain
was easy. Preserving it from over-zealous Cuban
patriots is another matter," commented the
accompanying editorial.

To the memory of

Ramón de Armas (1939–1997),

friend and colleague

CONTENTS

PREFACE

The war of 1898 has loomed large in national discourses of the twentieth century. All parties involved have come to understand 1898 as a watershed year, a moment in which outcomes were both defining and decisive, at once an end and a beginning: that special conjuncture of historical circumstances that often serves to delineate one historical epoch from another. It was special, too, in that the passage from one historical condition to another was discernible at the time, even as it was happening.

Most U.S. historiography commemorates 1898 as the moment in which the nation first projected itself as a world power, whereupon the United States established an international presence and global prominence. Spanish historiography has looked back on 1898 as *el desastre* (the disaster)—an ignominious denouement of a five-hundred-year-old New World empire, after which Spain plunged vertiginously into decades of disarray and disorder. For Cuba and the Philippine Islands, 1898 represents a complex point of transition from colony to nation in which the pursuit of sovereignty and separate nationality assumed new forms. For Puerto Rico, the transition was even more complicated, with central elements of nation and nationality persisting unresolved well into the next century.

• • •

The historical literature on 1898 in the United States has assumed vast proportions. It includes monographs and memoirs, published documents and unpublished dissertations, biographies and bibliographical guides, books, articles, and anthologies of all descriptions. The discussion of 1898 in various forms has loomed large in virtually every U.S. history textbook of the last one hundred years.

For all the importance traditionally accorded to 1898, and indeed the consensus has been one of the more notable characteristics of the historiography, generations of U.S. scholars have treated the war with Spain with ambivalence, uncertain as to where exactly to situate it: sometimes a war of expansion, other times an accidental war; an inevitable war or perhaps an unnecessary one; a war induced by public opinion or one instigated by public officials.

It is the thesis of this book that ambivalence in U.S. historiography is itself the product of a larger ambiguity, one that contemplates 1898 by way of such complex issues as motives and purpose, which in turn insinuate themselves into larger discourses on the nation: specifically, the way a people arrange the terms by which they choose to represent themselves. The meaning of 1898 in the United States is ambiguous precisely because what historical narratives understand the nature of the nation to be is itself constantly in flux in the form of self-interrogation as a means of self-definition. Far from detracting from the historical accounts, ambiguities shed light on the historiography as a form of national narrative and provide a way to gain insight into normative determinants of the historical literature. Modes of historical explanation have thus been simultaneously fitted within and derived from the moral hierarchies of the nation, fashioned in such a manner as to represent the ideals to which the nation has professed dedication. The telling of 1898—in historical discourses both popular and professional, repeated and refined—has served as a means of self-affirmation of what the nation is, or perhaps more correctly what the nation thinks itself to be, as past and present have been conjoined in the service of self-revelation. Representations of 1898 were early invested with the ideals by which Americans wished to define and differentiate their place in the international system.

A fuller understanding of 1898 must necessarily seek to expand its temporal reach and enlarge its spatial range. Advances must be sought in the reconfiguration of historiographical contours around categories shaped more by methodological considerations than national boundaries. U.S. historians whose livelihood has been the study of foreign relations have not typically been drawn to foreign archives. Nor do those who write about U.S. history ordinarily consult the historiography of other nations as a way to inform their own perspectives. This reflects a failure to take into account the part that others have played in outcomes of vital importance in U.S. history. The result has been a self-possessed— to say nothing of self-contained—historiography, given to the conviction that it alone has raised all the relevant questions and, of course, provided all the appropriate answers, and that the rest of the world has little useful to add.

The year 1898 occupies a special place in U.S. historiography. In one sense, the historical literature has assumed fully the proportions of a literary genre almost unique to the subject of 1898, best captured in the representation of the war—and indeed central to popular understanding of the war—through such phrasings as "Remember the *Maine!*" and John Hay's proposition of a "splendid little war." In another sense, the scholarship contains discernible traces of the ways that policy paradigms of 1898 have acted to shape the dominant historiographical formulations of the war: scholarship and policy converged and interacted and proceeded to assemble the familiarities by which the past was revealed.

This book is principally about one aspect of 1898: the complex relationship between Cuba and the United States and the ways that this complicated connection contributed to the coming of the war, no less than its conduct and consequences, as well as its subsequent representations and repercussions. This undertaking is informed primarily by Cuban historiography, steeped in the experience of decades of research in Cuban archives, of immersion in Cuban accounts of these years, as sources and scholarship, as first-hand accounts by participants and observers in the form of letters, journals, diaries, and official correspondence, published and unpublished. To this perspective is added years of consultation of U.S. archival and manuscript sources as well as the vast corpus of the U.S. historical literature on 1898. Attention is given to the ways that representations of Cuba have entered into the dominant historical narratives on the war. More specifically, and central to this discussion, the study that follows is about the historiography of 1898 in the United States, the accumulated historical scholarship of the last one hundred years and the degree to which historical narratives have reflected and reinforced notions of purpose and policy, many of which were first articulated and advanced in 1898 and served subsequently as the rationale of systems of domination. Cuba insinuated itself into one of the most important chapters of U.S. history. Indeed, what happened on the island in the final decade of the nineteenth century and the way that what happened has been subsequently represented and reproduced have had far-reaching repercussions, many of which continue to resonate in the final decade of the twentieth century.

Historical narratives have themselves played an important role in the transmission of explanations first advanced in 1898. The historiography has in large part persisted as an artifact of the war, a means by which to arrive at an understanding not only of 1898 but also of the ways that historical representations have sustained dominant paradigms that have to do with power and policy. This may not be exactly official history, but it is certainly national history. In an important sense, perceptions of 1898 matter even—and especially—when they can be demonstrated to be misconceptions or self-deceptions, for they suggest the means by which facets of national identity are formed and informed.

The expansion of national history onto an international stage has been a slow and complex undertaking. The scholarship early recognized 1898 and its aftermath as developments of global proportions, events that implicated peoples of Europe, Asia, and the Caribbean in direct and decisive ways. The representation of the place and purpose of others in the historiography has been influenced largely by the proposition of the Other, people who, as a result of ignorance or innocence, or perhaps mischief or malice, failed to appreciate the good that the Americans sought to visit upon them. In the United States, much of what has informed the analysis of the U.S. purpose abroad has usually been derived from generally shared if often unstated assumptions about motive and intent, which U.S. scholars tend to divine as generous and well-meaning. At the receiving end, where the analysis of the U.S. purpose is measured by actions and consequences, conclusions have typically been less charitable.

Historical scholarship in the United States has been slow to conceptualize 1898 within the larger framework of world systems. The proposition of empire has not fared well in mainstream historiography. Nor have themes of imperialism and colonialism developed into central concerns of U.S. historiographical traditions. Few historiographical propositions have persisted as unchanged and unchallenged as the interpretations of 1898, many of which were first formulated as a function of the war.

It began, of course, with the very construction of the conflict as the "Spanish-American War," which immediately suggested the purpose and identified the participants of the war. The representation of the war underwent various renderings—"the Spanish War," "the Hispano-American War," "the American-Spanish War"—before arriving at the "Spanish-American War." All shared a common exclusion of Cuban participation, palpable evidence of the power of dominant narratives to define the familiar and fix the forms by which the past is recovered, recorded, and received.

U.S. scholarship has displayed a number of notable characteristics, central to which has been a general lack of familiarity with Cuban historiography and neglect of Cuban archival sources and manuscript collections. The discussion of the Cuban place in 1898, when acknowledged at all, has been derived principally from U.S. sources and accounts, repeated and reproduced, again and again, with such authority that it soon assumed fully the force of self-evident truths.

yes, perhaps because the US gov't forbids Americans from travelling to Cuba

This study has to do with memory, incomplete and imperfect, transmitted and preserved in the popular and professional histories of the last one hundred years. Americans believed themselves to be benefactors of Cuba. They cherished a memory of having sacrificed life and treasure in 1898 in what they understood to be a noble undertaking in behalf of *Cuba Libre*, from which they perceived Cubans indissolubly linked to the United States by ties of gratitude and obligation. That this was not exactly what 1898 was about does not diminish in the slightest the resonance of those constructs. On the contrary, it has contributed to a historiography dense with contradiction and incoherence, in which historical narratives have blurred distinctions between interests and intentions, confused popular sentiment with official policy, and mistaken proclaimed objectives for actual outcomes. Much in the subsequent American understanding of the U.S. role on the world stage was influenced by misrepresentations of 1898, which in turn contributed to fashioning the purpose for which Americans used power. That Cubans developed profoundly different memories of 1898, from which they derived radically different meanings, goes a long way toward understanding the capacity of the past to shape the purpose of policy and the place of power.

• • •

The research and writing of this book could not have been completed without the support and assistance of many people and institutions. Friends and colleagues gave generously of their time and wisdom, in conversation and correspondence, especially in their reading of early drafts of the manuscript. Robert P. Ingalls subjected the manuscript to a careful review—and an occasional rewriting—and in the process contributed to making it a better book. Michael H. Hunt posed a number of thoughtful questions in the course of his reading of the manuscript, raising important issues that obliged me to reconsider and revise some of my original formulations into sharper arguments. I am especially grateful to Walter LaFeber and Thomas G. Paterson for their many helpful suggestions and criticisms. They provided valuable comments on the completed draft, but more important they have themselves, through their own work on some of the same issues, pointed to fuller understandings of 1898.

Many of the ideas that follow were first raised in conversations over the years with Rebecca J. Scott, John L. Offner, Oscar Zanetti, Jorge Ibarra, and Francisco Pérez Guzmán. In ways that were not always apparent at the time, these discussions had a decisive impact on shaping some of the directions taken by this study.

I am grateful to the Department of History at the University of North Carolina–Chapel Hill for the opportunity to teach a graduate seminar on 1898, and to the students in that course—Chris Endy, David Sartorius, and Benito Vilá—who engaged many of the propositions around which this book is organized. Their response to the historiographical formulations on 1898 helped clarify some of the principal lines of argument that follow.

My research was aided and facilitated by librarians and archivists at a number of research institutions. In the United States I have been the beneficiary of expert assistance and unfailing courtesy provided by the staffs of the Davis Library at the University of North Carolina–Chapel Hill, the Library of Congress, and the National Archives in Washington, D.C. Similarly, in Cuba I received courteous assistance from the personnel at the Biblioteca Nacional 'José Martí' and the Archivo Nacional in Havana.

It has indeed been a pleasure to work with Elaine Maisner of the University of North Carolina Press all the while the manuscript was being prepared for publication. Her support and enthusiasm from the outset contributed greatly to the completion of this book. The contribution of William Van Norman is acknowledged with appreciation. His assistance with the final phase of the research was characterized by both efficiency and thoroughness, which greatly expedited the completion of the manuscript. Rosalie Radcliffe provided vital assistance with the preparation of early drafts, for which I am most grateful. I owe a special note of gratitude to Deborah M. Weissman, who read early drafts of the pages that follow, responded with thoughtful inquiries, and offered helpful suggestions on matters all along the way.

This book, finally, is dedicated to the memory of Ramón de Armas, a friend of many years, whose death in Havana in June 1997 was keenly felt by everyone who knew him. His work combined intellectual passion with historical imagination and contributed greatly to a deeper understanding of the decisive decades of the late colonial and early republican periods of Cuban history. It will henceforth be considerably more difficult to contemplate the Cuban past without having his insights to draw upon. His thoughtfulness and genial temper, the kindness and the generosity of spirit that characterized his *manera de ser*, distinguished him as true *martiano* in the best possible sense. He will be missed.

Chapel Hill, North Carolina
November 1997
LAP

CHRONOLOGY

1895

February 24. *"Grito de Baire"*: Cuban war for independence begins.

1896

January. Generals Antonio Maceo and Máximo Gómez complete the insurgent invasion of the western provinces.

August 26. Filipino war for independence begins.

1897

March 4. William McKinley inaugurated as president.

1898

January 1. Autonomist home-rule government installed in Cuba.

January 25. Battleship *Maine* arrives in Havana.

February 9. De Lôme letter published in the *New York Journal*.

February 15. *Maine* destroyed by explosion in Havana harbor.

March 28. Naval court of inquiry releases report pronouncing that *Maine* explosion was caused by a Spanish mine.

April 11. President McKinley forwards war message to Congress.

April 19. Joint Resolution of Congress enacted.

May 1. U.S. Asiatic Squadron destroys Spanish fleet in Manila Bay.

June 22. U.S. expeditionary force lands at Daiquirí and Siboney.

June 24. Battle of Las Guásimas.

July 1. Battles of El Caney and San Juan Hill.

July 3. U.S. Flying Squadron destroys Spanish naval fleet outside Santiago de Cuba.

July 16. Spanish army command in Santiago de Cuba surrenders to the United States.

July 26. United States invades Puerto Rico.

August 12. Armistice suspends hostilities.

December 10. Treaty of Paris formally ends war between the United States and Spain.

1899

January 1. U.S. military occupation of Cuba begins.

1901

February. U.S. Senate enacts the Platt Amendment.

1902

May 20. U.S. military occupation of Cuba ends.

The War of 1898

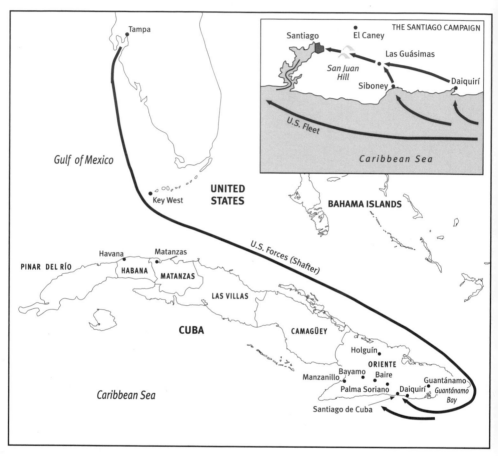

Cuba, 1898

On Context and Condition

I have always received as a political maxim the declarations made by our predecessors in regard to the annexation of Cuba. Every rock and every grain of sand in that island were drifted and washed out from American soil by the floods of the Mississippi, and other estuaries of the Gulf of Mexico. The island has seemed to me, just as our predecessors have said, to gravitate back again to the parent continent from which it sprang.
—William Seward (1859)

When the inability of Spain to deal successfully with the insurrection has become manifest and it is demonstrated that her sovereignty is extinct in Cuba for all purposes of rightful existence, and when a hopeless struggle for its reestablishment has degenerated into a strife which means nothing more than the useless sacrifice of human life and the utter destruction of the very subject matter of the conflict, a situation will be presented in which our obligations to the sovereignty of Spain will be superseded by higher obligations, which we can hardly hesitate to recognize and discharge.
—President Grover Cleveland (December 7, 1896)

what are those "higher obligations"?

No solution of this war can be thought of for an instant that is not based upon the absolute independence of the island. . . . We have accomplished too much to accept anything short of absolute freedom. The Cubans really control all of Cuba but the fortified towns, and the more artillery we receive the more of these we will take. . . . Why, then, should we lay down our arms for anything but the end for which we took them up: the freedom of the island and the people of Cuba?
—General Máximo Gómez (March 6, 1897)

The war was accepted by Spain when the island of Cuba was virtually lost . . . , when our troops lacked the most indispensable necessities. . . . Under these circumstances it was madness on our part to accept a conflict with an immensely wealthy

to be an active participant;
AND to actually create it /
construct it

nation. . . . Among the people of the United States the desire to make history stands above every other consideration, and we were incredibly stupid when we offered it to them gratis and at our own expense.

—Captain Víctor M. Concas y Palau, *La escuadra del almirante Cervera* (1899)

The war of 1898 was fought over and about a great many things: some were apparent and discernible then, others were not so clear—then or now. The war came in a decade of one of the most devastating economic depressions in U.S. history—curiously, years better remembered as the "gay nineties." These same gay nineties are also associated with places like Wounded Knee and Homestead; they were years of Populist revolt and nativist reaction, of labor conflict, of shifting gender boundaries and deepening racial strife; a time of ethnic diversity, of immigrants and migrants, with Frederick Jackson Turner lamenting the end of open land even as Americans abandoned the land for the cities, announcing—we know now—far-reaching demographic shifts from farm to factory, an economy in transition from agriculture to industry, implying also the need for new markets and new territories from which to defend them—all in all, very complicated times.

It is difficult to ascertain the meaning of 1898 under these circumstances, or even where and how to situate imperialism and colonial expansion in the larger realm of these experiences. Precisely how such conditions contributed to shaping the disposition for war may well lie beyond the explanatory reach of existing historical methods, although the convergence of circumstances certainly provides ample opportunity for creative conjecture. The 1890s are thus transformed into a point of imaginative departure, something of a transcendental divide after which everything and everyone is different. Frank Freidel attributed the war "to the American restlessness in the 1890s." Richard Hofstadter wondered about the impact of hard times, about the ways that conditions "brought to large numbers of people intense frustration in their economic lives and their careers," thereby resulting in "frustration with acts of aggression, and to allay anxieties by threatening acts against others." Robert L. Beisner pondered how "waves of doubt about America's strength, health, and purpose" contributed to "a need to reaffirm American strength: the United States could thrash some other country in a war or, more subtly, demonstrate its ability to govern 'inferior' peoples in an empire." David Healy detected in the imperialist impulse a people searching "to offset class struggles with a unifying nationalism" as a way "to combat a sordid and pervasive materialism." In similar fashion, Gerald F. Linderman suggested "a crisis of confidence," with Americans

US inferiority complex?

"worried about the fragility of their society" during which "elements essential to the [social] consensus disappeared." Something of a "psychic crisis" was the way that Daniel M. Smith characterized the 1890s, a condition that found "relief from internal economic and social tensions through a foreign crusade." Mary Beth Norton et al. wrote of the U.S. need for "more space, more land, more markets, and more power," of the "calls for war and foreign territory," when U.S. "power was sufficient to deliver both."[1]

On the other hand, it is also possible to contemplate 1898 as the denouement, possessed of an internal logic of its own that although perhaps not entirely predictable was highly probable, an eventuality foretold in pursuit of interests foreseen. The United States emerged from the war as a colonial power, seizing the far-flung remnants of the Spanish empire in the Pacific and Caribbean with remarkable efficiency of effort and economy of means. Whether or not empire was the object may matter less than that it was the outcome, as the United States acquired territories in the time-honored fashion of war and conquest—responsibilities, in any event, it assumed without protestation, without hesitation. Successively the Philippines, Guam, and Puerto Rico were seized. But it was Cuba that mattered most and, indeed, what the war was mostly about.

• • •

The sources of the war reached deeply into the nineteenth century. Americans began to contemplate Cuba very early in that century, mostly in the form of musings on possession. Some of these concerns were related to regional interests. The northeastern states prized the privileged access to Caribbean tropical agricultural products that Cuba promised in seemingly unlimited quantities at consistently low costs. Southern states wistfully contemplated the annexation of Cuba as a valuable addition to the political strength of the slaveholding South.

But the pursuit of possession of Cuba was more complicated. It had to do with a specific moment in the development of the nation, back to a time when Americans were beginning to define themselves as a nationality, as a people with common—that is, "national"—interests. Some of this, of course, was related to geography: Cuba was so near—"almost in sight of our shores," John Quincy Adams exaggerated to make the point.[2] Proximity did indeed seem to suggest destiny, and about destiny there was unanimity: it was manifest.

Almost from the outset, as Americans began to conceive of themselves as a cohesive nation, Cuba was a presence: capable under one set of circumstances of being a source of security and under another of becoming a source of vulnerability. In fact, it was precisely this uncertainty that drove Cuba deep into the realms of national consciousness. Cuba figured prominently in the meditations of nation, a means and a metaphor by which Americans took measure of their well-being, linked directly to the national concern for security and prosperity: "an object of transcendent importance to the political and commercial interests of our Union," Adams proclaimed, and more: "indispensable to the continuance and integrity of the Union itself." James Buchanan agreed, certain that "the acquisition of Cuba would greatly strengthen our bond of Union" and "insure the perpetuity of our Union." Secretary of State William L. Marcy expressed similar sentiments on more than one occasion. "The acquisition of Cuba by the United States," he insisted in 1854, "would be preëminently advantageous in itself, and of the highest importance as a precautionary measure of security." And in the following year, he declared: "The incorporation of Cuba into the American Union [is] essential to the welfare . . . of the United States." So much seemed to depend on Cuba, so much more was possible with Cuba. "Give us Cuba . . . ," Senator Robert Toombs exulted optimistically, "and we shall command all the . . . wants of the human race; we shall control their commerce in everything." With Cuba, Toombs predicted, "we can make first the Gulf of Mexico, and then the Caribbean sea, a *mare clausum*," whereupon the day would not be too distant "when no flag shall float there except by permission of the United States of America." It was only a matter of time, and indeed perhaps inevitable, that North Americans would persuade themselves that the well-being of the entire world depended on the U.S. possession of Cuba. "[T]he future interests not only of this country," proclaimed Senator James Bayard at midcentury, "but of civilization and of human progress, are deeply involved in the acquisition of Cuba by the United States."[3]

The destinies of both countries seemed not merely intertwined, but indissoluble. The future well-being of the United States could hardly be contemplated without implicating Cuba. Early in the nineteenth century, and all through the century, Cuba loomed large in U.S. meditations on security, as a people, as a nation. It is not certain that these concerns were wholly rational, but it is clear that they developed fully into a preoccupation, one embedded deeply in the national character. That the vision of nation formed around the expectation of inclusion of Cuba implied that the ideal of national integration would remain incomplete without Cuba. If possession of Cuba was to have made the United States stronger, more secure—and, in Buchanan's words, "insure the perpetuity of our

Union"—that Cuba remained outside the Union could not but have summoned uneasily a specter of uncertainty. Possession of Cuba became a fixed feature of U.S. policy. A sense of national completion seemed to depend on Cuba, without which the Union was unfinished and maybe even slightly vulnerable.

This disquiet insinuated itself into the dominant nineteenth-century narratives on the national interest. "[Cuba's] addition to our confederacy," Thomas Jefferson wrote to James Monroe as early as 1823, "is exactly what is wanting to round out our power as a nation to the point of its utmost interest." James Buchanan thought a great deal about the implications of Cuba and gave compelling expression to U.S. concerns: "If Cuba were annexed to the United States, we should . . . be relieved from the apprehensions which we can never cease to feel for our own safety and the security of our commerce whilst it shall remain in its present condition." Daniel Webster referred to the "danger to our security" and "danger, manifest and imminent danger, to our essential rights and our essential interests" as long as Cuba remained outside the Union. The Ostend Manifesto in 1854 addressed these apprehensions explicitly. "The Union," explained the manifesto, "can never enjoy repose, nor possess reliable security, as long as Cuba is not embraced within its boundaries."[4]

Several times in the nineteenth century the United States attempted to buy the island outright. James Polk offered $100 million for it in 1848, without effect. Six years later Franklin Pierce raised the purchase offer to $130 million, but with no greater success. The Grant administration also contemplated purchase, but nothing came of that project either.

The United States thus reconciled itself to continued Spanish sovereignty over Cuba and, indeed, resolved to defend Spanish rule as an adequate if temporary substitute for annexation. The presence of a weak Spain in decline, with more of a past than a future, without the means or the motives to challenge U.S. interests, was a tolerable alternative to U.S. control. Thomas Jefferson formulated one of the enduring tenets of U.S. policy, affirming that to guarantee Cuba's "independence against all the world, *except* Spain . . . would be nearly as valuable to us as if it were our own."[5]

But defense of Spanish sovereignty was not unconditional. Central to American policy formulations, derived in large part from the Monroe Doctrine, was the presumption of U.S. succession, a transaction that necessarily precluded transfer of sovereignty of the island to a third party. Thus it was that the status of Cuba suggested the circumstances under which to contemplate the eventuality of war. Secretary of State Edward Livingston outlined U.S. interests succinctly and directly. "The great objects of our Government in relation to Cuba," he stated in 1832, "are . . . to preserve it in the hands of Spain, even at the expense of a war, and only in the event of finding that impossible, to look to its annexation to our confederacy." The Van Buren administration communicated the U.S. position directly to the Spanish government several years later. "Permit me . . . to remark," U.S. Minister John H. Eaton explained to the Spanish minister of foreign affairs in 1838, "that while the United States are solicitous, that nothing may arise to disturb the jurisdiction of Spain over this Island, or to cause its transfer to other hands, they could not with indifference & unconcern look upon an attempt, to pass it, into the possession & ownership of another power." Minister Daniel Barringer reiterated the U.S. position at midcentury: "Our government [is] resolutely determined that the Island of Cuba should never be in the possession of any other power than that of Spain or the United States."[6]

Any modification of sovereignty that did not result in U.S. acquisition was unacceptable. War was the recourse the United States reserved for itself, explicitly and unabashedly, as the means to guarantee succession to sovereignty: war in the first instance as deterrent and as the last recourse defense.

There was no mistaking the meaning of what became known as the "no transfer" principle. Thomas Jefferson was unequivocal and in 1823 alluded to any number of different possibilities, all with the same result: "We will oppose, with all our means, the forcible interposition of any other power, as auxiliary, stipendiary, or under any other form or pretext, and most especially, [Cuba's] transfer to any power by conquest, cession, or acquisition in any other way." Minister to Spain Washington Irving emphasized the "determination" of the United States "to maintain Spain in the possession of Cuba by force of arms, if necessary, and to consider it a cause of war for any other power to attempt to possess itself of the Island." Concerned in 1840 that perhaps in the course of frequent Spanish cabinet changes U.S. interests would "be lost sight of," Secretary of State John Forsyth instructed the American chargé d'affaires in Madrid to communicate a warning to the new Spanish ministry: "Should you have reason to suspect any design on the part of Spain to transfer voluntarily her title to the island, whether of ownership or possession, and whether permanent or temporary, to . . . any other power, you will distinctly state that the U[nited] States will prevent it, at all hazard." A decade later Secretary of State John M. Clayton reaffirmed the U.S.

position. "This Government," he warned, "is resolutely determined that the Island of Cuba, shall never be ceded by Spain to any other power than the United States," adding: "The news of the cession of Cuba to any foreign power would, in the United States, be the instant signal for war."[7]

• • •

The war actually began on February 24, 1895, in the remote village of Baire at the eastern end of the island, announced by the celebratory *grito*—the cry for liberty and independence. Hardly anyone noticed. Separatist uprisings in the name of *Cuba Libre* during the last decades of the nineteenth century had become as commonplace as they were short-lived: typically localized affairs, confined mostly to the distant eastern province of Oriente, and rarely reported in the capital press as anything more than scattered incidents of lawlessness. The "Little War" of 1879–80 lasted eighteen months. A rebellion in Manzanillo in 1883 collapsed in weeks. Holguín was the site of another stillborn revolt in 1885. A separatist uprising in Guantánamo in 1892 ended ignominiously after only days of fighting. Another revolt in April 1893 collapsed in a matter of weeks. Six months later, an uprising in Las Villas ended abruptly with the quick capture of the principal leaders.

Rumors of new separatist stirrings in February 1895, understandably, failed to provoke undue concern among authorities in Havana. The conflict began in much the same fashion as others before it: localized skirmishes and scattered engagements, mostly in the remote mountain folds of the east. No one in power or with property had reason to believe that the *Grito de Baire* would end in any way other than its countless predecessors: a matter of no consequence.

But 1895 turned out to be different. Cubans were better organized in 1895. They had planned better and were better led, with effect. In the summer rebellious Cubans marched out of their eastern sanctuaries and onto the rich cattle-grazing ranges of Camagüey, by fall they had crossed the fertile sugar plateau of Matanzas and Havana, and by winter they had reached the lush tobacco fields of Pinar del Río. Within eighteen months, the insurrection had expanded across the entire length of the island, obtaining the support of Cubans of all classes, rural and urban, black and white, men and women, young and old. What began as scattered insurgent bands developed into an army of 50,000 officers and men organized into six army corps, distributed into twelve divisions and eighty-five regiments of infantry and cavalry.

Officials in the United States followed events in Cuba with deepening disquiet. Successive presidents, first the Democrat Grover Cleveland

and later the Republican William McKinley, doubted that Spain possessed either the material resources or the moral resolve to end the insurgency. "While the insurrectionary forces to be dealt with are more formidable than ever before," Secretary of State Richard B. Olney observed as early as September 1895, "the ability of Spain to cope with them has visibly and greatly decreased. She is straining every nerve to stamp out the insurrection within the next few months. For what obvious reason? Because she is almost at the end of her resources." Olney concluded that "Spain cannot possibly succeed." Nothing changed in the following six months, and Olney became even more certain of the outcome. "It can hardly be questioned," he observed in April 1896, "that the insurrection, instead of being quelled, is to-day more formidable than ever and enters upon the second year of its existence with decidedly improved prospects of successful results."[8]

By the second year of the war, the Spanish government was reeling from the combined effects of military reversals abroad and political resistance at home. Popular discontent and public opposition erupted into antiwar demonstrations, draft riots, and army mutinies. Simply the financial cost of the war was becoming unbearable as Spanish credit on the European money markets plummeted. In August 1896 an incredulous Spanish public, already weary of the eighteen-month campaign in Cuba, learned that the unthinkable had occurred: another colonial war in the tropics—now on the other side of the world—this one in the vast Philippine archipelago. The determination to preserve the integrity of empire abroad was threatening Spain with dissolution at home. In late 1897, as a last resort, the new Liberal ministry of Práxedes Mateo Sagasta introduced a series of far-reaching colonial reforms. The moderate Ramón Blanco was appointed governor general of Cuba. Amnesty was proclaimed and political prisoners were paroled. A new autonomist constitution was promulgated. On January 1, 1898, a Cuban home-rule government assumed power.

Colonial reforms had the net effect of sealing the doom of Spanish sovereignty in Cuba. Insurgent leaders denounced home rule and rejected accommodation with Spain on any terms other than complete independence. "It is the firm resolution of the army and people of Cuba," vowed General Máximo Gómez, "who have shed so much blood in order to conquer their independence, not to falter in their just cause until triumph or death crowns their efforts." Two weeks later Gómez reiterated the Cuban position: "We no longer ask for concessions. . . . Even were Spain's proposals bona fide, nothing could tempt us to treat with her. We are for liberty, not for Spanish reforms." The Cuban diplomatic representatives in the United States informed the State Department that colonial reforms were not an acceptable basis for the cessation of hostilities. "As the representative of the Cubans in arms, and under their instructions," Tomás Estrada Palma informed Secretary of State John Sherman in December 1897, "it is my duty to announce that nothing short of absolute independence will be accepted by us as the basis of peace.... We will never lay down our arms until we have freed ourselves from the sovereignty of Spain.... We will not renounce our objective."[9]

Rather than inducing conciliation, reforms actually encouraged intransigence. Cuban morale soared. The concessions were evidence of Spain's impending defeat, Cuban leaders concluded. "Spain's offer of autonomy is a sign of her weakening," Provisional President Bartolomé Masó proclaimed. General Calixto García agreed: "I regard autonomy only as a sign of Spain's weakening power and an indication that the end is not far off." The U.S. consul in Sagua la Grande reported exactly the same attitude among local separatist army commanders. "The insurgents . . . are every day more hopeful of forcing Spain to deliver the island to them," Walter Barker wrote in late 1897, "and the fact is that they are also more and more encouraged seeing that Spain demonstrating by offers of reform and autonomy her tendency of weakness."[10]

For the defenders of *Cuba española* colonial reforms assumed fully the proportions of treason. Reforms that were too little for separatists were too much for loyalists; the autonomy that was rejected in separatist camps was repudiated in loyalist circles. Conservatives denounced the establishment of a home rule government, publicly predicting that radicals would overwhelm moderates, revolution would overtake reform, and independence would overcome autonomy. The establishment of the new moderate government, moreover, convinced loyalists—Spaniards and Cubans alike—that Spain had lost the will to fight. The more thoughtful among loyalists understood, too, that the autonomist government lacked the means to wage war and was without the authority to make peace. The new government had been summoned into existence to preside over the liquidation of empire.

Rallies and demonstrations were organized across the island to protest autonomy. Rumors of conspiracies swirled and multiplied. The army that had ceased to fight in the countryside became the center of intrigue in the cities. On January 12, hardly two weeks after the installation of the new Cuban government, several units of Spanish troops and volunteers in Havana mutinied and stormed the editorial offices of two Havana newspapers sympathetic to home rule with cries "Death to Blanco!" and "Down with autonomy!" Rioting troops proceeded to destroy the presses and sack the offices of *La Discusión* and *El Reconcentrado*. The next day, U.S. Consul Fitzhugh Lee cabled Washington with an urgent request for the prompt presence of a U.S. warship. On January 25 the *Maine* moored in Havana harbor.

• • •

Spanish sovereignty in Cuba was coming to an end, or so it appeared. And appearances influenced outcomes. Of course, whether Cubans would have actually gone on to defeat Spain, then or thereafter, or even at all, cannot be demonstrated. What can be determined and documented, however, is that all parties involved had arrived at the conclusion that the days of Spanish rule in Cuba were numbered. This was the perception that, in the end, served as the basis on which the vital policy decisions were made and actions were taken.

Spanish authorities openly predicted defeat in Cuba. "Spain is exhausted," former president Francisco Pi y Margall concluded. "She must withdraw her troops and recognize Cuban independence before it is too late." The failure of autonomy, the Madrid daily *El Nuevo Régimen* editorialized, left only one alternative: "Negotiate on the basis of independence." *La Epoca* reached a similar conclusion. "In reality," observed the Madrid daily, "Cuba is lost to Spain."[11]

Cubans, too, sensed that the end was near. A new optimism lifted separatist morale to an all-time high. Never had they been so openly certain of triumph as they were in early 1898. "This war cannot last more than a year," Máximo Gómez exulted in January 1898. "This is the first time I have ever put a limit to it." Bartolomé Masó agreed; in a "Manifesto" to the nation he confidently proclaimed: "The war for the independence of our country is nearing the end."[12]

Even before the announcement of colonial reforms, Cuban army commanders noticed a decline in Spanish morale and a decrease in Spanish military operations. "The Spanish are tired," Máximo Gómez reported as early as the summer of 1897, "and in these days when the heat suffocates even us, I do not see how those troops move." This view was corroborated in Havana by the British consul, who reported that Cubans retained "possession of the interior of the Island, from end to end, and Spanish jurisdiction and authority are only capable of being enforced within the cities."[13] In the closing months of 1897 Spanish troops lay prostrate, sapped by illness, disease, malnutrition, and the unrelieved tropical heat. The Spanish army had lost the will to fight.

Conditions deteriorated markedly—and rapidly—after January 1, 1898. Military operations came to a virtual standstill across the island. Spanish commanders simply refused to fight in behalf of the new colonial government. Army units were withdrawn from smaller interior towns and concentrated in the larger provincial cities, then redeployed to prepare for the defense of the provincial capitals and major ports. In January 1898 Máximo Gómez wrote of a "dead war." The collapse seemed complete. "The enemy is crushed," Gómez reported from the field, "and is in complete retreat from here, and the time which favored their operations passes without them doing anything." Spanish failure to mount a new winter offensive convinced the Cubans that Spain was exhausted and lacked the means and the motivation to continue the war. "The enemy," Gómez disclosed from central Cuba in March 1898, "has departed, ceasing military operations and abandoning the garrisons and forts which constituted his base of operations. Days, weeks and months pass without a column of troops appearing within our radius of action."[14]

Preparations for what were generally expected to be the final desperate battles had begun. In late 1897 the Cuban army command completed the organization of artillery units and arranged to carry the war to the cities. Gómez wrote confidently about making ready for the final assault against the remaining Spanish urban strongholds. With "cannons and a great deal of dynamite," he predicted from Las Villas in March 1898, "we can expel them by fire and steel from the towns." In Oriente province, General Calixto García mounted a stunning and successful artillery attack in August 1897 on the city of Victoria de las Tunas. In the next six months, town after town in Oriente fell to Cuban control, including Guisa, Guáimaro, Jiguaní, Loma de Hierro, and Bayamo. In early 1898, the port city of Manzanillo was threatened. In April, General García prepared to lay siege on Santiago de Cuba.[15]

U.S. officials were also among those who concluded that the Spanish cause was hopeless. "Spain herself has demonstrated that she is powerless either to conciliate Cuba or conquer it," former U.S. minister to Spain Hannis Taylor wrote in late 1897; "her sovereignty over [Cuba] is . . . now extinct." Secretary of State John Sherman agreed: "Spain will lose Cuba. That seems to me to be certain. She cannot continue the struggle." Assistant Secretary of State William Day warned grimly that the end was imminent. "The Spanish Government," he observed, "seems unable to conquer the insurgents." In a confidential memorandum to the White House, Day went further: "To-day the strength of the Cubans [is] nearly double . . . and [they] occupy and control virtually all the territory outside the heavily garrisoned coastal cities and a few interior towns. There are no active operations by the Spaniards. . . . The eastern provinces are admittedly 'Free Cuba.' In view of these statements alone, it is now evident that Spain's struggle in Cuba has become absolutely hopeless. . . . Spain is exhausted financially and physically, while the Cubans are stronger."[16]

The Spanish army was disintegrating, Consul Lee reported from Havana. "The disparity between the contending forces is daily decreasing. I do not think the Spaniards can now muster more than 75—or 80,000 soldiers who have strength enough to carry a rifle and a haversack, while it is certain—with the exception of the seaports and a few interior towns, the Insurgents occupy the whole island." When asked if Spanish authorities possessed the means of ending the insurrection, Lee responded unequivocally: "I do not think there is the slightest possibility of their doing it at all in any way." In a passage of frank if perhaps unintended admission, Senator Henry Cabot Lodge noted that the proposed April armistice could not have succeeded without the agreement of both parties, "and the Cubans, on the eve of victory, of course, would not consent." Naval attaché George L. Dyer, assigned to the U.S. legation in Madrid during the final months of negotiations, reflected on the proposed armistice, and wrote on April 1: "If the insurgents would ask for an armistice I am sure we would have it at once. But would they? With their independence in sight will they risk it for long drawn out negotiations which may fail in the end?"[17]

• • •

In early 1898 the McKinley administration contemplated the impending denouement with a mixture of disquiet and dread. If Spanish sovereignty was untenable, Cuban pretension to sovereignty was unacceptable. The Cuban insurrection threatened more than the propriety of colonial administration; it also challenged the U.S. presumption of succession, for in contesting Spanish rule Cubans were advancing the claim of a new sovereignty. For much of the nineteenth century, the United States had pursued the acquisition of Cuba with resolve, if without results. The success of the Cuban rebellion threatened everything. In 1898 Cuba was lost to Spain, and if Washington did not act, it would also be lost to the United States. The implications of the "no transfer" principle were now carried to their logical conclusion. If the United States could not permit Spain to transfer sovereignty to another power, neither could the United States allow Spain to relinquish sovereignty to Cubans.

Opposition to Cuban independence was a proposition with a past, possessed of a proper history, one that served to form and inform the principal policy formulations of the nineteenth century. Only the possibility of the transfer of Cuba to a potentially hostile foreign country seemed to trouble the United States more than the prospect of Cuban independence. Cuba was far too important to be turned over to the Cubans. Free Cuba raised the specter of political disorder, social upheaval, and racial conflict: Cuba as a source of regional instability and inevitably a source of international tension. Many had long detected in the racial heterogeneity of the island portents of disorder and dissolution. "Were the population of the island of one blood and color," John Quincy Adams affirmed in 1823, "there could be no doubt or hesitation with regard to the course which they would pursue, as dictated by their interests and their rights. The invasion of Spain by France would be the signal for *their* Declaration of Independence." However, Adams continued, in "their present state . . . they are not competent to a system of permanent self-dependence." Secretary of State Henry Clay gave explicit definition and enduring form to U.S. opposition to Cuban independence. "The population itself . . . ," Clay insisted, "is incompetent, at present, from its composition and amount, to maintain self government." This view was reiterated several decades later by Secretary of State Hamilton Fish, who looked upon a population of Indians, Africans, and Spaniards as utterly incapable of sustaining self-government.[18]

The cause of Cuba Libre found little support inside the Cleveland administration. Opposition to independence was registered early and often. The withdrawal of Spain, the administration feared, would be the signal for the onset of desultory and destructive civil strife. Even the "most devoted friend of Cuba and the most enthusiastic advocate of popular government," Secretary of State Olney brooded, could not but look at developments in Cuba "except with the gravest apprehension." Olney continued:

> There are only too strong reasons to fear that, once Spain were withdrawn from the island, the sole bond of union between the different factions of the insurgents would disappear; that a war of races would be precipitated, all the more sanguinary for the discipline and experience acquired during the insurrection, and that, even if there were to be temporary peace, it could only be through the establishment of a white and a black republic, which, even if agreeing at the outset upon a division of the island between them, would be enemies from the start, and would never rest until the one had been completely vanquished and subdued by the other.[19]

At one point the Cleveland administration contemplated purchasing the island—not, however, to establish an independent republic. On the contrary: "It would seem absurd for us to buy the island," President Cleveland declared, "and present it to the people now inhabiting it, and put its government and management in their hands."[20]

Nor was the McKinley administration any more sympathetic to the prospects of Cuban independence. "I do not believe that the population is to-day fit for self-government," McKinley's minister to Spain, Stewart L. Woodford, commented in early March 1898. Woodford characterized the insurgency as "confined almost entirely to negroes," with "few whites in the rebel forces." Under the circumstances, he asserted, "Cuban independence is absolutely impossible as a permanent solution of the difficulty, since independence can only result in a continuous war of races, and this means that independent Cuba must be a second Santo Domingo." Several days later Woodford again invoked the specter of racial strife: "The insurgents, supported by the great majority of the blacks, and led by even a minority of enterprising and resolute whites, will probably be strong enough to prevent effective good government. . . . This would mean and involve continuous disorder and practical anarchy. . . . Peace can hardly be assured by the insurgents through and under an independent government." He concluded: "I have at last come to believe that the only certainty of peace is under our flag. . . . I am, thus, reluctantly, slowly, but entirely a convert to the early American ownership and occupation of the island. If we recognize independence, we may turn the island over to a part of its inhabitants against the judgment of many of its most educated and wealthy residents." Woodford predicted: "I see nothing ahead except disorder, insecurity of persons and destruction of property. The Spanish flag cannot give peace. The rebel flag cannot give peace. There is but one power and one flag that can secure peace and compel peace. That power is the United States and that flag is our flag."[21] The proposition of possession of Cuba persisted as a singular theme. "The ultimate acquisition of Cuba," affirmed Senator Donald Cameron in December 1896 in a pronouncement reminiscent of language used earlier in the century, "has been regarded as the fixed policy of the United States—necessary to the progressive development of our system. All agree that [it] is not only desirable but inevitable."[22]

Both the Cleveland and McKinley administrations acted vigorously against Cuban efforts to support and supply the insurgency from the United States. Repeatedly government authorities warned Cubans to observe U.S. neutrality laws. President Cleveland vowed to "enforce observance to our neutrality laws and to prevent the territory of the United States from being abused as a vantage point from which to aid those in arms against Spanish sovereignty."[23] The U.S. government committed its full resources to interdict expeditions to the island. "Expedition after expedition was circumvented or captured," Secretary of the Treasury Lyman J. Gage boasted after the war. "The coast of Florida was patrolled by revenue cutters of the Treasury Department and collectors of customs were under strict orders to take the most effective steps at their command to prevent the violation of the law." Indeed, Navy captain French Ensor Chadwick acknowledged in his 1909 account of the war that "American ships were, in fact, doing the duty which should have been done by the Spanish navy on the Cuban coast."[24] Tomás Estrada Palma was disheartened by the continued U.S. interdiction of Cuban expeditions. "I despair in the face of the enormous difficulties associated with evading what the government of this country calls 'neutrality law,' " he wrote from New York in late 1895, "which is really a one-sided law: loosely defined for the Spanish, strictly applied to us." Conditions worsened the following year. "Every day it becomes more difficult to send expeditions," Estrada Palma complained in 1896, "and those that do leave carry only the number of men strictly needed to unload supplies." Between 1895 and 1896 U.S. authorities intercepted over half of the Cuban expeditions fitted in the United States. Of the seventy expeditions organized from the United States during the Cuban insurrection, only one-third reached the island.[25]

• • •

Thus it was that the McKinley administration contemplated the impending defeat of Spain in early 1898 with concern and consternation. A settlement had to be reached before the summer, prior to the onset of the rainy season. "The awful condition of affairs in Cuba can not continue forever," Minister Woodford warned Spanish authorities on March 9 and exhorted: "End it at once—*end it at once—end it at once*."[26]

But Woodford's admonitions were to no avail. One week later the minister to Spain arrived at a dismal conclusion, an "evident fact," he stressed, which he communicated directly to President McKinley: "I do not think that any thoughtful man in Madrid now believes that [Spain] can practically suppress the rebellion *before the rainy season begins*." The prospects, he concluded, were bleak. "It now seems almost certain," he reported to the White House in mid-March, "that autonomy cannot succeed before the rainy season begins." On April 1 Woodford confirmed what the administration had feared: "They know that Cuba is lost."[27] Cubans were preparing for the final offensive operations, and few doubted that they would succeed. The summer of 1898, many sensed, would be decisive.

At the same time, and no less distressing, the cause of Cuba Libre had obtained widespread popular support in the United States, manifested most dramatically in periodic congressional resolutions calling for the recognition of Cuban independence and threatening war in its behalf. A new urgency now joined the administration's concern about the outcome of the approaching rainy season. Cubans were nearing the end of their war while Congress threatened to start a new war, both in the name of Cuba Libre.

These were difficult times. All through late winter and early spring, President McKinley sensed the urgency of the moment and pursued ways to foreclose or otherwise forestall the impending Cuban triumph. This was not always easy, to be sure, for noteworthy and unforeseen distractions intervened and frustrated even the best laid plans. On February 9, 1898, a private letter written by the Spanish minister in Washington, Enrique Dupuy de Lôme, characterizing McKinley as a "cheap politician," was purloined and subsequently published in the *New York Journal*, creating something of a sensation in the press and adding new stress fractures to strained U.S.-Spanish relations. A week later, the destruction of the *Maine* in Havana harbor called further attention to deteriorating conditions in Cuba.

The administration moved quickly. On one hand, President McKinley explored the idea of buying the island directly from Spain. "Some way must be found," Woodford proposed to colonial minister Segismundo Moret in March, "by which Spain can part with Cuba without loss of self-respect and with certainty of American control." Woodford proposed to offer a "fixed sum for the purchase of the island," part of which would be retained as a fund for the payment of war claims. Minister Moret pledged to consider the offer seriously.[28]

At the same time, McKinley sought to devise a way to suspend hostilities on the island as a means of averting the anticipated Spanish collapse. On March 27 the administration presented Spain with an ultimatum demanding an armistice until October 1, an immediate revocation of the reconcentration policy, authorization to distribute U.S. relief supplies on the island, and the acceptance of President McKinley as arbiter if the conflict resumed after October 1. "If Spain agrees," Assistant Secretary of State William Day cabled Woodford, "[the] President will use friendly offices to get insurgents to accept the plan." On April 5

Woodford cabled stunning news: the queen regent of Spain had personally interceded and was at that very moment preparing a proclamation ordering a unilateral cease-fire in Cuba, effective immediately and lasting to October 5. Spain had acquiesced. "Can you prevent hostile action by Congress?" Woodford asked anxiously, adding hopefully: "I believe this means peace."[29] Five days later Governor General Ramón Blanco in Cuba ordered an immediate and unilateral cease-fire.[30]

But it was a concession without consequence. In fact, McKinley already knew his plan had failed. Whether or not Spain had fully acquiesced to U.S. demands, long at the center of an ongoing historiographical debate, was in fact irrelevant. Cubans settled the issue. The president had failed to persuade the Cubans to halt military operations during the rainy season. The Cuban army command refused to observe the cease-fire. In early April McKinley had summoned Horatio Rubens, the legal counsel of the Cuban delegation in New York, to the White House to discuss the terms of the proposed settlement. Rubens recalled the meeting:

> "You must," he clipped out at me, "accept an immediate armistice with Spain."
> "To what end, Mr. President?"
> "To settle the strife in Cuba," he cried.
> "But is Spain ready to grant Cuba independence?" I asked.
> "That isn't the question now," he exclaimed, his voice rising. "We may discuss that later. The thing for the moment is an armistice."

Rubens rejected outright the terms of the cease-fire. Such an arrangement, he countered, would benefit only Spain and have calamitous consequences on the Cuban war effort. He explained to McKinley:

> The reason is a practical one, Mr. President. Nothing you could propose would be so beneficial to Spain and so detrimental to Cuba as an armistice. If an armistice is carried out in good faith, it means the dissolution and disintegration of the Cuban army. There is no commissary for it even now; it must live, poorly and precariously, on the country. If an armistice is accepted the army cannot obtain its food supplies; it will starve. Furthermore, in the natural uncertainty pending negotiations, the men would scatter, going to their homes. . . . If, on the other hand, having accepted the armistice, the Cubans continued to live on the country, they would be loudly charged with breach of faith.[31]

On the island, Cuban leaders denounced the Spanish cease-fire and ordered army units to continue operations. President Bartolomé Masó reacted to the cease-fire immediately and categorically: "Such a decision does not change in the slightest the situation of Cuban forces nor in any manner does it affect our condition of open hostility against the Spanish government and its army nor does it modify in the least our system and procedure of war." General Calixto García exhorted his troops to continue operations. "They have to be hit hard and at the head, day and night," García demanded. "In order to suspend hostilities, an agreement is necessary with our Government and this will have to be based on independence." Máximo Gómez explained to his officers in a "General Order":

> Whereas the enemy has clearly proclaimed an armistice, without prior official notice or even as much as proposing such a condition to our Government, I am ordering the following:
> 1. We should not or shall we accept such a resolution.
> 2. The chiefs and officers of the army under my command will strike at the enemy in whatever situation he is found, without the slightest modification of our method of war.
> 3. For that reason, all the decrees and circulars previously issued and by which the war for independence has been waged remain in force.[32]

Several days later, reflecting on his General Order, Gómez wrote in his diary: "More than ever before the war must continue in full force."[33]

• • •

By early spring the Cuban triumph appeared inevitable. Negotiations between Spain and the United States were becoming increasingly irrelevant to the outcome in Cuba, for events were being determined by forces beyond their control. Cubans were dictating the pace and the place of events. The failure of Spain to obtain separatist support of autonomy and the inability of the United States to secure separatist compliance with the cease-fire signified that Spain and the United States had nothing further to discuss with each other. The consummation of Cuban independence was precisely the outcome that Spain and the United States were determined to resist but seemed powerless to prevent. By spring 1898, as the summer neared, President McKinley faced only two choices: Cuban independence or U.S. intervention.

There was nothing further to be gained by delay. On the contrary, continued postponement could only benefit the Cubans. On April 11

McKinley forwarded his message to Congress. The portents of his purpose were clear: no mention of Cuban independence, nothing about recognition of the Cuban provisional government, not a hint of sympathy with Cuba Libre, nowhere even an allusion to the renunciation of territorial aggrandizement—only a request for congressional authorization "to take measures to secure a full and final termination of hostilities between the Government of Spain and the people of Cuba, and to secure in the island the establishment of a stable government, capable of maintaining order and observing its international obligations." The U.S. purpose in Cuba, McKinley noted, consisted of "forcible intervention . . . as a neutral to stop the war." The president explained: "The forcible intervention of the United States . . . involves . . . hostile constraint upon both the parties to the contest."[34]

The war was thus directed against both Spaniards and Cubans, a means by which to neutralize the two competing claims of sovereignty and establish by force of arms a third one. This was the outstanding virtue of the "neutral intervention" to which the United States had committed itself in April 1898. "We have already canvassed recognition of independence," the State Department reported in an internal memorandum on April 7, only days before the release of the war message, "with an adverse conclusion." The "neutral intervention" offered the greatest likelihood of guaranteeing U.S. control of the island. "It would make a notable difference in our conduct of hostilities in Cuba if we were to operate in territory transiently ours by conquest, instead of operating in the territory of a recognized sovereign with whom we maintain alliance." On the same day, the pro-administration *New York Tribune*, owned by Republican Whitelaw Reid, reflected White House thinking editorially. "It must be frankly stated," the *Tribune* insisted, "that [Cubans] have not yet sufficiently established their authority to entitle them to recognition." Separatists represented only a "small minority of the whole population"—a minority "guilty of many acts of which this Government could never approve." The destruction of property, the conduct of guerrilla war, and Cuban indifference to the interests of foreign property, concluded the *Tribune*, hardly "inspired confidence in Washington that they possess the attributes necessary to qualify for independence." Having submitted the message to Congress, the White House let it be known that the president would veto any resolution according recognition to Cuban independence.[35]

Cubans looked upon the impending U.S. intervention with a mixture of fear and foreboding. They had not sought U.S. intervention but, rather, had solicited belligerency status and recognition of the provisional government. Indeed, there were many reasons to resist U.S. intervention. José Martí feared that the Cuban insurrection would provide the United States with the pretext to intervene—"and with the credit won as a mediator and guarantor keep [Cuba] for their own." And, Martí asked rhetorically, "once the United States is in Cuba, who will drive them out?" General Antonio Maceo similarly opposed U.S. intervention. "I expect nothing from the Americans," he explained to a friend in 1896. "We should entrust everything to our own efforts. It is better to rise or fall without help than to contract debts of gratitude with such a powerful neighbor."[36]

News of McKinley's April 11 message to Congress, proposing intervention without recognition, immediately provoked hostile reactions from the Cuban leadership. "We will oppose any intervention which does not have for its expressed and declared object the independence of Cuba," Gonzalo de Quesada vowed. Horatio Rubens released a statement bluntly warning the U.S. government that an intervention such as McKinley had proposed would be regarded as "nothing less than a declaration of war by the United States against the Cuban revolutionists." The arrival of a U.S. military expedition to Cuba under such circumstances, Rubens predicted, would oblige the insurgents to "treat that force as an enemy to be opposed, and, if possible, expelled." He added: "[T]he Cuban army will . . . remain in the interior, refusing to cooperate, declining to acknowledge any American authority, ignoring and rejecting the intervention to every possible extent. Should the United States troops succeed in expelling the Spanish; should the United States then declare a protectorate over the island—however provisional or tentative—and seek to extend its authority over the government of Cuba and the army of liberation, we would resist with force of arms as bitterly and tenaciously as we have fought the armies of Spain."[37] The State Department, in fact, had dreaded this reaction. As early as March 24, Secretary Day indicated that unless the United States recognized the Cubans, "or make some arrangement with them when we intervene, we will have to overcome both the Spaniards and Cubans."[38]

The cause of Cuba Libre had wide support in Congress, and defenders of the Cuban cause mounted sustained efforts to secure recognition of Cuban independence. Seven days passed between the arrival of the president's message and the final war resolution on April 18, almost all of which were given to acrimonious debate and intense political maneuvering by the administration and its congressional supporters to defeat pro-independence resolutions.[39] Compromise was reached when Congress agreed to forgo recognition of independence in exchange for McKinley's acceptance of a Joint Resolution in which Article Four, the Teller Amendment, served as a disclaimer of mischievous intentions:

> First. That the people of the Island of Cuba are, and of right ought to be, free and independent.
>
> Second. That it is the duty of the United States to demand, and the Government of the United States does hereby demand, that the Government of Spain at once relinquish its authority and government in the Island of Cuba and withdraw its land and naval forces from Cuba and Cuban waters.
>
> Third. That the President of the United States be, and he hereby is, directed and empowered to use the entire land and naval forces of the United States and to call into the actual service of the United States the militia of the several States to such extent as may be necessary to carry these resolutions into effect.
>
> Fourth. That the United States hereby disclaims any disposition or intention to exercise sovereignty, jurisdiction, or control over said island except for the pacification thereof, and asserts its determination, when that is accomplished, to leave the government and control of the island to its people.[40]

The Joint Resolution calmed Cuban misgivings. Persuaded that the intervention made common cause with separatist objectives, Cubans prepared to cooperate with their new allies. No matter that the United States refused to recognized the republic, as long as Washington endorsed the goals for which the republic stood. "It is true," Calixto García conceded, "that they have not entered into an accord with our government; but they have recognized our right to be free and independent and that is enough for me."[41]

The chronology of the war was brief. The naval battle of Manila Bay commenced at dawn on May 1 and was over by the early afternoon, a total of seven hours. Six weeks later U.S. armed forces landed at points along the southeastern coast of Cuba wholly unopposed, first at Guantánamo Bay on June 14 and eight days later at Daiquirí and Siboney. The battles at Las Guásimas (June 24), El Caney (July 1), and San Juan Hill (July 1) prepared the way for the siege of Santiago de Cuba. On July 3, the naval battle of Santiago de Cuba resulted in the destruction of the Spanish fleet. On July 16, Spanish forces in Santiago de Cuba surrendered. Ten days later, a U.S. expeditionary force landed at Guánica, on the southern coast of Puerto Rico, and promptly seized control of the island. On August 12, an armistice announced the suspension of hostilities, almost two months after the first landing in Cuba. In December 1898, Spain and the United States completed negotiations for the Treaty of Paris, formally ending the "Spanish-American War."

Intervention and Intent

We are coming, Cuba, coming: we are bound to set you free!
We are coming from the mountains, from the plains and inland sea!
We are coming with the wrath of God to make the Spaniards flee!
We are coming, Cuba, coming; coming now!
—Evan M. Jones, *We Are Coming, Cuba, Coming!* (1898)

Cheers and waving handkerchiefs and laughing girls sped the troops on their way....
The atmosphere of the country was one of a great national picnic where each one
was expected to carry his own lunch. ... For youth the Spanish-American War was a
great adventure; for the nation it was a diversion sanctioned by a high purpose.
—Carl Russell Fish, *The Path of Empire* (1919)   *a diversion from what?*

None of us thought that [the U.S. intervention] would be followed by a military
occupation of the country by our allies, who treat us as a people incapable of acting
for ourselves, and who have reduced us to obedience, to submission, and to a
tutelage imposed by force of circumstances. This cannot be our ultimate fate after
years of struggle.
—Máximo Gómez (June 1899)

We have taken the responsibility of freeing them from Spain; we are equal to the
responsibility of deciding whether they are capable of governing themselves. If they
can maintain government as we understand the term,—that is, if they can give
security to persons and property, assure religious toleration, and guarantee freedom of thought and expression,—our specific obligations to them are at an end; if
not, then we shall have to continue to regard ourselves as their guardians.
—Andrew S. Draper, *The Rescue of Cuba* (1899)

[The Platt Amendment] if carried out, would inflict a grievous wrong on the people of
Cuba, would rob them of that independence for which they have sacrificed so much
blood and treasure, and would be in direct violation of the letter and purpose of the

solemn pledge of the people of the United States to the world as consigned in the Joint Resolution.
—Salvador Cisneros Betancourt,
An Appeal to the American People on Behalf of Cuba (1900)

Politically, the people are quite untrained; for, during the long rule of Spain, there was practically no opportunity of learning how to work free institutions. . . . They have had hardly any means of learning who are their own best men, and, in this respect, it is unfortunate for them that they did not achieve their liberty by their unaided exertion, for, in the process of winning it, the men of the most natural capacity for politics would probably have been brought to the front.
—*North American Review* (April 1902)

The United States entered into war amid great excitement and enthusiasm. It was a popular war, it has been affirmed often. That the public imagination could persuade itself that the call to arms represented a summons to deliver an oppressed New World people from the clutches of an Old World tyranny served to consecrate the virtue of the U.S. purpose. Off to war Americans went in defense of Cuba Libre, they believed, a lofty and selfless undertaking, in a spirit of exalted purposefulness, confident in their mission of liberation.

The proposition of war in behalf of Cuban independence took hold immediately and held on thereafter. Such was the sense of the public mood. Such, too, was the power of the Teller Amendment to insinuate the intent of liberation as the dominant representation of the U.S. purpose. Certainly contemporary popular narratives celebrated the call to arms as a project of deliverance. "The war between the United States of America and Spain," exulted schoolteacher James Henry Brownlee in 1898, ". . . will be known in history as the War for Humanity." *Harper's Weekly* described the "popular movement in this country" and the "wild frenzy of desire" to free Cuba, adding: "The horrible tales . . . have fired the imaginations of our people, and have made them ready to incur the miseries and horrors of war in behalf of a struggling people."[1]

There is no reason to doubt the authenticity of popular perceptions of purpose in 1898. Americans did appear to feel personally and collectively addressed by the plight of the Cuban people. In the realm of public discourse the war was indeed about the right of the "people of Cuba . . . to be free and independent." Popular music of the time is rich with allusions to war in behalf of Cuban independence. Titles alone are suggestive. "Cuba Shall Be Free," "Set Cuba Free," "Fighting for Cuba," "Columbia," "Make Cuba Free," and "For the Boys Who Have Gone to Set Cuba Free" are only some of the many hundreds of songs written to celebrate the cause of Cuba Libre. The lyric of "Cuba Must Be Free!" proclaimed the mission of liberation explicitly:

'Tis ours to take up Cuba's plea.
'Tis ours to snap the tyrant's chain,
'Tis ours to make the Cubans free,
'Tis ours to break the yoke of Spain.[2]

The voice of "We Are Coming with Old Glory" addressed Cuba directly:

We have heard you, Cuba, heard you,
And your cry is not in vain;
We are coming now to free you
From the tyranny of Spain!
We are coming!
We are coming!
We are coming with Old Glory
To o'er turn the rule of Spain![3]

"Cuban Battle Song" announced that "Ev'ry boom of ev'ry gun / Tells an hour of tyrants done; Tells an hour of Freedom won: Cuba Shall be Free!" The "Song of Our Nation" exulted:

Yes, we'll fight and we'll die with stars and stripes on high
We fight for the cause of Cuba.
She shall nevermore belong to the Spaniards ever wrong
That we fight and die for Cuba."[4]

In "Freedom for Cuba" the sacrifice of American lives was proclaimed worth the cost:

We will rally at the call boys,
And Cuba shall be free.
   Shouting the battle cry, "Free Cuba!"
Though it cost our life and blood
We will give her liberty,
   Shouting the battle cry, "Free Cuba!"[5]

The pages of newspapers and magazines were filled with solemn outpourings in the form of poems and odes eulogizing the cause of Cuba Libre. The poem "War" appeared in the *Cincinnati Commercial Tribune*:

Now, once again, the great sword awes
   The despot—flames o'er land and sea—

> A volunteer in Cuba's cause:
> Spain falls and Cuba rises free![6]

In "Hail Our Glorious Banner," Thomas Sullivan identified freedom for Cuba as the central issue of the war:

> We hold one purpose, steadfast, sure; this war
>   shall never cease
> Till Cuba's isle shall Freedom know: but, when
>   our task is done,
> With joy we'll crown our battle flags with garland
>   wreaths of peace,
> With charity for all, and malice toward none.[7]

George E. Woodberry made the purpose of liberation explicit in his poem "The Islands of the Sea":

> Be jubilant, free Cuba, our feet are on your soil;
> Up mountain road, through jungle growth, our
>   bravest for thee toil;
> There is no blood so precious as their wounds pour
>   forth for thee
> Sweet be thy joys, free Cuba—sorrows have made
>   thee free.[8]

The letters, diaries, and journals of the men who rushed to volunteer for military service in Cuba similarly provide powerful corroboration of the extent to which the cause of Cuba Libre moved a people to action. Among the reasons Corporal Harry Ross cited for volunteering was "to assist in freeing these half-half starved, half-clad Cubans." Captain Joseph H. McDermott used his time at sea en route to Cuba to reflect on his role in the larger national purpose and concluded: "We can't fully realize that we are taking part in one of the greatest undertakings ever instigated by this country." Many years later, poet Carl Sandburg recalled wistfully his decision to volunteer for military service in the Sixth Infantry Regiment of Illinois. "I read about the . . . people of Cuba who wanted independence and a republic," he wrote. "I read about Gómez, García, the Maceos, with their scrabbling little armies fighting against Weyler. They became heroes to me. I tried to figure a way to get down there and join one of those armies." Sandburg continued: "I was going along with millions of other Americans who were about ready for a war to throw the Spanish government out of Cuba and let the people of

Cuba have their republic. If a war did come and men were called to fight it, I knew what I would do." More than thirty years later, editor Oswald Garrison Villard recalled how "we were naturally all in favor of the Cuban demand for self-government, sympathized with the rebels, and severely criticized the Spanish offer of autonomy made in the fall of 1897."[9]

The popular fiction of the time and later years similarly evoked Cuba Libre as the salient story line. In the Gertrude Atherton novel *Senator North* (1901), the protagonist proclaims astonishment at the extent of popular enthusiasm for the Cuban cause. "The pressure upon us has been intolerable," Senator North comments and adds: "Both Houses have been flooded with petitions and memorials by the thousands: from Legislatures, Chambers of Commerce, Societies, Churches, from associations of every sort, and from perhaps a million citizens. The Capitol looks like a paper factor. . . . The average Congressman and even Senator does not resist the determined pressure of his constituents, and to do them justice they have talked themselves into believing that they are as excited as the idle minds at home who are feeling dramatic and calling it sympathy." In the Edward Stratemeyer novel *Young Volunteer in Cuba* (1898), the narrator describes protagonist Ben Russell as "patriotic to the core, and [who] from the very start had taken a deep interest in the struggles of the people of Cuba to throw off the yoke of Spanish tyranny and oppression." Ben speaks for himself on volunteering for military service: "We owe it to the Cubans and to the cause of humanity to expel the Spanish from Cuba. The poor fellows down there have been fighting for their freedom for three years, and they deserve to have it." At another point, he says: "I've been reading up on this war trouble every day, and I'm going to help the Cubans to freedom and help give Spain the thrashing she deserves." In *Shackles Cast* (1912), novelist Alvan Elmar Clarendon attributes Chester Fenton's decision to volunteer for the Rough Riders to the desire "to serve his country and help Cuba—to set it free." In the novel *Crittenden: A Kentucky Story of Love and War* (1911), John Fox Jr. speaks through his protagonist: "It was, he said, the first war of its kind in history. It marked an epoch in the growth of national character since the world began. As an American, he believed that no finger of mediaevalism should so much as touch this hemisphere. The Cubans had earned their freedom long since, and the cries of starving women and children for the bread which fathers and brothers asked but the right to earn must cease." This theme serves as the story line in Joseph Hergesheimer's *The Bright Shawl* (1922), where the protagonist proclaims: "I came to Cuba to fight the cursed Spanish. . . . Cuba ought to be free; this oppression is horrible."[10]

• • •

These were powerful images, as irresistible as they were incontrovertible. The cause of Cuba Libre could not but have inspired noble hearts. The Cuban struggle was in full public view, reported in the press daily, exploited on the front pages and exalted in editorials. Much of what passed for "yellow journalism" was, in fact, highly charged and sensational support of the Cuban cause.[11] Cuba Libre had indeed captured the popular imagination and served as a potent means by which to rally public support for war.

The Teller Amendment reflected the popular mood in 1898, a way to give form to moral support to the cause of Cuba Libre. It would be unduly facile, however, to conclude that the McKinley administration would have suddenly renounced nearly a century-long policy, one based on the proposition that Cuban independence was inimical to U.S. interests, solely as a result of a self-denying resolution adopted by, many felt, an overzealous Congress in a moment of war fervor. "Personally . . . ," explained Whitelaw Reid, publisher of the *New York Tribune*, "I have always regarded the resolution of Congress, at the outbreak of the war a grave mistake." He continued: "Seventy-five years of our diplomacy on this subject has pointed steadily to this—the absolute necessity of controlling Cuba for our own defense. To announce at the outset that we were going to drive Spain out and then preclude ourselves from this control was a self-denying ordinance possible only in a moment of national hysteria and as little likely to be kept to the letter as was Mr. Gladstone's pledge, twenty years ago, to leave Egypt."[12] Former secretary of state Richard Olney denounced the Teller Amendment as "ill-advised and futile," adding that "no such resolution can refute the logic of the undisputed facts or should be allowed to impede the natural march of events." For Olney, the anomaly of a free Cuba could only end—"the sooner the better"—when Congress made "Cuba in point of law what she already is in point of fact, namely, United States territory." Senator Albert J. Beveridge quickly repented his support of the Teller Amendment, passed "in a moment of impulsive but mistaken generosity," and predicted that "it will not be kept." In a "personal and confidential" letter to U.S. planter Edwin Atkins in 1901, Senator Orville Platt fumed against "that foolish Teller resolution" that "stands not only in the way of [annexation], but all other action which we might take if it had never been passed." General James H. Wilson, the military governor of Matanzas province during the U.S. military occupation of Cuba (1899–1902), insisted that the Teller Amendment was "an unnecessary and serious mistake," an impediment that required the United States to seek a "different course" by which to acquire Cuba. Wilson urged a policy of "Americanization [of] the island" and predicted: "If my views are carried into effect, Cuba will be in the Union within ten years."[13]

The McKinley administration had vigorously opposed any recognition of Cuban independence but in the end understood the necessity of yielding to congressional demands. Acquiescence to the Teller Amendment, however, did not signal acceptance of the proposition of Cuban independence. On the contrary, the administration never wavered in its determination to resist, restrict, or otherwise reduce the possibility of Cuban independence, by way of either a military victory by the insurgent army or a political resolution of the U.S. Congress.

In fact, the purpose of 1898 was consummated in 1901, and it was in the course of the intervening three years that the larger implications of 1898 emerged in sharp relief. The vogue of Cuba Libre soon waned after the war. Spain had been roundly defeated and expelled from Cuba, and insofar as "independence" had been associated with the expulsion of Spain, it did indeed appear that good intentions had yielded good results.

The question of Cuban independence, of course, had not been resolved. In the weeks and months that followed the cessation of hostilities, the McKinley administration moved determinedly to evade, circumvent, or otherwise nullify the purpose if not the purport of the Teller Amendment. Cubans were simply not ready to govern themselves, U.S. officials proclaimed after the war. "Self-government!" General William Shafter thundered in response to a reporter's question. "Why those people are no more fit for self-government than gunpowder is for hell." General Samuel Young insisted that "the insurgents are a lot of degenerates, absolutely devoid of honor or gratitude. They are no more capable of self-government than the savages of Africa." General William Ludlow agreed. "We are dealing here in Cuba," he reported to Washington, "with a relatively uninstructed population, whose sensibilities are easily aroused but who lack judgment, who are wholly unaccustomed to manage their own affairs, and who readily resort to violence when excited or thwarted. . . . The whole structure of society and business is still on too slender and tottering basis to warrant putting any additional strain upon it."[14]

The implications were clearly drawn. The United States could hardly release Cuba into the family of nations so utterly ill-prepared for responsibilities in self-government. One cabinet member announced bluntly that President McKinley did not intend to expel Spain only to turn the island "over to the insurgents or any other particular class or faction." General Leonard Wood, the U.S. military governor of Cuba, articulated administration thinking succinctly. "When the Spanish-American war was declared," he insisted, "the United States took a step forward, and assumed a position as protector of the interests of Cuba. It became responsible for the welfare of the people, politically, mentally and morally."[15]

• • •

The rationale to retain control over Cuba was established immediately after the war and found justification in the very congressional resolution that had promised independence. The Joint Resolution was reexamined and reinterpreted. Had not the Teller Amendment stipulated the necessity for "pacification"? Swift and striking, the new consensus formed around the proposition that "pacification" implied more than simply the cessation of hostilities. It also meant stability. "It is true," editorialized the *Philadelphia Inquirer*, "that the Congressional resolutions . . . set forth that we, as a nation, had no designs upon Cuba, and that our sole object was to free it. But these resolutions went further. They also declared it to be our intention to see to it that a stable government should be formed." The *New York Times* made a similar point, but with far more ominous implications: "The pledge we made by no means binds us to withdraw at once, nor does full and faithful compliance with its spirit and letter forbid us to become permanent possessors of Cuba if the Cubans prove to be altogether incapable of self-government. A higher obligation than the pledge of the resolution of Congress would then constrain us to continue our government of the island." The United States, insisted the *New York Tribune*, "is not repudiating, but is scrupulously and exactly fulfilling the obligation it assumed in the Act of Intervention. It did not then recognize the independence or sovereignty of the so-called Cuban Republic. It did not promise to establish that republic, or to put the insurgents in control of the island. It avowed the intention of pacifying the island." The implications if not the intention of these propositions were not lost on McKinley confidant Charles Dawes. " 'Until pacified' "— Dawes reflected privately in his diary. "The latter logically under conditions now and hereafter to exist in Cuba means ultimate annexation."[16]

The meaning of the Teller Amendment, which once had seemed so explicit and so clear, now became ambiguous and vague. "Pacification" soon came to mean many different things, as circumstances warranted. "What does 'pacification' mean in that clause?" Senator Orville Platt asked rhetorically two years after the war had ended. "We became responsible for the establishment of a government there, which we would be willing to endorse to the people of the world—a stable government, a government for which we would be willing to be responsible in the eyes of the world." And at another point, Platt insisted: " 'Pacification' of the 'island' manifestly meant the establishment in that island of a government capable of adequately protecting life, liberty and property." Attention—and emphasis—shifted from "independence" to "pacification." "The master-factor of the whole problem lies in the phrases already quoted, 'except for the pacification' and 'when that is accomplished,' " the *New York Tribune* explained as early as August 7, 1898, adding: "We have gone into Cuba to pacify it, and we are under no obligation, legal or moral, expressed or implied, to leave it until it is fully pacified. On the contrary, we under the strongest possible obligation, legal and moral, expressed and implied, not to leave it until it is fully pacified."[17]

There was, perhaps, no clearer explanation of the original intent of the Joint Resolution at the time of its passage than that offered by Senator Joseph Benson Foraker in an article dated April 28, 1898, and published in *The Forum* the following June. "The resolutions meant the absolute and unqualified independence of the Cubans," Foraker explained ten days after the passage of the Joint Resolution, "with the right to establish their own government without let or hindrance from us or anybody else." But Foraker, too, seems to have had a change of mind or possibly a lapse in memory. Writing almost two decades later, he recalled that although "we had pledged to the Cubans a free and independent government . . . that did not mean that we would or should be indifferent as to the kind of government they established; nor did it mean that the relations between the two countries should not be clearly defined and properly and permanently established."[18]

Many reasons were given to fear Cuban independence. Cuba had to be protected from pernicious forces, whether they originated from the outside or especially from those that might arise from within. "If it is our business to see that the Cubans are not destroyed by any foreign power," Senator Beveridge asked in 1901, "is it not our duty to see that they are not destroyed by themselves?" "We have pledged ourselves to give Cuba independence," conceded journalist Herbert P. Williams in 1899. But the results, he predicted grimly, "will be disorder, fierce contention between the leaders, and then civil war of the old familiar guerrilla kind, degenerating into butchery," and thereby "expose" large sectors of the law abiding residents "to the fury of the negroes, and the other inflammable elements . . . which the demagogues will stir up." Congressman Town-send Scudder made the point explicitly:

> Our dominant purpose [in 1898] was that of destroying a regime under which savagery flourished . . . and setting up instead the machinery of a true and lasting civilization. We shall not discharge in honor the duty we have voluntarily assumed by a mere technical observance of the Teller resolution. We have promised to Cuba peace, order, equal rights, security for life and property, justice, and material progress. Does any sane man believe that these results are likely to be attained by . . . surrendering the destinies of the island to the former insurgent leaders?[19]

Once stability was subsumed into the meaning of the Teller Amendment, independence itself became a condition over which the United States claimed authority to recognize, restrict, or regulate, as circumstances warranted. Stability, like pacification, underwent repeated redefinition. It did not signify simply political order. It came to imply a condition capable of inspiring public confidence and encouraging private investment. General Leonard Wood characterized stability wholly as a condition of "business confidence." "The people ask me what we mean by stable government in Cuba," he explained to Secretary of War Elihu Root in early 1900. "I tell them that when money can be borrowed at a reasonable rate of interest and when capital is willing to invest in the island, a condition of stability will have been reached." Wood offered a similar definition to President McKinley: "When people ask me what I mean by stable government, I tell them 'money at six percent.'"[20]

By 1901 the definition of pacification had undergone final transfiguration as an extension of U.S. interests. What circumstances would satisfy U.S. notions of "pacification," the *Philadelphia Inquirer* asked—and answered: "As soon as the Cubans show themselves able and ready to govern the Island in accordance with American principles of order, liberty, and justice, it is to be assumed that this Government will be ready to fulfill its pledge and relinquish control to them. It is not to be assumed that it will do so one day before that time." Leonard Wood was unequivocal. To end the occupation without having established prior control over Cuba, Wood predicted, would be tantamount to inviting European powers to occupy every harbor of the island. The United States demanded some definition of a "special relationship" as a precondition for the completion of "pacification," and hence compliance with "independence." And this "special relationship" necessarily required defining the terms by which the new government of Cuba would be obliged to act in a manner consistent with U.S. interests, even if this meant violating the spirit of the Teller Amendment. The United States, Secretary of War Elihu Root explained years later, insisted on "vitalizing the advice" to be offered to the Cuban government. " 'Advice' meant, in this connection, more than the advice a man might give to his client; it meant 'enforceable advice,' like the advice which Great Britain might give to Egypt." Senator Platt expressed his preference for "very much more stringent measures" but understood, too, that "when they concede to us the right of intervention and naval stations . . . that the United States gets an effective moral position, and which becomes something more than a moral position." Platt was categorical. "All that we have asked," he responded in defense of the amendment that would bear his name, "is that the mutual relations [between Cuba and the United States] shall be defined and acknowledged coincidentally with the setting up of Cuba's new government. In no other way could a stable government be assured in Cuba, and until such assurance there could be no complete 'pacification' of the island, and no surrender of its control."[21]

The passage of the Platt Amendment in 1901 fulfilled the U.S. purpose. The new Cuban republic was to be shorn of all essential properties of sovereignty prior to its creation. The Cuban government was denied authority to enter into "any treaty or other compact with any foreign power or powers," denied, too, the authority to contract a public debt beyond its normal ability to repay, and obliged to cede national territory to accommodate a U.S. naval station. Lastly, Cubans were required to concede to the United States "the right to intervene" for the "maintenance of a government adequate for the protection of life, property and individual liberty."[22]

News of the Platt Amendment provoked widespread protests in Cuba. Anti-U.S. demonstrations spread across the island. Cubans took to the streets in organized demonstrations and rallies to denounce the Platt Amendment. Municipalities, civic associations, and veterans organizations on the island cabled their protests to U.S. authorities. "Representatives of all social classes in impressive manifestation," Mayor Leopoldo Figueroa of Cienfuegos appealed directly to President McKinley, "ask me to transmit to you the persistent desire for absolute independence of Cuba." The Sancti-Spíritus Council of Veterans registered its "profound displeasure" with the Platt Amendment, and the Regla municipal council pleaded with Secretary Root "to comply with the terms of the Joint Resolution." Federal Party president Pelayo García called for the "complete fulfillment of the Joint Resolution which embodies the constant aspiration of the Cuban people, that for which they have sacrificed so many lives and wasted so much property."[23] This display of public opposition strengthened the resolve of the constituent assembly, to which the task of approving the Platt Amendment was presented, to reject the amendment. A naval squadron was prepared for a "courtesy call" to Havana. General Wood became uneasy and cabled Root for instructions: "Can you indicate our action in case convention refuses to accept Platt Amendment?"[24]

North American authorities remained unmoved. Acceptance of the Platt Amendment, Cubans were told, was the minimum condition for ending the military occupation. "We should . . . make our requests and desires known to Cuba," Representative Scudder insisted, "and thereafter, if necessary, these requests should be put in the form of an ultimatum. . . . The probability is that Cuba will yield; but if she does not do so readily, then our troops must remain until an absolute understanding is reached." Elihu Root was equally adamant. "Under the act of Congress they can never have any further government in Cuba, except the intervening Government of the United States until they have acted," Root pronounced. "No constitution can be put into effect in Cuba, and no government can be elected under it, no electoral law by the Convention can be put into effect, and no election held under it until they have acted upon this question." Root's point was unambiguous: "There is only one possible way for them to bring about the termination of the military government and make either the constitution or electoral law effective; that is to do the whole duty they were elected for."[25]

Cubans eventually acquiesced. The choice before the assembly, delegate Manuel Sanguily understood, was limited independence or no independence at all. "Independence with restrictions is preferable to the [U.S.] military regime," he explained in casting his vote to accept the Platt Amendment. Enrique Villuendas agreed. "There is no use objecting to the inevitable," he conceded. "It is either annexation or a Republic with an amendment."[26] The Platt Amendment was incorporated into the Cuban Constitution of 1901 as an appendix and subsequently ratified into fixed bilateral relations by way of the Permanent Treaty of 1903.

• • •

This, then, was the final form in which the "independence" pledged by the Joint Resolution of Congress was delivered. The conditions imposed on the exercise of Cuban nationhood rendered meaningless all but the most cynical definition of independence. The Platt Amendment deprived the republic of the essential properties of sovereignty while preserving the appearance of independence, permitting self-government but precluding self-determination. "There is, of course, little or no independence left in Cuba under the Platt Amendment," Leonard Wood acknowledged to Theodore Roosevelt in a moment of private candor in late 1901. And more to the point, he advised: "The only consistent thing to do now is to seek annexation."[27] A disconsolate General Máximo Gómez understood well what had happened. "The Republic will surely come," he wrote to a friend in May 1901, "but not with the absolute independence we had dreamed about."[28]

The Platt Amendment thus brought the U.S. purpose in 1898 to a successful conclusion. National interests were guaranteed, not—to be sure—by way of the direct succession of sovereignty so long foreseen. On the other hand, neither did sovereignty pass to a third party. The United States went to war, as it always said it would, to prevent the transfer of sovereignty of Cuba, in this instance to the Cubans themselves. "I am constrained to vote for the [Platt] amendment . . . ," Congressman John B. Corliss announced as he cast his vote, "because I believe that the adoption thereof will insure the continuance of our sovereignty. I am unalterably opposed to the surrender of the sovereignty of the United States over the island of Cuba. . . . I voted for that [Teller] resolution and intend thereby to extend to them the same liberty, freedom, and independence enjoyed by the citizens of our own territory. What greater liberty, freedom, and independence can be obtained than that enjoyed under the protection of our flag?"[29]

The United States thus acted in defense of long-standing national interests. Cuba had insinuated itself into some of the most important policy initiatives of the nineteenth century, explained and expounded, again and again, and passed into those spheres of policy where assumptions shaped anticipations. They assumed the power of a larger logic that ceased to be apprehended as anything other than self-evident truths.

The perceptions of war in 1898, however, did not enter the realm of public comprehension as a defense of national interests but rather as the discharge of moral responsibilities, of ideals upheld, of sentimental formulations—a war for humanity, for example—which early seized hold of the popular narratives and professional discourses as the dominant representations of the U.S. purpose. Central and essential to these formulations was the proposition of intervention undertaken explicitly in pursuit of a higher purpose, principally in the form of Cuban independence.

The proposition of Cuban independence as objective and outcome of

1898 has long enjoyed a dominant position in the historiography of the war. Indeed, war as a deliberate undertaking, if admitted at all, possessed of rationale and rationality, a war willed and waged with forethought of purpose and object, has found its most enduring representation as an act in behalf of Cuban independence. The difference between, on one hand, the end of Spanish rule and, on the other, the exercise of Cuban sovereignty early lost all distinction, as if to imply that the latter was synonymous with the former. Americans then and thereafter could celebrate the self-proclaimed selflessness with which the nation went to war and obtained Cuban independence. Fifteen years later Theodore Roosevelt could unflinchingly continue to sustain the proposition of Cuban independence. "We made the promise to give Cuba independence," he proclaimed in his *Autobiography*, "and we kept that promise."[30]

Explanatory narratives of 1898 have not typically represented the war as a defense of national interests, in which intervention sought to obstruct the Spanish relinquishment of sovereignty to Cubans, that is, war as a response to specific circumstances, precisely as the United States had always threatened. On the contrary, the war has been represented largely as an undertaking to obtain Cuban independence.

In fact, the proposition of war in behalf of Cuba Libre lacks coherent logic. The depiction of the United States as undertaking national mobilization for war to obtain independence for Cubans runs directly counter to the central tenets of nearly one hundred years of U.S. policy. If, in fact, this was the U.S. purpose in 1898, then it would have represented a remarkable reversal of long-standing policy tenets of the nineteenth century, of such magnitude that it would itself demand explanation. What factors, in short, would have persuaded the United States to abandon one hundred years of strategic thinking?

That Cuban independence was neither the objective of the intervention or the outcome of the war has not found a place in U.S. historiography. The imposition of the Platt Amendment in 1901 as both a condition of and a constraint on the "independence" pledged in the Joint Resolution has passed largely unnoticed in the historical literature. Indeed, it is not at all clear that U.S. historians have fully understood the extent to which the Platt Amendment restricted the independence to which the United States committed itself in 1898. There have been a number of notable exceptions, to be sure, but in the main historians have routinely propounded the fiction that the pledge of "independence" had been fulfilled, apparently unmindful of or indifferent to the ways that the Platt Amendment negated the project of Cuba Libre.[31]

With the end of the military occupation, R. D. W. Connor proclaimed, "Cuba was at last free and independent." Mabel B. Casner and Ralph Henry Gabriel similarly insisted that, "according to its promise, the United States withdrew the American soldiers and made Cuba independent." John Holladay Latané and David W. Wainhouse were unabashedly exuberant: "Never has a pledge made by a nation under such circumstances been more faithfully carried out." James Ford Rhodes affirmed in 1922 that the "pledge contained in the Teller amendment was faithfully kept." Seventy years later Gary Nash et al. continued to insist that the "United States honored Cuban independence, as it had promised to do in the Teller Amendment." The military occupation of Cuba ended in 1902, affirmed William Wood and Ralph Henry Gabriel, whereupon "the pledge of the nation, given at the time of the declaration of the war on Spain, had been redeemed." Randolph Greenfield Adams pointed with pride to "one of the most creditable pages in American foreign policy," when the United States kept its promise to make Cuba "a free and independent nation," and Ralph Henry Gabriel on another occasion could characterize the military occupation (1899–1902) as a "period of aid," whereupon Cuba "was established as an independent nation." H. Wayne Morgan was categorical. "In 1902 the Cuban Republic became independent," he affirmed, although he did acknowledge in the next sentence that a kind of "supervision" lasted until 1934, without mentioning the Platt Amendment by name. Robert E. Welch Jr. wrote in similar terms, depicting the U.S. purpose in 1898 as "necessary to end an intolerable situation, free Cuba from Spanish misrule, and put the island on its feet as an independent nation." But Welch also felt obliged to acknowledge in a passing but otherwise unobtrusive caveat that "independence . . . should be obtained under American tutelage so that Cuba would have a government stable and sensible as well as independent." John A. S. Grenville and George Berkeley Young could, on one hand, refer to McKinley's devotion to "his duty to the Cubans" and the demand that Spain "grant Cuba its independence," and yet in another paragraph give historiographical credibility to policy constructions of the McKinley administration: "Many knowledgeable Americans doubted whether the Cubans were really ready for self-government and feared that immediate independence would create fresh problems for the United States. McKinley shared these fears and inclined to the view that the Cubans would first have to pass through a period of American tutelage before they could be trusted to make wise use of a representative government."[32]

Nor is it simply or solely that the implications of the Platt Amendment on the exercise of sovereignty have not been fully understood. In fact, considerable energy has been expended to reconcile the constraints of the Platt Amendment with the commitment of the Teller Amendment. John A. Garraty disposed of the contradiction in peremptory fashion, but only after having first ignored the "free and independent" clause in the Joint Resolution as the proclaimed purpose of the intervention, to suggest instead that "the purpose of the Spanish-American War" was "to bring peace and order to Cuba." Garraty concluded that "[t]he Platt Amendment was a logical step." Richard H. Collin sought to reconcile the obvious contradiction between the promise (Teller) and the product (Platt) by arguing both sides of the issue. "Americans were both idealistic and practical," he suggested. Collin, in fact, began with the assumption that independence was untenable, whereupon he proceeded to fashion an imaginative but implausible rationale. "Most businessmen shrank from giving Cuba absolute freedom," he argued, "for fear that Cubans would seize American property or, equally onerous, that revolutionaries would take control of trade relations between the United States and Cuba." What Collin may have had in mind by alluding to revolutionaries taking "control of trade relations" is not clear. The proposition that Cubans threatened to "seize American property," moreover, was utterly fatuous. With these dubious propositions in place, however, Collin could complete his case by arguing that "[l]imited autonomy and responsibility were good pragmatic American solutions for maintaining enough control for practical purposes." Frederic L. Paxson argued that "Cuba came into possession of an independence limited only by restrictions against self-destruction and an American guarantee of law and order." Paul L. Haworth conceded that the "general effect" of the Platt Amendment was "to make Cuba a protectorate of the United States," but he hastened to add: "The United States has never . . . exercised its protectorate in a manner contrary to the interests of the Cuban people." And still, even after having conceded, in a fashion, the condition of protectorate, Haworth could conclude: "On May 20, 1902 . . . the last American troops sailed from the island, and the new republic formally entered upon her independent existence. Thus closed one of the most admirable chapters in human annals."[33]

These have been among the most compelling historiographical representations of 1898: a nation aroused by a noble mission, inspired to defend the cause of Cuban independence. That these are, in fact, debatable if not dubious formulations does not, of course, reduce the authenticity of popular support of Cuba Libre. On the contrary, vast numbers of men and women who were party to and participants in 1898 acted in good faith, persuaded that the U.S. purpose was both righteous and rightful. Indeed, careful and nuanced studies of 1898 have been careful to draw fine but important distinctions between popular persuasions and policy purpose. There is, in fact, little reason to disagree with Julius W. Pratt's observation that "[a]s far as the American public was concerned, intervention, if it came, should be intervention for *Cuba libre*—for a Cuba free and independent, not a Cuba transformed from a colony of Spain to a colony of the United States." In the same way, David F. Trask's observation that the "American people went to war convinced that they had embarked upon an entirely selfless mission for humanity" was well-founded, as was John M. Dobson's assertion that "public opinion in the United States swung behind the rebel cause." J. Rogers Hollingsworth was absolutely correct in his carefully phrased observation that "the American people were convinced that the nation had entered the war for purely humanitarian reasons, and they immediately rallied behind the government."[34]

That public opinion seemed so powerfully arrayed on the side of Cuba Libre, in behalf of Cuban independence, however, has also served as a means by which to take a larger leap of faith and validate the proposition of a policy designed as a project of liberation. Cognitive thresholds were crossed in subtle fashion, almost imperceptibly, as public sentiment was rendered as official policy. Popular narratives and political pronouncements seemed possessed of the capacity to validate themselves and passed directly into the collective memory and thereupon proceeded to inform the assumptions from which historical scholarship was derived. The purpose pronounced in 1898 developed easily enough into the principal explanatory formulations of the war. This necessarily and not surprisingly conceded privileged narrative space to beneficent representations of the U.S. purpose. These were perhaps, under the circumstances, inevitable pronouncements, the stuff by which the national purpose was ennobled and duly consecrated: no sordid imperialist impulses here, no mischievous motives or insidious intentions—rather, selfless service to the cause of humanity and confirmation of the deepening conviction of American exceptionalism.

The historical literature is rich with allusions to popular support for Cuban independence and in the aggregate constitute one of the dominant narratives of 1898. "The Spanish-American War," affirmed Walter T. K. Nugent, "began as an American attempt to bring about the independence of the Cuban people." Foster Rhea Dulles used a similar argument, declaring that "the nation embarked, idealistically, enthusiastically, on its war to establish the independence of Cuba." The war, asserted Wayne S. Cole, "expressed American determination to throw off Old World control in the Western Hemisphere and win independence for the Cubans." Daniel M. Smith forced the argument even further, insisting that McKinley himself "sympathized deeply with the Cuban rebel cause, on humanitarian grounds and because of an ideological aversion to Old World rule and a belief in the virtues of independence and democracy." John Garraty maintained in 1993 that the "Spanish-American War was fought to free Cuba." Two years later Maldwyn A. Jones argued that the United States embarked upon war "to free a colonial people from Old World oppression." David Trask made a similar point: "A humanitarian crusade had attained its prime object, Cuban independence."[35]

The invocation of idealism as a source of war emerged as one of the dominant representations of the U.S. purpose in 1898. For contemporaries, it made for self-validating notions about the nobility of the nation, the higher moral ground by which the United States defined its purpose in world affairs. The proposition of war in defense of freedom and liberty was not without self-confirming appeal, of course. Political leaders especially were fond of proclaiming the generosity of purpose with which the United States went to war. The war, Secretary of War Russell A. Alger maintained, was inspired by the need of the United States to "discharge . . . its responsibilities to civilization." McKinley confidant Charles G. Dawes years later wrote that the president's purpose was "in accord with the dictates of humanity." It was a war that "was as necessary as it was righteous," asserted John Hay, and "a remarkable altruistic performance," Champ Clark later exulted. Carl Schurz wrote with heartfelt sincerity of a "war of liberation, of humanity, undertaken without any selfish motive, . . . a war of disinterested benevolence." Senator John Spooner was eloquent in his appeal to conscience. "We intervene to put an end to savagery," Spooner maintained during the debate over the Joint Resolution. "We intervene because, as a Christian nation at the end of the nineteenth century, we cannot stand it any longer in the sight of God." He concluded: "We intervene . . . not for conquest, not for aggrandizement, not because of the Monroe doctrine; we intervene for humanity's sake; we intervene to gain security for the future; we intervene to aid a people who have suffered every form of tyranny and who have made a desperate struggle to be free. . . . We intervene upon the highest possible ground."[36]

President McKinley in particular invoked humanitarian motives as the source of U.S. policy. It was, in the end, "in the name of humanity" and "in the name of civilization" that he requested congressional authority "to secure a full and final termination of hostility between the Government of Spain and the people of Cuba." "We took up arms only in obedience to the dictates of humanity," the president insisted, "and in the fulfillment of high public and moral obligations." Repeatedly, he explained the U.S. purpose in the name of "humanity and the advance of civilization." On one occasion, he said: "We went to war, not because we wanted to, but because humanity demanded it." McKinley asserted: "We went [to war] only that we might relieve the Cuban people of an oppression under which they had been suffering for years—our neighbors, close to us, almost on our very borders. We went to war that we might give them relief. . . . [W]e must carry the burden, whatever it may be, in the interest of civilization, humanity, and liberty."[37]

Certainly this was a view with which most contemporary writers agreed. "The war between the United States and Spain was, in brief," proclaimed Alexander K. McClure and Charles Morris two years later in their biography of McKinley, "a war for humanity, for America could no longer close her ears to the wails of the starving people who lay perishing, as may be said, on her very doorsteps. It was not for conquest or gain, nor was it in revenge for the awful destruction of the *Maine*." Woodrow Wilson was especially receptive to this formulation, and in his *History of the American People* (1902) he maintained that the war was "not for the material aggrandizement of the United States, but for the assertion of the right of the government to succor those who seemed hopelessly oppressed."[38] "If ever there was a war that was entered into purely from motives of humanity and with no thought of conquest," affirmed A. D. Hall in 1898, "it was this one." He continued: "The entire people of the United States were agreed that their purpose was a holy one. . . . War is justifiable, when waged, as the present one unquestionably is, from purely unselfish motives, simply from a determination to rescue a people whose suffering had become unbearable to them and to the lookers-on. The United States, by its actions, has set a lesson for the rest of the world, which the latter will not be slow to learn and for which future generations will bless the name of America."[39] William James was equally emphatic. "The basis of it all is . . . ," he wrote in June 1898, "perfectly honest humanitarianism, and an absolute disinterested desire on the part of our people to set the Cubans free." Novelist Jack London was certain that the war was "a stroke against monarchy & for political democracy."[40]

The purpose proclaimed in 1898 passed directly into the historical literature. In the successive telling and retelling of 1898, the place of noble intentions assumed an ever larger prominence. The literature assumed unabashedly self-congratulatory tones, as the dominant historiographical discourse commemorated selflessness and sacrifice, magnanimity of intention and generosity of purpose, as the source of the U.S. policy. Idealism—not interests—inspired U.S. actions. The Teller Amendment in particular served as a powerful corroboration of the U.S. objective, to which the U.S. scholars could point confidently as proof of purpose. "It reflected both America's idealistic and humanitarian motives in [the] intervention," asserted Daniel M. Smith. Randolph Greenfield Adams rejoiced over the Teller Amendment as a "burst of generous enthusiasm." In the "very declaration of war," Adams exulted, "Congress did a thing which will forever mark the dawn of a new era in international relationships, a thing to which every American may point as an evidence of the fact that America had a mission in world politics which was not sordid, nor materialistic nor merely land-grabbing." The war was waged "in the great cause of humanity," H. Addington Bruce proclaimed. Harold and Margaret Sprout characterized the war as "a crusade to liberate Spain's Cuban colony." Using slightly different imagery, Albert Shaw conveyed the same idea. "We undertook the war as a relief mission," he contended. "Our own grievances were slight and incidental, and we were embarking upon an adventure that was essentially altruistic." Howard Jones agreed, insisting that intervention "in behalf of Cuba's independence seemed justified as a crusade" and that the "the war with Spain was a crusade to free Cuba from Old World Oppression." Arthur Hendrick Vandenburg swelled with pride as he wrote in 1926 of a war undertaken as "one of the loftiest purposed acts in the history of civilization." The gesture," he continued, "compliments the altruism of a nation which . . . is prepared to serve human-kind in its own way and on its own initiative with a purity of dedication unmatched in any other government on earth." More than twenty-five years later Frank Freidel employed elegant prose to celebrate the generosity of the U.S. purpose. "It was a nation innocent of the nature of modern warfare," he wrote in 1958, "and with little inkling of world-power politics that so boldly and idealistically set forth to punish Spain for her mistreatment of her Cuban colony." At another point Freidel insisted that the United States entered into war "to rescue the Cuban people from the Spanish malefactors," for the purpose of "setting forth to right great wrongs, to rescue Cubans from the cruel and wicked grasp of the Spaniards."[41]

Ruhl Bartlett characterized the war as an "act of liberating Cuba from an iniquitous Spanish empire" and "not the acquisition of territory, nor economic advantage, nor imperialism in any form"; A. F. Pollard insisted that "[n]o one imagines that the United States went into the war of 1898 in order to annex the Philippines, or Cuba, or Puerto Rico. The motive was rather humanitarian sentiment." Robert Endicott Osgood affirmed the U.S. purpose in categorical terms: "Americans began the war not out of a realistic calculation of national advantage but largely as an idealistic crusade to free the Cubans from Spain's imperial shackles."[42]

Eventually the representation of the U.S. purpose in 1898 went beyond independence for Cuba to include even loftier objectives. H. Wayne Morgan gave perhaps one of the fullest expressions to this line of argument. The suffering in Cuba, he described the U.S. purpose in 1898, "inevitably and understandably aroused humanitarian sympathy in the United States." This notion of inevitability provided the occasion for Morgan to expound on the national character of the American and its influence on U.S. policy: "generously and honestly endowed with the desire to relieve suffering and to extend to others what he considers the blessings of his way of life." In the conviction that the United States "is history's chosen child," the American believes that it is "not merely a right but a duty" to extend assistance "to the less fortunate." Some "fight for their countries boundaries or to add a province to their nation's domains"; the American, Morgan insisted, is "more easily moved to liberate the provinces of the heart and mind," even when such actions are "averse to his own country's immediate best interests." He added: "But these feelings, so deeply and honestly a part of the nation's history and thought, have been the greatest single force in American foreign policy. Cuba in 1898 was a classic example of their operations." At another point Morgan characterized McKinley's intentions: "Humanitarian desires to relieve the island's suffering, to make it free, and to establish a Latin-American democracy were uppermost in his own mind." Morgan's conclusion was a stirring tribute to the national purpose:

> The nation's movement toward world power and participation in international events, which the Spanish-American War symbolized rather than caused, carried in it potent ideas and ideals that captured the allegiance of most Americans. It promised to carry the dream of freedom to all corners of the world. . . . It fed pride in America's greatness; not merely in military or diplomatic might, but in the goodness of her institutions. . . . Honest indignation at the thought of misery in other lands, and the earnest desire to end cruelty and oppression fortified the general public's belief in the American mission.[43]

These themes appeared often as the dominant historiographical formulations of 1898, as unassailable as they were unquestionable. Allan Keller linked the war to McKinley's angst "that a democratic, freedom-loving nation like the United States could not sit by forever while tyranny and stupidity destroyed the Cuban people." Sam Acheson gave colorful expression to the U.S. purpose: "The Spanish-American War was . . . a natural child of American emotionalism, conceived in that loosely sentimental pocket of the mass mind out of which from time to time issue crusades against the Saracens, attacks on windmills, and wars to end war: in short, the altruistic idealism of civilized beings."[44] Tony Smith suggested that the war was "largely inspired by a [U.S.] determination to stop Spain's repeated abuse of human rights in Cuba" and rescue "Cubans suffering at the hands of the Spanish."[45]

Soon even the Platt Amendment was celebrated as an act of beneficent magnanimity. It was, in the end, in Cuba's best interest. Once more, policy paradigms served to drive historical narratives. It would have been irresponsible for the United States to have conceded complete independence to a population "made up of some pure-blood Spanish, and a mass of negroes and mixed bloods, to a great extent illiterate," contended John Truslow Adams. "There was no 'public,' in the Anglo-Saxon sense, educated and fit for self-government, but there were plenty of the unfortunate type of South Americans who take naturally to political agitation and insurrection." Adams drew the obvious moral: "The Platt Amendment was . . . for the good of the Cuban people, and if we threw to the wind the idealism with which we had started the war, we at least maintained it with regard to Cuba, and gave an example of restraint in leaving the rich 'Pearl of the Antilles' to work out its own destiny in comparative freedom if it could." For John Schutz, it was a matter of Congress defining relations with Cuba "by laying down some apparently sensible restrictions on Cuban independence that permitted North Americans to supervise island affairs," whereas Robert H. Ferrell characterized the Platt Amendment as an "improvement upon [Cubans'] constitutional labors." John S. Bassett observed that "turbulent methods had become habitual to the Cuban masses who were without experience in self-government. Congress, accordingly, devised a restraining mechanism in 1901 in the Platt Amendment."[46]

• • •

The resonance of idealism as an explanation of 1898 had other sources. It could assume a place of prominence in the historical literature precisely because the possibility that the success of the Cuban independence struggle might threaten or in any other way adversely affect U.S. interests was never contemplated. The historiography, in fact, could not imagine that U.S. interests were in any way implicated in the outcome of the Cuban insurrection. The narrative framework of 1898 has thus tended to favor modes of historical explanations derived principally from "realist" paradigms. George F. Kennan argued that the Cuban insurrection "was none of our business," and the United States could "have let things take their course." Kennan added: "Our national security, as we think of it today, was not threatened." David Trask formulated a variation of this argument, insisting that "irrational impulses rather than calculated strategic, economic, ideological, or religious considerations moved [the United States] to a great crusade in defense of *Cuba Libre*." The war of 1898, claimed Norman Graebner, "was not the result of any deliberate weighing of interests and responsibilities," affirming specifically that "the United States had no legitimate cause for declaring war on Spain." Ruhl Bartlett likewise maintained that "the United States had no just cause for war against Spain," and Bernard Bailyn et al. argued that the United States embarked upon war "for no particularly compelling reasons of national interest." William E. Leuchtenburg made the same point with equal directness: "We entered a war in which no vital American interest was involved." The United States, affirmed James C. Bradford, went to war "for an abstract principle [and] out of a sense of moral obligation." Bradford concluded: "The Spanish-American War was the first brought on by consideration for the lives of others, and entry into it marked the first step in what was to constitute a revolution in American foreign relations."[47]

These formulations were themselves a product of the assumptions around which the dominant historiographical representations of 1898 took form. That these narratives passed fully as conventional wisdom about the U.S. purpose—war explicitly in behalf of idealism and moral imperatives—eventually produced a counternarrative in the form of a realist critique of U.S. foreign policy. Accordingly, 1898 was represented as the point at which the United States went astray, when the nation abandoned policy based on rational articulation of national interests to pursue ambiguous and abstract moral principles at the expense of strategic interests. Hans J. Morgenthau was among the first to represent 1898 as the decisive point of deviation at which the United States broke with nineteenth-century traditions. "The intoxication with moral abstractions," Morgenthau wrote, "which as a mass phenomenon started with the Spanish-American War and which in our time has become the prevailing substitute for political thought, is indeed one of the great sources of weakness and failure in American foreign policy." Whereas Thomas Jefferson and John Quincy Adams were represented as upholders of the "realist tradition," acting principally on the basis of "interests," McKinley was depicted as having inaugurated the era of the "moralistic tradition," acting on the basis of sentiment. Morgenthau asserted: "McKinley leads the United States as a great world power beyond the confines of the Western Hemisphere, ignorant of the bearing of this step upon the national interest, and guided by moral principles, completely divorced from the national interest."[48]

Robert Welch made a similar argument, insisting that the war "undoubtedly hastened America's acceptance of international responsibilities, but in equal measure American military successes encouraged a national tendency to confuse the promotion of United States interests with the progress and well-being of other peoples." James M. McCormick agreed, holding in 1992 that the war resulted from Spanish "alleged moral violations," in which "a variety of moral arguments was advanced to justify American actions," adding: "Few arguments for American participation were advanced on the basis of how it might affect the national interest; instead, moral arguments provided the dominant rationale." Robert Endicott Osgood pointed to 1898 as the juncture at which U.S. policy lost its clarity of purpose. The need to guarantee "the nation's ability to survive," Osgood affirmed, required a policy based on "a disposition to perceive and act upon the real conditions under which a nation may achieve its ends in international society." These principles were compromised in 1898, Osgood insisted, in the belief that "standards of personal conduct, including even altruism, were entirely applicable to national conduct; and that these standards were quite compatible with national self-interest." The United States entered the war with a mixture of "self-righteousness and genuine moral fervor," in the form of a "crusade" and a combination of "knight-errantry and national self-assertiveness," in response to "the pitiful plight of the Cuban revolutionists." Osgood argued: "A war to free Cuba from Spanish despotism, corruption, and cruelty, from the filth and disease and barbarity of General 'Butcher' Weyler's reconcentration camps, from the devastation of haciendas, the extermination of families, and the outraging of women; that would be a blow for humanity and democracy." However much this impulse may have been a "product of a compelling conviction, rooted solidly in American character and tradition," the war was also a "product of a policy that militated against a more realistic and wide-spread recognition of the conditions for a stable and effective foreign policy." Osgood concluded: "The nation entered and fought the war with Spain out of a combination of self-assertive egoism and altruistic idealism which was inconsistent with its long-run scale of priorities among national ends and motives."[49]

Norman Graebner depicted 1898 as "a turning point in the history of the Republic," the point at which the United States "deserted . . . those principles of statecraft which had guided it through its first century of independence" and in which "moral abstraction as a mass phenomenon was substituted for the political realism which had circumscribed all previous diplomacy." Graebner maintained that "[f]ew Americans attempted to justify the war against Spain except in humanitarianism." Although such motives were "not strange to American liberal thought," he argued, "before 1898 they had never governed action"; with the "Spanish-American War, moral abstraction as a mass phenomenon was substituted for the political realism that had circumscribed previous American diplomacy." Graebner continued:

> This defiance of American diplomatic experience lay . . . in the decision to anchor such unprecedented national behavior to abstract moral principles rather than to the political wisdom and common sense of the past. This newly acquired sense of moral obligation which propelled the nation on its twentieth-century course in world affairs was totally incompatible with the assumptions and methods which had permitted earlier generations of Americans to defend the perennial interests of the United States with style and distinction. After the events of 1898, the nation no longer possessed an unblurred diplomatic tradition which reached deeply into its own history or which could enlighten the thought and decisions of the future.[50]

In fact, the realist critique was itself derived from and based on a literal if uncritical reading of the dominant historiographical narratives by which 1898 became generally known and comprehended. So well had the story of idealism as the source of U.S. policy been told and retold, that it assumed a logic of its own, self-evident and self-validating. Critics, too, appeared to have made the same normative leaps of faith and proceeded to give new resonance to the old historiographical formulations of 1898.

This scholarly consensus overlooked the long history of North American preoccupation with Cuba. All through the nineteenth century, successive policymakers shared a common view about the future disposition of Cuba. The central policy tenets were defined precisely in terms of national interests, driven by propositions that were perceived as pragmatic. Strategic interests and security, not sentiment, and matters of vital trade and commercial interests, not idealism, informed the dominant policy formulations of the nineteenth century. Policymakers contemplated the prospects of calamity and catastrophe associated with Cuban independence. These were propositions so deeply embedded in U.S. strategic thinking, so universally endorsed and commonly understood, that they passed as self-evident assumptions of U.S. policy.

What changed in 1898 was that an established policy canon having to do with vital national interests entered into the public discourse, subject to political mediation and popular debate. More specifically, popular sentiment did indeed endanger security interests, for rising public sympathy for Cuban independence threatened to undermine a policy with antecedents deep into the nineteenth century. Interests, not idealism, guided the McKinley administration. The president had vigorously opposed the Teller Amendment, and when it seemed that its passage could not be prevented, he settled on alternative means through which to advance U.S. interests. McKinley's war message was noteworthy on several counts. His silence on the question of Cuban independence was striking. He distanced himself from public sentiment. Nor was this simply an oversight. The president defined the role of the United States in the conflict as a "neutral third party" at the precise moment that the public was demanding support of Cuba Libre—not neutrality.

Policy officials associated prominently with the defense of U.S. strategic interests, including Elihu Root, Theodore Roosevelt, Captain Alfred Thayer Mahan, and Senator Henry Cabot Lodge, understood well the strategic and political importance of Cuba to the long-standing project of the Isthmian canal; they also feared for the future stability of the region with a free and independent Cuba. Elihu Root repeatedly invoked "interests" as the driving consideration behind defining the terms of Cuban-U.S. relations, which included the right of U.S. intervention "to maintain a government adequate for protect life, liberty and property" and the establishment of a U.S. naval base on the island. Root was blunt. He understood exactly what "the most obvious meaning" of the Teller Amendment signified and bristled that Congress had "thus so tied the hands of the President by its resolution" that it would have forced the president to abandon "American interests by literal compliance with the obvious terms of the resolution." The United States, Root affirmed categorically, must "insist upon provisions essential to our interests and to the maintenance of international obligations and the protection of property and life in Cuba." He conceded privately that the "most obvious meaning" of the Joint Resolution called for the establishment of an independent government in Cuba to be followed in the ordinary course of events with the negotiation of a treaty of mutual relations. But, Root pondered, what if the Cubans could not be "induced to do voluntarily whatever we think they ought to do?" The administration would find itself forced "to abandon American interests by a literal compliance with the obvious terms of the resolution or must engage in a controversy with Cubans in which they shelter themselves under the resolution of Congress against the Executive." To withdraw in strict compliance with the terms of the Teller Amendment, Root declared, was to place the United States "in a worse condition in regard to our own vital interests than we were while Spain was in possession."[51]

The exercise of power in pursuit of interests in 1898 found its most efficacious representation in appeals to noble instincts and the lofty principles on which Americans understood their political institutions and public transactions to be based. Yale law professor Theodore Salisbury Woolsey, writing only weeks after the passage of the Joint Resolution, contemplated war in terms that would have delighted the realists. "We shall require a foothold in China to compete in trade facilities with other powers," Woolsey affirmed in May 1898. "We should insist upon the exclusive control of a Central American inter-oceanic canal. . . . We should need Cuba as the key to the eastern approach of this canal. We should need coaling stations and dry docks—in other words, fortified and garrison ports—at convenient points in the Pacific and south Atlantic."[52] Senator Stephen Elkins understood the implications of the war in ways that were fully alive to U.S. interests:

> When Cuba shall become a part of the American Union and the isthmian canal shall be completed, which is now assured, Porto Rico, Cuba, Hawaii and the Philippines will be outposts of the great Republic, standing guard over American interests in the track of the world's commerce in its triumphant march around the globe. Our people will soon see and feel that these island possessions belonging to the United States are natural and logical, and in the great part we are to play in the affairs of the world we would not only not give them up but wonder how in the working of our national destiny we could get on without them. This splendid chain of island possessions, reaching half-way around the world, would not be complete without Cuba, the gem of the Antilles.[53]

What, in fact, changed in 1898 was not so much purpose as presentation. Almost all parties to the decision for war seemed determined to subsume strategic interests and security needs into formulations of idealism and altruism. No one less than Theodore Roosevelt, among the most outspoken defenders of "interests," seemed to have persuaded himself—or at least sought to persuade others—of the beneficence of the U.S. purpose in 1898. "Our own direct interests [in Cuba] were great...," Roosevelt remembered years later. "But even greater were our interests from the standpoint of humanity. Cuba was at our very doors. It was a dreadful thing for us to sit supinely and watch her death agony. It was our duty, even more from the standpoint of National honor than from the standpoint of National interest, to stop the devastation and destruction." Captain Mahan, long associated with the pursuit of bases and the defense of trade routes as vital to national interests, who defended publicly and in print the need for an interoceanic canal with Cuba and Hawaii as territories indispensable for the security of such a canal, insisted that "the avowed purpose and cause of our action" were "to enforce the departure of [Spain] from Cuba . . . as its deliverance from oppression was the object of the war." Senator Henry Cabot Lodge had a clearly defined notion of "interests." In 1895 he had invoked "the interests of our commerce and of our fullest development" as the basis on which to urge the development of a canal in Nicaragua, which in turn would require "at least one strong naval station" in the Caribbean. With the completion of the canal, "the island of Cuba, still sparsely settled and of almost unbounded fertility, will become to us a necessity." Lodge pointed out the "vast interests which lie just outside our borders," which were "not only of material importance" but which concerned "our greatness as a nation and our future as a great people." One year later he referred to "broader political interests in the fate of Cuba," adding that "she commands the Gulf, she commands the channels through which all our coastwise traffic between the Gulf and our Northern and Eastern States passes. She lies right athwart the line which leads to the Nicaragua Canal." None of these issues were subsequently mentioned in relation to the war. On the cause of the war, Lodge was transformed into a sentimentalist. He was downright moving in writing about the "gathering strength" of "popular sentiment" and about how the Cubans' "brave fight for liberty and against Spain presently aroused the sympathy of the American people."[54]

The realists' critique of 1898, best represented in the work of Morgenthau, Osgood, and Graebner, was itself a product of the larger normative assumptions from which the historiography was derived. Their work served to further confuse the issues of the U.S. purpose in 1898. The proposition of morality as the source of U.S. policy in 1898, the focus of the realist critique, in fact, acted to validate its place in the historiography. Having accepted the argument that idealism was the source of U.S. policy, realists moved the debate one step further away from its historical bases, away from a discussion in which premises were tested to a debate where assumptions were shared and only outcomes were debated. In accepting as valid war in behalf of the long-suffering Cuban people, out of sentiment and sympathy, and debating these formulations as policy truths, the realist critique contributed to reinforcing the privileged place of idealism as the dominant historiographical canon.

• • •

The proposition of a U.S. war in behalf of Cuban independence, as an act of idealism and altruism, necessarily required the construction of corroborating interpretations of 1898. Once these formulations assumed a place of prominence in the historical literature, historiographical advances were registered less in the form of new research than new inferences on old assumptions. The logic of historical arguments thus constructed summoned into existence a sequence of corollary propositions that seemed to "fit" within the larger discursive framework. If the United States went to war in behalf of Cuban independence, the obvious inference to draw was because the Cubans had revealed themselves ill-equipped for the task of their own liberation. These deductions were made early, and the moral was unambiguous. Trumbull White insisted in 1898 that the Cuban Liberation Army was "a distinctly inferior body" and added: "If the Cuban soldier had been the equal of the American mentally and physically, if he had been as well armed, well clothed, and well fed, he would not have needed our aid. It was because he was distinctly inferior that we gave our assistance."[55] "After they had been fighting for three years," wrote Herbert H. Sargent in 1907, "they held no important city, had captured no important stronghold, had won no important battle."[56]

Once these propositions entered into historiographical narratives, it became further necessary to characterize the insurgents and the insurgency as unfit for, if not unworthy of, success. This argument, in turn, required the presumption of Cuban setback and failure. Consultation of Cuban sources was rarely deemed necessary, for apparently the inferences seemed as incontrovertible as they were inescapable. John D. Hicks and George F. Mowry proclaimed that it was an "exaggeration" to "speak of the disorder in Cuba that broke out in 1895 as a revolution," and David Saville Muzzey characterized the Cuban war for independence as hardly more than "ambush, assassination, and devastation." Cubans were "poorly organized" and "poorly disciplined," George Kennan argued. John L. Offner maintained that insurgent "military efforts" were "inadequate to win Cuban independence," further branding the 50,000 Cubans in arms as "a small army . . . divided into small, poorly armed units scattered across the island," unable to "confront the Spanish in a decisive battle or force them from their entrenched fortifications associated with towns and cities." Offner concluded: "Cuban developments were stalled." Harry T. Peck described the Liberation Army as "prowling bands of ill-armed peasants," adding: "A Cuban Republic had been proclaimed; but it had no capital and had organized no government. It had not even an army, in the proper sense of the word." David Gawronski dismissed the three-year Cuban campaign as "hardly a full-scaled rebellion"; rather, "it consisted mostly of part-time insurgents who periodically looted and raided the villages and then hid out in the mountains." Ellis Paxson Oberholtzer portrayed Cubans as "little above banditti" engaged in "bushwacking and banditry, assassination and massacre," whose "pradaceous spirit [and] cruelly vindictive measures were a disgrace to the profession of arms." The Cuban army, Joseph Smith argued, had been "unable to capture any city or important center of local government." Smith concluded: "In reality the [Cuban] 'army' was disorganized and widely dispersed throughout the island. It consisted mainly of roving bands of soldiers led by individual chiefs who assumed the titles of 'general' and 'colonel.' Lacking training and more often armed with machetes than rifles, these men adopted the tactics of guerrilla warfare in which skirmishes and ambushes were preferred to large-scale battles."[57]

The condition of the Cuban campaign in 1898, moreover, was represented in a variety of ways, almost all of which were predicated on the proposition that the Cuban cause had stalled if it was not altogether hopeless—exactly the opposite of the views that had prevailed during the early months of 1898. The Cuban insurrection, John W. Chambers affirmed, had "bogged down in a bloody stalemate." Frank Freidel provided the rationale for U.S. intervention by contending that the Cubans "were not strong enough to win, yet not weak enough to capitulate, and the entire island suffered." A similar argument was made by Walter Karp, who described the Cuban army as "chiefly black ex-slaves" who were "half-beaten . . . confined largely to the wilder eastern portion of the island, and reduced to mere roving bands more frightening to the neutral population—the *pacíficos*—than to the Spanish army." Sidney Lens characterized the Cuban campaign as something that "sputtered along, with rebels fighting only small harassing actions," and Charles S. Campbell observed that the "beautiful island seemed to be foundering in a welter of bloodshed." Foster Rhea Dulles insisted that "it had become apparent that neither side could prevail in the fighting in Cuba"; Albert Shaw proclaimed that the U.S. intervention was designed "to end a three-year struggle that had become deadlocked and increasingly disastrous." This was also the situation as depicted by H. Wayne Morgan, who wrote of "insurgents [who] could not defeat the Spanish, nor could the Spanish defeat the insurgents." The year 1898 was a decisive moment, asserted Lately Thomas, for Cubans "were reported to be in desperate straits, their forces threatened with collapse unless help came soon." Alan Brinkley et al. actually suggested that by the end of 1897 "the insurrection [was] losing ground." Richard Collin argued that "Cubans did need help" and drew the predictable inference: "The Americans were their only likely allies."[58]

Inevitably, one last corollary explanation was required to complete the logic of intervention-for-independence narratives. The argument also required Cubans to be desirous of U.S. intervention to assist them in achieving what they themselves were alleged to be incapable of. Cubans were thus represented as welcoming U.S. intervention, for in the larger explanatory schema it was necessary to represent the U.S. decision to intervene as wholly consistent with, and indeed in behalf of, Cuban interests. Norman Graebner suggested that "Cuban leaders knew from the beginning" that they were "unable to mount a successful revolution" and hence that "their success hinged on American support." Cuban strategies throughout the war were represented less to defeat Spain than to draw U.S. intervention to rescue the flagging separatist effort. "The insurgents," wrote John Schutz, "trying to involve the United States in the dispute, destroyed North Americans' property, compromised the neutrality laws by running arms, and spread propaganda." Robert Ferrell made a similar point directly: "In the hope of [U.S.] intervention the revolutionaries did their best to disrupt the island's sugar production." Walter Karp insisted that Cubans "did not expect their scorched-earth tactics to drive the Spanish from Cuba or their revolt to win widespread popular support." Rather, Karp proposed, the "main objective . . . was to create conditions so atrocious in Cuba that the United States in due course would intervene." Over and over historians in the United States persisted with the proposition of a campaign waged by Cubans not to defeat Spain directly but to obtain U.S. intervention. "Rebel tactics in 1895," William Miller suggested implausibly, "included deliberate attacks on American property with the objective of forcing the United States to intervene to restore order that Spain was too weak to maintain." Harry J. Carman, William G. Kimmel, and Mabel Walker made the point ex-plicitly: "By destroying the sugar plantations, many of which were owned by Americans, the rebels hoped to provoke American intervention." Dumas Malone and Basil Rauch argued that Cubans "destroyed sugar plantations and mills, some of which were owned by Americans, hoping to induce intervention." Walter LaFeber also interpreted Cuban tactics as undertaken "in the hope of forcing McKinley's intervention." In what was at one time the standard text of U.S. diplomatic history, Thomas A. Bailey argued that the "*insurrectos* put the torch to Yankee property in the hope that the United States would be forced to intervene." H. Wayne Morgan made the same observation: "Gomez destroyed property to keep the issue alive in the United States and to provoke American inter-vention." A similar argument was advanced by Daniel Boorstin and Brooks Mather Kelley, who insisted that Cubans destroyed U.S. property "to prod the United States to intervene." In a slightly different variation of this theme, William Leuchtenburg could write that Cuban leaders rejected the April cease-fire because "they were confident of ultimate American intervention."[59]

The presumption of Cuban desire for U.S. intervention served log-ically and perhaps inevitably to implicate Cubans in the destruction of the *Maine* for, within this reasoning, they would have had the most to gain from U.S. intervention. This proposition was derived by way of inference, of course, and was always unabashedly speculative, because everyone knew that nobody knew. What could not be corroborated by evidence was thus offered as conjecture and with the desired effect: a way to suggest a point without having to assume responsibility for it. In other words, it was sufficient simply to suggest possibilities, not prove them. "The Cuban revolutionaries—perhaps—made their supreme effort to secure American intervention," Robert Ferrell theorized in 1975. He continued: "No one to this day has discovered who or what in 1898 blew up the *Maine*. One can say only that the vessel's destruction greatly benefitted the Cuban revolutionaries, already distinguished by the aban-don with which they conducted their guerrilla actions against the Span-ish." If, in fact, the explosion was not internal, John Richard Alden conjectured, "it is more likely that the Cuban insurgents were responsible for it," for "presumably rebels stood to gain from American action against Spain." Thomas Bailey similarly speculated that the "Cuban insurgents may have sunk the vessel to force America into the war on their side." Harold Underwood Faulkner implicated the Cubans just by musing on the possibility: "Was it set off by insurgents eager to embroil the United States?" This occurrence was also suggested by John Holladay Latané, who speculated that the destruction of the *Maine* "may have been the work of Cuban insurgents, whose object was to bring on war." Arthur S. Link and Stanley Coben argued that "to this day no one knows who planted the mine, although the most likely culprits would seem to be either the Cuban rebels, ruthless in their pursuit of American intervention; or else one of the groups of Spanish nationalists in Havana." Gerald R. Baydo arrived at a similar conclusion in similar language, acknowledging that "no one knows who planted the mine"; he could see only two possibilities: "Either Cuban rebels anxious for American intervention or Spanish nationalists protesting the softening of Spanish policy." Wayne Cole suggested that Cubans had motives to destroy the *Maine* but "probably would have lacked the technical requirements for the task."[60]

What is particularly remarkable about these propositions, advanced as formulations on which larger arguments are derived and developed, is that they pretend to represent the Cuban purpose without even the pretension of examining Cuban sources. In fact, Cuban tactics were not designed to draw U.S. intervention. Cubans conducted military operations against property, U.S. and non-U.S. alike, as a means to deny Spain the resources to wage war on the island and to force a realignment of social forces in such a manner as to reduce Spanish support inside Cuba. Indeed, the burning of cane fields as a method of colonial resistance was as old as sugar production itself. The premise that Cubans sought to force a North American intervention, so central in U.S. historiography, was wholly contrived—and subsequently repeated and repeated—because it was an element necessary to corroborate the equally unfounded suggestion that Cubans desired U.S. intervention. The genealogy of these propositions, so central in U.S. historiography, can be traced to assumptions derived from historiographical formulations of U.S. policy, from which the Cuban purpose was in turn inferred.

It was a short and perhaps inevitable step, finally, to portray Cubans as culpable in 1898. Cubans were thus held responsible for apparently forcing the United States into war with Spain by their insistent and presumably unreasonable demand for independence. H. Wayne Morgan contemplated the "blame" and reflected on the conditions that might have "saved the peace"—the U.S. peace, supposedly—and concluded that war might have been averted "if the Cubans had not been so irksome and had no influence in Congress and the press." Samuel Flagg Bemis affirmed outright that Cubans were "more to blame than the Spaniards for the character of hostilities" and that Cubans were "more inhuman in their warfare than the Spaniards"; Nelson Manfred Blake and Oscar Theodore Barck Jr. maintained that "rebel terrorism provoked the Spaniards." Lester D. Langley implied a critique of the Cubans in noting that the failure of the autonomist government "was the fault of the insurrectionists" due to their "absolute rigidity." John Offner rendered a particularly severe judgment of the Cubans. "Whereas the Spanish made some attempts to end the colonial war and to prevent an American conflict," he argued, "the Cubans were inflexible." In Offner's view, the Cubans were to blame for the "Spanish-American War." They were "unyielding." Máximo Gómez—"not known for compromise"—was guilty of "stubbornness [and] kept the revolutionary forces in the field despite a staggering cost in lives and property." The Cuban commitment to independence was thus at the heart of Offner's causal explanation. "The result was inflexibility as the Cubans adhered to one position that all could agree on: independence from Spain at all cost." Offner was eloquent in wondering "what might have occurred if the Cubans had attempted to cooperate" and speculated: "They might have respected American property and obeyed the neutrality laws; when they obtained the de Lôme letter, they might have taken it to the State Department rather than spread it across the front page of the *Journal*. More important, they could have helped the McKinley administration to establish an armistice in Cuba in order to prevent a Spanish-American war."[61] All of this was undoubtedly true. But it was also undoubtedly true that Cubans would likely have remained under Spanish rule—and that is precisely what they had set out to change.

Meaning of the *Maine*

She had been destroyed, by deliberate and fiendish treachery, and her destroyers must be brought to account. That was the verdict rendered by a public opinion so strong, so unanimous, so earnest, that no official authority, however anxious to avoid a conflict so long as an honourable way of escaping it was to be found, could restrain the voice of national indignation.
—Richard H. Titherington, *A History of the Spanish-American War of 1898* (1900)

To arbitrate the liability for the loss of the Maine—that would have been the ideal, the logical course. But there are moments in the life of nations, as well as of individuals, when logic does not point the road. The youth of to-day, like his savage ancestor centuries ago, chooses his mate when the supreme passion flames up in his breast, and considerations of fortune and position are forgotten. The man vindicates his rights when his blood is up, and pays a five-hundred-dollar fee to recover a five-dollar claim. The nation, stirred beyond endurance, throwing logic and economy to the winds, interprets its duty to suit its passion, and rushes into war.
—Theodore Salisbury Woolsey, *America's Foreign Policy* (1898)

It looks as though we were to have war. . . . If the Spaniards back down now, it would be the source of the very bitterest disappointment. They will have to kneel and crawl in a manner that history has never before seen. Why did they blow up our Maine? No matter what pretext any or all of the members of Congress can give for war, *we must have it*. The cause of the war lies in a set of American colors blown up in an explosion, and with the colors the men who served to protect them; blown up at night while asleep—evidence in itself sufficient to show that a contemptible Spaniard did it. The blood almost fills my head when I think of this; it makes me almost wild with anger.
—Ensign Worth Bagley to Mother (April 3, 1898)

Remember the *Maine*!
To hell with Spain!
—Popular refrain (1898)

On the evening of February 15, 1898, the battleship *Maine* exploded in Havana harbor. The explosion occurred in the forward part of the vessel, near the port side, almost directly under the enlisted men's quarters. The loss of life was staggering: out of a total complement of 354 officers and men, 266 perished in the explosion.

The destruction of the *Maine* had immediate repercussions and lasting implications. Relations between the United States and Spain, already strained by mutual suspicions and mounting tensions, deteriorated rapidly thereafter. American impatience with Spain's conduct of the war in Cuba was increasing. So was popular support for Cuba Libre. For almost three years public officials and public opinion acted upon one another in such a fashion as to make the insurrection in Cuba an unsettling intrusion in domestic politics. These conditions were exacerbated by the excesses of "yellow journalism," in which sensational news stories about the Cuban war had become the stock-in-trade of the circulation rivalry between William Randolph Hearst's *New York Journal* and Joseph Pulitzer's *New York World*. Anti-Spanish sentiment was on the rise. Only one week before the destruction of the *Maine*, ill will toward Spain had flared over the publication of the de Lôme letter.

But the impact of the *Maine* was not only a matter of timing. The explosion was also a question of circumstances. That a U.S. warship exploded in Havana harbor, waters nominally under Spanish jurisdiction, invited immediate and obvious conclusions. "The *Maine* was sunk by an act of dirty treachery on the part of the Spaniards," Theodore Roosevelt concluded the day after the tragedy—a suspicion that gained currency in many quarters.[1]

Events moved quickly after February 15. On the following day President McKinley convened a naval court of inquiry to investigate the cause of the explosion. Two weeks later Congress appropriated $50 million for war preparations. On March 25 the naval court completed its investigation and three days later released its findings. Two explosions were responsible for the destruction of the *Maine*, the naval inquiry concluded. An initial external explosion—one that "could have been produced only by the explosion of a mine situated under the bottom of the ship"—detonated a second internal blast in "two or more of the forward magazines."[2] The court of inquiry declined to fix responsibility for the disaster, but the determination that the first explosion originated externally, attributed explicitly to a submarine mine, could mean only one of two things: the explosion was either the result of criminal negligence or the work of malicious intent. In either case, the implication was clear: Spain was responsible.[3]

• • •

The destruction of the *Maine* developed almost immediately into one of the dominant narrative vehicles for the explanation of 1898. The mysterious coincidence and unforeseen consequences, matters of chance and circumstance, combined intriguingly to provide more than ample material with which to contemplate the imponderables of 1898: a presumed random casus belli of unverifiable if not unknown origins, apparently a case of bad timing at a bad place, and of such far-reaching consequences. These have been some of the subplots that have made the *Maine* the object of such enduring appeal: a wholly fortuitous event to which is attributed the cause of a war that altered the course of U.S. history.

There is some charm to this narrative structure. In the hands of a skilled storyteller the destruction of the *Maine* is rendered rich with layers of far-reaching meaning, moral and metaphysical, epistemological and existential, from which to ponder weighty consequences, continuously revealing themselves, always transcending temporal bounds and spatial boundaries. The story appeals to the delights of private meditations on irony and invites contemplation on what otherwise might have been only if. . . . Causal relationships are drawn by supposition, deduced by inference, and advanced by implication. Why did the *Maine* explode at that moment, at that place, G. J. A. O'Toole asked rhetorically: "The answer to such questions lies beyond the realm of chemistry, physics, or naval architecture. Each must find it within his own personal understanding of the universe. However, there seem to be but three answers to choose among: God, chance, or the impatient hand of destiny." For Peggy and Harold Samuels, the destruction of the *Maine* "contributed to the outbreak of the Spanish War and thus to the rise of American imperialism." But that was only the beginning. The Samuels's added: "The history of the turn of the last century, and of much that has taken place since then, was affected by what happened after the battleship exploded."[4]

The explanatory function of the *Maine*, moreover, is often set within a larger conceptual framework in which the deeper meanings of the war serve as the larger, if not always stated, object of historical narratives. To a remarkable degree, the historiography of 1898, and specifically the explanation of the war, have been a function of and fashioned by parameters suggested by the causal role attributed to the *Maine*. Indeed, the use of the *Maine* as an explanation has sustained larger assumptions about the war. That the *Maine* has enjoyed enduring historiographical preeminence underscores the conceptual appeal of treating the war as a function of chance, not choice. War with Spain is represented as the result of an "incident" and aberration, a chance event—a random occurrence that just as easily might not have happened.

The consensus developed immediately out of the events of 1898, with policymakers and political leaders among the first to proclaim the causal role of the *Maine*. Theodore Roosevelt was categorical: "When the *Maine* was blown up in Havana Harbor, war became inevitable." Senator Shelby M. Cullom agreed. "I have no doubt at all," he wrote a decade later, "that war would have been averted had not the *Maine* been destroyed in Havana harbor." Champ Clark characterized the *Maine* as "the straw that broke the camel's back," and Secretary of War Russell A. Alger believed that the incident "swept away forever" all likelihood of a peaceful settlement. Army commander General Nelson A. Miles later affirmed flatly that the *Maine* "precipitated the war with Spain."[5]

Early historical accounts of 1898 similarly emphasized the causal role of the *Maine*. "The sinking of the *Maine* meant war between the United States and Spain," Richard R. Titherington wrote in 1900. "But for the destruction of the *Maine*," John R. Musick observed in the same year, "war might have been averted." Horace Edgar Flack argued that "it was largely due to the *Maine* that intervention took place" and that, "in all probability, there would have been no war, had our battleship not been destroyed." For Theodore E. Burton, "peace might have been obtained had it not been for the blowing-up of the . . . *Maine*." "After the *Maine*," Trumbull White insisted, "the logic of events was irresistibly drawing the country toward war with Spain."[6]

Subsequent historical narratives of the war have departed only slightly from interpretations first formulated at the turn of the century. The *Maine* has persisted as a factor of singular importance and the principal cause of war, proclaimed by three generations of historians in terms as categorical as those employed in 1898. William A. Robinson insisted that "the explosion shattered the hope of preserving peace as completely as it had shattered the vessel itself." "Hopes for peace sank with the *Maine*," proclaimed David Burner, Robert D. Marcus, and Emily S. Rosenberg. "On the night of February 15, 1898," William Leuchtenburg asserted, "came the terrible blow which ended all real hope for peace." "The *Maine* incident," wrote A. E. Campbell in terms strikingly reminiscent of Theodore Roosevelt's phrasing, "made war all but inevitable." Robert Welch similarly argued that the tragedy "not only heightened the war hysteria in certain sections of the American press and public but persuaded McKinley that events had overtaken the possibility of putting an end to the struggle in Cuba by means of Spanish reforms and limited autonomy."

Elmer Plischke speculated that "had President McKinley not sent the battleship *Maine* into Havana harbor. . . the war with Spain might not have broken out." "If any one event was responsible for the Spanish-American War," Charles Campbell posited, "it was not the mere destruction of the *Maine* but her destruction by an outside explosion as attested by a responsible board of inquiry." For Turnbull White, the *Maine* was the "culminating influence for American intervention." "An affair of tremendous importance," wrote Herman Reichard Esteves, "the disaster was unquestionably first among the immediate causes of the Spanish-American War." Allan Nevins and Henry Steele Commager declared that the explosion "rendered war almost unavoidable," and for Thomas Bailey the destruction of the *Maine* "was unquestionably the most important single precipitant of the war with Spain."[7]

The particular usefulness of the *Maine* as an explanatory device has been the ease with which it has lent itself to corollary causal categories. Explanations first formulated at the turn of the century have displayed remarkable endurance and indeed have persisted as central elements of the major historiographical narratives of 1898. The functions attributed to the *Maine* have over time undergone periodic reinterpretation and revision, to be sure. However, the primary explanations of 1898 have derived much of their internal coherence and larger logic from possibilities suggested, and most of all rendered plausible, by the *Maine*. The war is made to make sense and is situated in a larger sequence of events that implies an underlying design, even if the design is informed by the notion of randomness. The *Maine* has thus enabled contradictory and otherwise conflicting possibilities to be linked together into a seemingly coherent and creditable explanatory framework. The *Maine* has discharged various historiographical functions, central to which has been the proposition of chance as a principal explanation of 1898.[8]

The actual weight assigned to the *Maine* as the cause of the war, no less than the means by which it was perceived to have precipitated the war, has remained the subject of divergent and often conflicting interpretations. To the *Maine* has been variously attributed, and often at the same time, the predominant and immediate cause of the war, the necessary as well as the sufficient cause; the *Maine* has been represented as having made war at once possible and inevitable. Opinion also differs on whether it was one of many causes or chief among all, whether it precluded an obtainable peace or merely accelerated an inevitable war.

For the most part, however, differences have been less of kind than of degree and emphasis, generally in the form of variations on a common theme. Taken together, they represent a larger consensus about the origins of the war, from which have been derived the principal explanations of 1898. The argument assumed fully the properties of an article of faith and early developed into one of the enduring historiographical truths of 1898.

Whether or not Spain was actually responsible for the destruction of the *Maine* was, in fact, of marginal significance. In fact, the justification of war was not related directly to a determination of Spanish guilt. That the explosion occurred at all raised issues at least as important as questions of Spanish complicity and offered no less compelling grounds to undertake war as an appropriate response. The need to establish Spanish guilt was unnecessary, even if possible—and particularly because it was not. No matter what or who may have caused the explosion, Spain was responsible simply for tolerating conditions that resulted in the loss of U.S. lives and property, thereby justifying the expulsion by arms of an unsettling Spanish presence so near the United States.

The historiography is rich with consequences attributed to the destruction of the *Maine*. Thus, under one set of circumstances, the *Maine* exposed the weakness of Spanish authority in Cuba, a condition that could only prolong regional instability and endanger U.S. interests. The "condition of affairs in Cuba was a constant menace to our peace," declared Marrion Wilcox. He continued: "The destruction of the *Maine*, by whatever exterior cause, was a patent and impressive proof of a state of things in Cuba that was intolerable. That condition was thus shown to be such that the Spanish Government could not assure safety and security to a vessel of the American navy in the harbour of Havana on a mission of peace and rightfully there." In similar fashion, James Morton Callahan argued that the "feeling in the United States was strong that it was time to remove medievalism from our front doors, so that our ships could safely enter Havana." Expelling Spain from Cuba, hence, "appeared to be a necessary act of duty for the health of civilization." Callahan concluded: "If Cuba had been in other hands the *Maine* might have been safe, and the blood of American citizens might not have caused the foul waters of Havana to blush with shame." The argument of Willis Fletcher Johnson was much the same: the destruction of the *Maine* was "proof of the worthlessness of the Spanish administration and was an additional reason for turning it out, bag and baggage." Robert L. Jones pointed out that the "American government took the position that Spain failed to exercise proper police supervision in the harbor and was therefore culpable," and Nelson Blake and Oscar Barck carried the argument one step further: "Even were Spanish complicity never proved, many Americans argued that the explosion had demonstrated Spain's inability to protect foreign lives and property in Cuba. Did the United States not therefore have an obligation to intervene on behalf of the civilized world?" According to Charles Campbell, the explosion of the *Maine* demonstrated the collapse of Spanish sovereignty; he thereby suggested that the approaching extinction of colonial authority precipitated the war. It was not that Spain had direct responsibility for the destruction of the ship, but rather that its "crumbling authority in Cuba had made it possible." Campbell added: "No nation had the right to claim sovereignty in an area where its control had disappeared, where disorder had become chronic, where it had no chance of regaining control."[9]

More than providing moral justification to declare war, the destruction of the *Maine* has been represented as having forged the political consensus required to wage war. "The loss of the *Maine*," suggested Trumbull White in 1898, "had focused American attention upon the Cuban situation as it had never been before, and . . . people began to realize as they had not before, the horrors that were being enacted at their thresholds." Thomas Bailey made a similar point: "Nothing could have brought home to the American republic more forcibly the disordered conditions in Cuba and the proposed solution that the island be freed." David Trask agreed. "Prior to this," he wrote, "the Cuban question had been but one of a number of public issues of interest to the American people; but after the *Maine* went down the fate of Cuba dominated the public consciousness."[10]

After the *Maine*, hence, political opposition to war could hardly be sustained. Differences between Republicans and Democrats, expansionists and anti-imperialists, northerners and southerners, administration foes and friends were set aside in the face of the national crisis. The result was the popular support and public consensus necessary to make war a politically acceptable instrument of foreign policy. J. Rogers Hollingsworth described a "nation united," and with "the country ablaze with patriotic emotion, pacifists and doubters were silenced; partisanship and sectional hostility were temporarily laid aside." Sectional divisions were replaced by national unity, Paul H. Buck suggested, as the "South at once responded to the national excitement which followed the sinking of the *Maine*"; he added: "For a time all people within the country felt the electrifying thrill of a common purpose. When it subsided a sense of nationality had been rediscovered, based upon consciousness of national strength and unity." John Weems agreed, insisting that the sinking of the *Maine* "did beyond a doubt unify Americans for the war." Weems also suggested that the incident "served to unify the North and the South, whose Civil War differences were still apparent." No less important, he suggested, the *Maine* had the net effect of neutralizing opposition to war. After March 28, "the voice of the pacifist was generally stilled." Elbert Benton made a similar point, insisting that an "ultimate pacific settlement had become improbable when the American world was startled by the blowing up of the *Maine*," and added: "It only required such an event as that in Havana harbor and the recriminations which grew out of it to fix the wavering convictions of both parties and render diplomacy impotent." Jack Cameron Dierks maintained that "the country was united as it hadn't been for decades," observing: "The common enemy provided an excuse to heal the old bitternesses between Yankee and Confederate that thirty-three years of peace since 1865 had been unable to do."[11]

• • •

The persistence of the *Maine* as a dominant explanatory element underscores some of the more enduring characteristics of the historical literature. Historiographical advances have been conspicuously few; indeed, the principal conceptual formulations of 1898 have remained largely unchanged. Narratives have relied primarily on contradictory and inconclusive evidence. Causal arguments based on the *Maine* have always been far easier to propound than to prove. The importance of the *Maine* has been presumed self-evident and self-explanatory, derived more from a reworking of the historical literature than from a reexamination of historical evidence.

If there has been general agreement about the causal role of the *Maine*, there has been no comparable consensus about specifically how the *Maine* acted to cause the war. Central to the explanatory functions of the *Maine* have been derivative arguments about the role of public opinion. In fact, public opinion has served as the historiographical device of choice and has played an important part in making explanatory formulations "work." The relationship of public opinion to the coming of the war has undergone repeated presentations and representations in the course of one hundred years of historical writing. So, too, have the ways public opinion has been measured. Whatever else may separate the varieties of usages of the notion of "public opinion," however, the historical literature has been all but unanimous in the conclusion that popular sentiment figured prominently in propelling the United States to war.[12]

The historiography has long pointed to the destruction of the *Maine* as a source of public wrath, whereupon a climate of opinion developed in which war became an acceptable if not inevitable course of action. This proposition has appeared in a variety of narrative formulations but over time has remained substantially constant. The historiographical consensus has indeed been striking. "The disaster to the *Maine* was but a match touched to the powder of public sentiment," stated Charles Morris a year after the war ended; "an unparalleled wave of horror and indignation swept over the United States," Russell H. Fitzgibbon agreed. Thomas Bailey similarly insisted that "the explosion of the *Maine* was matched by an explosion of public opinion." George Kennan wrote that "the American public was profoundly shocked and outraged to hear that the battleship *Maine* had been sunk," and Daniel Smith noted that "the sinking of the *Maine* aroused the public to a fighting temper."[13]

The electorate was thus depicted as having entered directly into the decision-making process, transforming an issue of foreign policy into a concern of domestic politics. The public did not merely resign itself to the possibility of hostilities; on the contrary, it demanded the prosecution of war. Implicit in this argument was the proposition that once public opinion began to influence the course of events, the drift to war became irreversible. The "effect of the *Maine* disaster on the American public opinion," David F. Healy contended, "seemed to make war inevitable." The incident "so affected American opinion," George Kennan argued, "that war became inevitable with the sinking of the *Maine*. From that time on no peaceful solution was really given serious consideration in the American government." Alluding to "public pressure," Dorothy Burne Goebel concluded that "popular opinion determined foreign policy." Dexter Perkins stated the argument succinctly: "Never was there a clearer case of a war brought about by public opinion."[14]

The role attributed to public opinion, from which a number of corollary generalizations have been derived, serves several functions—some conceptual, some theoretical, some methodological. Public opinion provides a plausible causal factor without the necessity of explanation or evidence. Accordingly, the onset of the war in 1898 was portrayed as a function of an aroused public opinion that, as commonly acknowledged, did not need to be rational and therefore required no explanation. The inference was inescapable: the United States was propelled to war by an agitated citizenry, overcome by stirred passions and at the brink of mass hysteria. Represented as a powerful undercurrent, public opinion was thus depicted as an unseen, relentless force that, once aroused, assumed an inexorable logic of its own, one that could be calmed by nothing less than war. Responsibility for war was attributed to the aroused masses, who, it was suggested, had taken collective leave of their senses.

The literature is rich with such characterizations: "an ungovernable burst of popular emotion"; "war hysteria swept the country"; "public opinion outran . . . sober judgment"; the "lid was now off" as a result of "the unthinking American masses"; "the nation had gone mad"; the "pressure generated by the ensuing emotional outburst swept away all reason and hesitation"; "hysteria seized upon a large part of the American people"; "in response to the clamorous war spirit aroused by the sinking of *Maine* in the harbor of Havana, the United States was about to go to war with Spain"; "a hurricane of emotion swept the country"; "across the country, thousands gave themselves up to emotional excesses like those of tent-meeting revivals"; "the people, acting out of powerful irrational impulses, dictated the decision of April 1898."[15]

War thus found one of its most enduring representations as a result of spontaneous emotional reaction to a random incident—armed retribution brought on by the caprice of public opinion anxious to avenge the *Maine*. Indeed, public clamor for revenge was represented as the force that propelled the country inexorably into war. "It cannot be denied," Alexander K. McClure and Charles Morris argued in 1901, "that this unparalleled outrage intensified the war fever in the United States, and thousands were eager for the opportunity to punish Spanish cruelty and treachery." The destruction of the *Maine*, Morris wrote elsewhere, "gave rise to a natural feeling of resentment in the minds of the American people, which quickly deepened to a thirst for revenge." The explosion, suggested Oscar Doane Lambert, "created a storm for retribution." Charles E. Chapman agreed, writing: "People nearly went out of their heads in a wave of patriotic feeling that was mingled with a call for vengeance against Spain." John Grenville and George Young indicated that "patriotic fervor now demanded vengeance for the *Maine*." "The American people were calling for blood," wrote James A. Henretta et al. E. Berkeley Tompkins similarly suggested that the public "clamored for revenge," and John Dobson asserted that the public "considered avenging the American deaths a matter of national honor."[16]

• • •

The linkage between the *Maine* and public opinion, on one hand, and war, on the other, is not, however, without historiographical anomalies. The contradictions have not been simply a matter of conflicting interpretations, although at times differences in interpretation have been sufficiently great to raise larger questions about attention to accuracy and use of evidence. There are, in fact, at least two substantially different and irreconcilable accounts of the timing and character of public reaction, both of which appear to share a congenial and untroubled coexistence in the historiography. In one version, public opinion is depicted as having been aroused immediately after and in direct response to the explosion, that is, immediately after February 15. This formulation is best represented by Foster Rhea Dulles: "When it mysteriously blew up . . . an already worked-up public went wild. There were occasional cautionary voices urging that judgment should be withheld until an official investigation could determine the cause of the *Maine*'s destruction, but they were scarcely heard in the noisy clamor demanding immediate retaliation against Spain as without question being responsible for the disaster."[17]

Other accounts agree. "An already war-conscious American public opinion was still further aroused when, on February 15, 1898, the *Maine* blew up. . . ," Hollis W. Barber wrote, adding: "When word of this blast reached the United States it seemed that war might be only minutes away." Samuel W. McCall made a similar point, noting that "the country was at once stirred from one end to the other. . . . The popular impulse was to rush into war." William Roscoe Thayer wrote that the following morning a "tidal wave of anger surged over this country." In his account of these days, Donald Barr Chidsey declared that "papers back and forth across the land—not only the yellow press—were screaming for war." A "wave of belligerent enthusiasm . . . swept at once throughout the country," Walter Millis noted. According to Charles Morris, "indignation was extreme on learning of the terrible event."[18]

A second version, however, describes a public reaction substantially different in chronology and character. In this account the citizenry is represented as having remained calm during the days and weeks following February 15, and not until March 28, when the naval court of inquiry implicated Spain in the explosion, did public wrath erupt. Henry Watterson wrote in 1898 that citizens "awaited patiently the report of their commission. No more than the President did they wish to perpetuate any injustice against Spain." "There was no violent demand for vengeance," Harry Peck maintained. "The gravity of the situation gave steadiness and poise to public opinion. The nation displayed a universal willingness to suspend judgment until a full and vigorous inquiry should be made. The tone of the press through the country was admirable." Roscoe Lewis Ashley insisted that "for five weeks, with rare self-control, the nation waited." Thomas Bailey wrote that it was "to the credit of the

American people that on the whole they were inclined to suspend judgment. . . . This fact is all the more remarkable when one considers the surcharged atmosphere." But, Bailey added, "following the official report on the *Maine*, the masses were on fire for war." "When the court of inquiry reported that the explosion was caused by a mine," wrote John Holladay Latané, "the American people, who had displayed great self-control, threw aside all restraint and the country witnessed an outburst of patriotic fervor such as had not been seen since 1861."[19] Other accounts concur: "public judgment was restrained"; "most of the public withheld judgment pending the findings of the official inquiry," after which "the cry for war rose over the land"; "American public opinion was restrained and dignified"; "there was no instantaneous and unanimous outcry for war"; "the American public had suspended judgment until the investigation was over."[20]

Discrepancies of this type suggest ambiguities of other kinds. The linkage of public opinion to the coming of the war, a causal formulation long associated with explanations of 1898, stands as one of the more problematical constructs of the historical literature and, indeed, sets in sharp relief the degree to which interpretations of 1898 have often tended to operate independently of the requirements for evidence. Public opinion arguments derive plausibility more from normatively derived democratic theory than from a body of assembled evidence. A vast literature has formed around arguments for which adequate verification is either incomplete or unavailable, or both. Explanations have relied freely if implicitly on the theoretical functions of public opinion in a political democracy: the electorate, from which emanates political legitimacy and to which elected officials are presumed responsible, is represented as dictating the pace of events and the course of policy.

War as a product of public opinion has long relied on the proposition of functional democratic structures, mandated by political considerations and sanctioned by constitutional injunction. Attributed as it is to the will of the people, war stands as a metaphor for the triumph of popular democracy. Historiography as national narrative itself serves at one and the same time to form and inform notions of nation, to foster a sense of past and place congruent with the normative structures around which the nation defines itself. Accordingly, elected officials are obliged to acquiesce to public pressure, perhaps against their better judgment if not against their will. Popular demand for war thus legitimizes war as an imperative of democratic processes. The argument suggests an element of choicelessness on the part of elected officials, who presumably have no alternative and for whom war becomes the means by which to discharge their constitutional responsibilities to the electorate. An unwilling Congress and a reluctant president appear thrown on the defensive, resorting to war to meet the demands of an aroused citizenry.

These propositions were first advanced by elected officials themselves, many of whom subsequently justified the war resolution as the expression of popular democracy. "It was this public sentiment," wrote Senator Henry Cabot Lodge in 1899, "that drove Congress forward to meet the popular will, which members and Senators very well knew could be fulfilled by war and in no other way." "Thousands of petitions came to Congress demanding war," recalled L. White Busby, private secretary of Representative Joe Canon. Busby concluded that "the Government was being forced into war." Senator Joseph Foraker later explained that "public sentiment was so aroused that it was impossible longer to delay positive action to put an end to the trouble," and Champ Clark recalled that "the American people cried out with one accord for vengeance and forced the gentle and kind-hearted President's hand." Senator Shelby Cullom was no less unequivocal about the consequences of the *Maine*: "The country forced us into it after that appalling catastrophe."[21]

These propositions entered the historiography early and, with only slight interpretative variations, have subsequently flourished as the principal thematic staples of the 1898 scholarship. "All well-meaning sophistries were brushed aside by the rude hand of a popular demand for reprisal," wrote Henry Watterson in 1898, "and Congress was admonished that it disobeyed the summons at its peril." The "verdict rendered by a public opinion [was] so strong, so unanimous, so earnest," agreed Richard R. Titherington, "that no official authority, however anxious to avoid a conflict so long as an honorable way of escaping it was to be found, could restrain the voice of national indignation." The "temper of the people" was so "distinctly belligerent," declared Harry Peck, that it was "obvious to those in power that war could not be long averted." "After the *Maine* episode," T. Harry Williams, Richard Current, and Frank Freidel asserted, "there was little chance the government could keep the people from war." As Mary Mander put it, "when the *Maine* blew up . . . a tidal wave of public clamoring for intervention washed over all sentiments to the contrary."[22]

The role attributed to public opinion makes for an appealing causal construct on several counts. It provides a plausible explanation for a war that many scholars have judged harshly or otherwise represented as having lacked both clear reason and compelling purpose. A war depicted often as senseless and irrational—described variously in the historiography as "unfortunate," "unnecessary," "unnecessary and perhaps even avoidable," "foolish and unnecessary," "totally unnecessary," and "needless"—is thus rendered comprehensible.[23] George Kennan made the point explicitly, insisting that the United States "resorted to war for subjective and emotional reasons" and at another point describing the war "as an example of superficiality in concept as well as the power of chauvinistic rhetoric and war hysteria." Robert E. Riegel and David F. Long characterized the conflict as the "strangest war in American history," one of "sheer military aggression against a hopelessly outclassed and conciliatory adversary."[24] In this way, the explanation of acts that fail to conform to preconceived and generally implicit norms of political rationality can be attributed to the recklessness of the public. It was not the leaders who failed, or their policies that fell short, but the body politic that was derelict.

Attributing the war to the demands of aroused public opinion suggests a subtext of another kind. The proposition of war by design, deliberate and intentional, is thus by implication rendered inadmissible. Political leaders are presumed innocent of willing war and thereby absolved of responsibility for it. They are overtaken by events, or they are weak or incompetent. But they are not represented as willing war in the defense of national interests.

The proposition of war as unwarranted and even unnecessary thus proceeds to arrange explanatory categories around alternative causal modalities. The *Maine* fits perfectly into this order of things, for it makes possible—and plausible—war as a function of chance and happenstance, as an improvised response to an unforeseen circumstance. But it is public opinion that connects the random event to the needless outcome. That the war is proclaimed irrational while political leaders are presumed rational further places the causes of the war more in the realm of chance than of choice.

The subtext of public opinion as a prime mover in this instance invites a moral of another kind: a statement on how mass politics often acts to undercut enlightened policy choices. War "did not take place because of the failure of American diplomacy," wrote John Hicks, George Mowry, and Robert Burke. "War came in spite of the complete success of American diplomacy, and primarily because the American people wanted to have a war." Thomas Bailey agreed, insisting that the people "were determined to have their war . . . , and they got it."[25] William Leuchtenburg briefly considered William Randolph Hearst as the culprit but then focused on "the people," noting that "no newspaper can arouse a people that is not willing to be aroused"; he concluded: "At the root lay the American gullibility about foreign affairs. . . . The American people were not led into war; they got the war they wanted." Randolph Greenfield Adams wrote about the "fascinatingly interesting evidence of the popular control of foreign policy," affirming that "the populace clamored for war" and the "will of the masses overbore the judgment of the President and had its way." This was indeed a momentous occasion, Adams proclaimed: "From the depths of lethargy about their foreign policy and from an appalling abyss of ignorance on the subject, the American people suddenly determined to control their own destinies in international relations." Norman Graebner characterized the conflict as "a people's war," and James Bradford described the U.S. resort to military action as "a people's war pressed on a reluctant administration." "The masses warmed to the prospect of new adventure," was the way Harold Underwood Faulkner portrayed the momentum behind the war.[26]

These circumstances suggested, too, a hint of the irrational, for a war proclaimed as unnecessary could hardly be explained except as irrational in some manner. "The United States went to war," Carl Degler concluded, "because the body of its citizens, overwrought, highly moralistic, and heedless of the consequences, insisted upon it." Thomas Bailey wrote of "the war-mad masses" forcing "the nation into an unnecessary clash with Spain, in spite of McKinley, Mark Hanna, and Big Business." David Trask argued that "the people, acting out powerful irrational impulses, dictated the decision of April, 1898." George Brown Tindall had a similar view: "The ultimate blame for war, if blame must be levied, belongs to the American people for letting themselves be whipped into such a hostile frenzy."[27]

The role attributed to public opinion as an explanation of 1898 is itself derivative of generally implicit and culturally determined notions about the nature of political democracy. The proposition works without need of verification precisely because it draws inferentially from shared assumptions about democratic theory and implicitly corroborates dominant views about the practice of democracy in the United States. It is as self-evident as it is self-validating. Public opinion influences public officials because it is supposed to. There are thus no evidentiary requirements in this formulation. The normatively presumed influence of public opinion in public affairs substantiates itself, corroborated primarily by the belief system that produced it and is, in turn, validated by it.

The formulation of public opinion as the source of the war was stated explicitly by Thomas A. Bailey and David M. Kennedy: McKinley "believed in the democratic principle that the people should rule, and he hesitated to deny the American masses what they demanded—even if it was not good for them." Carl Russell Fish condemned the haste with which the United States went to war; "responsibility rested immediately upon the American people themselves, all too eager for a war which they were not prepared and for a speedy victory at all costs." Carl Degler drew a larger moral. "The war . . . ," he argued, "revealed that a democracy's foreign policy was peculiarly and especially vulnerable to the threat of an irresponsible citizenry." Wolfgang Drechsler provided one of the clearest expressions of this formulation. "It is probably safe to say that neither Congress, nor the president, nor business interests were to blame," he affirmed. "All of them viewed such a war as foolish and unnecessary." Who, then, was "to blame"? The people were, concluded Drechsler. The war was thus explained as the result "of a system that is too democratic: a system in which the leaders' good reason is swept aside by an unscrupulous yellow press and an ill-advised fanatical public." The role of the president and Congress was "to exercise the will of the people of the United States," and "In this case, presidential as well as congressional action in the . . . war would actually exemplify a well-functioning representative government."[28]

The role of the press was also central to the discussion of public opinion. Public ire was represented not so much as a spontaneous response to the destruction of the *Maine* as it was the result of deliberate and cynical manipulation by prowar elements, principally the yellow press and expansionist politicians, who seized the opportunity to advance larger policy goals. "Whipped on by unscrupulous journalists," Samuel Flagg Bemis wrote, "the public hastily held Spain responsible for the vengeful destruction of an American warship." James P. Warburg stated that the "yellow press held Spain responsible and whipped up a frenzy," and Louis Martin Sears suggested that public opinion "succumbed to the arts of yellow journalism." "Public sentiment had been worked up by the sensational press, frequently called the 'yellow press,'" James Ford Rhodes wrote; "it had manipulated the real news, spread unfounded reports, putting all before their readers with scare headlines." W. E. Woodward insisted that "the war was created by the newspapers. They put it on the market just as a soap manufacturer makes a market for a new brand of washing powder. . . . It was an advertising campaign of the most lavish character." Roger Burlingame suggested that it was "doubtful . . . that the war would have developed without the agency of the most vicious and cynical behavior of a part of the American press that our nation had yet seen." Joseph E. Wisan was categorical: "The Spanish-American War would not have occurred had not the appearance of Hearst in New York journalism precipitated a bitter battle for newspaper circulation." Richard W. Leopold carried the argument one step further: "Popular indignation was kept at a boiling point by an irresponsible press whose disgraceful practices were not confined to any one city."[29] H. Wayne Morgan held the press directly responsible for the war. "Newspaper pressure," Morgan argued, "helped cause the war by keeping diplomacy unsettled in the face of mounting public opinion and ranting congressmen." Cuba was a "godsend to popular newspapers," Oscar Handlin affirmed. "Exciting stories set forth in horrifying detail the record of Spanish atrocities and whipped sentiment to a boiling point."[30]

Historiographical formulations of public opinion, aided and aroused by yellow journalism, as the explanation for 1898 have not, however, always been convincing or conclusive. Certainly not all narratives accord the same prominence to the press. Lewis Gould argued quite the opposite, insisting that the press "reflected what the public wanted, rather than shaping it." John Offner similarly insisted that "there is no evidence" to indicate that the "sensational press" influenced McKinley's policy, suggesting that "its impact on changing public opinion may have been limited."[31]

But even if it were possible to demonstrate the relationship between policy and public opinion, the larger and perhaps more important question involves precisely the character of popular opinion. What, in short, was the opinion of the public that was said to have moved political leaders toward a specific course of action? On this question there does exist scattered if admittedly anecdotal evidence. In fact, "public opinion" by all accounts had arrayed fully in support of Cuban independence. As early as September 1895, Secretary of State Richard Olney prepared an internal memorandum on the Cuban insurrection, submitted for "the careful consideration of the Executive," warning about "public opinion." Olney wrote: "The contest [is] attracting the attention of all our people as well as enlisting their sympathies, if for no other reason, than because the insurgents are apparently the weaker party—politicians of all stripes, including congressmen, either already setting their sails or preparing to set them so as to catch the popular breeze—it being not merely probable but almost certain that next winter Washington will swarm with emissaries of the insurgents demanding at least recognition of their belligerency."[32] Years later Senator Foraker reflected on his support for recognizing the insurgent provisional government: "In entertaining the opinion by which I was governed that the Government known as the Republic of Cuba was entitled to recognition, I was but in harmony . . . with the majority of my colleagues, and an overwhelming majority of the American people."[33]

If, indeed, public opinion in a democracy acted in such a decisive fashion to determine the course and conduct of policy, the steadfast opposition of both the Cleveland and McKinley administrations to Cuban independence in the face of "public opinion" poses an apparent problem. In fact, public pressure in behalf of Cuba Libre, including the call for the recognition of the Cuban provisional government and granting belligerency status, was rejected at every turn. Cleveland and McKinley were unabashed in their resistance to "public opinion." On the contrary, opposition to popular clamor was celebrated at the time as evidence of courageous presidential leadership. Occasionally this point is acknowledged in the historical literature. James MacGregor Burns took note of the "popular sympathy for the Cuban revolution" but stressed that the Cleveland administration "had resisted these pressures." A similar argument was made by Gerald C. Eggert in his biography of Richard Olney. "When guerrilla warfare in Cuba became more savage," Eggert affirmed, "and public sympathy for the rebels increased, the administration refused to alter course." In truth, at the time President McKinley was congratulated for standing up against public opinion. The *Philadelphia Inquirer* praised McKinley for resisting popular support of the Cuban cause: "The President was wise when he fought valiantly against the recognition of a Cuban republic." The *Hartford Post*, published by McKinley's private secretary, John Addison Porter, was openly exultant. "President McKinley," the *Post* editorialized, "was right when with all his power he successfully resisted the demand of Congress and of a large section of people that these cowardly, good-for-nothing insurgents be recognized as an independent government." The *Journal of Commerce* also reflected official exaltation. "There is great gratification in the Cabinet," the *Journal* affirmed, "that the United States have escaped from the ridiculous and embarrassing position in what they would have found themselves if they had been compelled to recognize Gomez. . . . The firmness of the President saved the country from such a situation."[34]

• • •

Public opinion further implicated the actions of President McKinley. The representation of the war has often been personalized and linked to the character of the president, his temperament and disposition. Formulation of policy has often been eclipsed by formation of personality; questions of the national interest are overshadowed by individual idiosyncrasies. In one view, McKinley is depicted as standing up courageously against mounting pressure from an aroused public and a bellicose Congress. The White House is a bastion of reason during a time of irrationality, but eventually is obliged to capitulate to the will of the people and the demands of their elected representatives. James Henretta et al. argued that "President McKinley did not seek war. He had no stomach for the martial spirit sweeping the country. . . . But, in the end, McKinley had no choice." "The destruction of the *Maine*," John Spencer Bassett concluded, "increased the feeling against Spain and strengthened the hands of those who were trying to press McKinley into war." According to Wolfgang Drechsler, after February 15 "public opinion rapidly turned against those who wanted to exercise caution, particularly against McKinley."[35] "The administration was unable to stem the tide which both the Congress and the country was making for war," Herbert Croly insisted. He continued: "Up to the last moment the President sought to find some middle ground. He sought to placate American public opinion by acting energetically on behalf of American citizens in Cuba, and by pressing Spain to improve its conduct of the war and to redress the grievances of its Cuban subjects. If the *Maine* had not blown up, he might have succeeded. . . . As it was, the President risked his popularity and the confidence of the country by his reluctance to abandon a peaceful solution."[36]

There are variations on this theme, of course, and not all of them are favorable to McKinley. Indeed, his role in the events of 1898 has been one of the more controversial aspects of a literature otherwise noteworthy for the prevalence of consensual narratives. Sympathetic accounts portray McKinley as personally committed to peace, but in the end obliged to acquiesce to events beyond his control. The president emerges in these accounts as a pragmatic politician, attentive to political considerations, and mindful of the need to defend the constitutional prerogatives of the executive branch of government. He is depicted as having understood, too, that he could not long ignore public opinion or resist congressional pressure—not, at least, without calamitous political consequences or a monumental constitutional crisis, or both. McKinley has thus been represented as finding himself in an impossible situation and finally bowing to the inevitable. The *Maine* produced an "extraordinary burst of public opinion to which a struggling President could find no effective antidote," argued David Trask. McKinley was "desperate to avoid hostilities" but was "ultimately responsive to the voice of the people"; what "compelled [McKinley] to act against his deepest desire for peace was the irresistible popular demand welling up everywhere in America after the destruction of the *Maine*."[37]

"By the spring of 1898," asserted Thomas Bailey, "the pressure of herd hysteria had become so overwhelming that it could not have been stemmed by any ordinary mortal." Richard Welch contended that the destruction of the *Maine* "not only heightened the war hysteria in certain sections of the American press and public but persuaded McKinley that events had overtaken the possibility of putting an end to the struggle in Cuba by means of Spanish reforms and limited autonomy." "McKinley could not resist the growing pressure to intervene," wrote Irwin Unger, and Oscar Handlin believed that "McKinley had to act, much as he was reluctant to do so." "McKinley, despite his personal desire to avert war, did not feel he had freedom of action," was how Alexander DeConde saw it; E. Berkeley Tompkins concluded that McKinley "had come to feel that it was best to acquiesce and give the people the war they were demanding." John Spencer Bassett also spoke of "popular demand," a "feeling [that] grew so strong that it swept away McKinley's resistance and made war inevitable." George Tindall agreed, speculating that McKinley "might have defied Congress and public opinion, but in the end the political risk was too high."[38] That McKinley resisted pressure for war as long as he did, the argument concludes, was in itself no small tribute to his leadership ability. "It would be easy to condemn McKinley for not holding out against war," contended William Leuchtenburg, "but McKinley showed considerable courage in bucking the tide." "McKinley . . . exhibited commendable restraint," asserted Richard Leopold.[39]

Not all observers agree, however. Other interpretations of 1898 question the inevitability of the war and reject the proposition that McKinley was without choices. That he capitulated to public pressure, the inflammatory press, and jingoes in Congress, some have argued, says more about the character of the president than the constraints on his options. The logic of the school of thought that represents the war as unnecessary often leads directly to the president, to whom the inexplicable war is attributed. McKinley was incompetent and ineffective, and thus the war was his fault. By implication, war became possible because of a weak president who, at a decisive moment of a deepening political crisis, failed to assert executive leadership. "Possibly a strong President might have headed off the rush to war by openly denouncing the clamor for intervention," speculated T. Harry Williams, Richard Current, and Frank Freidel, "but McKinley was not a strong executive." The *Maine* so emboldened jingoes, Wayne Cole suggested, that it "would have required a stronger President than McKinley to resist their war-making influence." McKinley "had not the nerve and power to resist the pressure for war," argued James Ford Rhodes, and Frederick Merk observed that "moral courage . . . was not part of the kindly make-up of this President." Roger Burlingame, who persisted with his indictment of the press, maintained that pressured by "the press-inflamed Congress, goaded by the press-inflamed people, breathing down his neck, [McKinley] was frightened into sending his war message," adding: "It was a compelling pressure, surely, but a strong leader would probably have resisted it." "McKinley exhibited neither the determined leadership nor the moral courage that might possibly have restrained his impatient, war-minded countrymen," declared Foster Rhea Dulles. "His failure did not lie in the field of diplomacy . . . but in national leadership at home."[40] "In a period of acute national crisis the executive was paralyzed," asserted Gerald Linderman. Ruhl Bartlett wrote of "a weak President," and Charles and Mary Beard noted that McKinley was perceived as "weak-kneed." "A kindly soul in a spineless body," was the way Samuel Eliot Morison described him, and Leland D. Baldwin stated: "McKinley, had he been a strong leader, might conceivably have won his ends by diplomatic ends." "Congress wanted war," Harold Underwood Faulkner indicated, "and McKinley was not the man to resist."[41]

In still another explanation of 1898, the relationship between the *Maine* and public opinion, on one hand, and Congress, the president, and the coming of the war, on the other, have been modified and transformed into a proposition from which significantly different causal hierarchies have been arranged. With a slight change of sequence and a shift of emphasis, the *Maine* was represented as the occasion contrived as a pretext for war rather than a chance precipitant. The incident was thus exploited by expansionist politicians to mobilize public opinion in behalf of a policy of territorial expansion. It was not an aroused public that pressured unwilling politicians into war but, on the contrary, unscrupulous politicians who manipulated the unsuspecting public into war. The *Maine* simply played into the hands of expansionist elements in Congress and the administration. "Our government," wrote Horace Edgar Flack, "had practically decided on war . . . the *Maine* question was considered the best thing to arouse popular enthusiasm." "The shocking disaster was a stroke of good fortune for America's interventionists," insisted

Walter Karp, "a stroke of good fortune" that "drastically shortened the road to war." Ruhl Bartlett characterized the de Lôme letter and the *Maine* as the "fortuitous circumstances and events" that increased "the influence of those who wanted war with Spain for imperialistic reasons." He continued: "There existed a small, influential group of politicians with imperialistic ambitions who seized an opportunity they partly created to further their designs." D. A. Graber described the *Maine* as one of the incidents "used by the yellow press and by expansionist Americans such as Senator [Henry Cabot] Lodge and Assistant Secretary of the Navy Theodore Roosevelt to inflame public opinion." William Appleman Williams similarly argued that the *Maine* incident "significantly increased the tension and did encourage those, like Roosevelt, who had been 'hoping and working ardently to bring about our interference in Cuba.'" Horace Merrill and Marion Merrill agreed, affirming directly— but without naming names—that "the Senate warmongers, employing the *Maine* episode in particular, pushed the nation relentlessly toward war." This view was shared by J. Rogers Hollingsworth, who argued that by "deliberately creating a war sentiment, the expansionists were rapidly producing an atmosphere in which the voices of sanity could hardly be heard." "Pro-annexationists in the Administration," Philip Foner also suggested, "could not let such an opportunity pass without taking as much advantage of it as possible." In a careful study of policy and public opinion, Robert C. Hildebrand concluded that as early as 1897, President McKinley had formulated a Cuban policy that could only lead to war. Public support was "made certain" by the destruction of the *Maine* and "rendered superfluous any efforts of [McKinley] to prepare the public for war." Hildebrand concluded: "The president could . . . predict the direction of the public's drift, and he saw little reason to guide a public opinion that was moving—parallel to his own diplomacy—inexorably toward war."[42]

This interpretation produced a substantially different assessment of McKinley. No longer characterized as weak and ineffectual, buffeted by forces he neither controlled nor comprehended, McKinley was portrayed as an expansionist, calculating and clever, steadfastly pursuing clear objectives and skillfully exploiting a fortuitous event to embark on an expansionist policy. With the naval court report completed, Karp wrote, "McKinley's difficulties were at an end." It was now only necessary to "bring his diplomacy with Spain to a crisis—never very difficult in dealing with a fifth-rate power." Karp concluded: "Had McKinley been seeking a peaceful solution, the Spanish concessions certainly provided the basis for one. Instead, McKinley rejected the offer. . . . With the official release of the *Maine* report on March 28, he now had overwhelming popular support for armed intervention."[43]

Conspicuously absent from most accounts of 1898 has been the possibility of U.S. intervention as a response to the imminence of a Cuban triumph. Some of the conflicting and otherwise contradictory explanations of U.S. policy acquire far greater coherence when set against the prospects of an insurgent victory. Julius Pratt argued that the war would have been avoided "if McKinley had been resolute enough to exercise a little more patience with Spain and defy Congress." No doubt, too, James Ford Rhodes was correct in suggesting that had McKinley not succumbed to public pressure and "abandoned his policy and went over to the war party," Spain "might have been led to grant independence to Cuba." But that was precisely the one eventuality McKinley was seeking to foreclose. Thus, on one hand, a rebellious Congress responded to public pressure to intervene in behalf of Cuban independence and, on the other, rebellious Cubans within a measurable distance of military victory defined the necessary policy course in defense of U.S. interests. Henry Bamford Parkes came slightly closer to the mark by noting that Spanish capitulation to the March 27 ultimatum "would probably have led to the liberation of Cuba without war; but a peaceful settlement would not have . . . enabled the United States to acquire bases overseas."[44]

Perhaps the most persistent criticism of McKinley has centered on his decision to proceed with war despite Spanish acquiescence to the U.S. ultimatum of March 27. Without an acknowledgment of the Cuban role in these events, U.S. historians have been left to improvise an explanation to account for McKinley's actions. One line of argument has maintained that the Spanish concessions were, in fact, suspect, and that McKinley lacked confidence in Spain's commitment to peace. "Spanish evasion and delay had destroyed confidence in the good faith of the Spanish government," was the way that William MacDonald saw it. W. E. Woodward speculated that McKinley "may have thought the Spaniards were insincere and playing for time." Nelson Blake and Oscar Barck suggested that McKinley "could thus shrug off the Spanish concession . . . as insincere and worthless." Richard Leopold indicated that Spanish concessions were rejected by "contemporaries who had grown weary of broken promises and the inevitable Spanish *mañana*." It was Thomas Bailey's belief that Spanish acquiescence did not matter, for Spain "had pursued such a tortuous course that McKinley had little faith in her promises, or in her ability to carry them out." According to Arthur M. Schlesinger, McKinley "doubted Spain's good faith in comply-ing," and John Bassett argued that the administration believed that last-minute concessions "would be evaded, as in the past."[45]

Various types of weaknesses have been attributed to McKinley: weak-ness of character, or of courage, or of conviction were all offered as explanations of why he proceeded to war even after Spain had appar-ently capitulated to his demands. "Any President with a backbone would have seized this opportunity for an honorable solution," pronounced Samuel Eliot Morison. Randolph Greenfield Adams arrived at a similar conclusion: "left alone, McKinley would probably have avoided a war, as he was a peaceful and gentle man." James Warburg agreed, suggesting that McKinley "was not a man who would stand out resolutely for a lit-tle more patience when a peaceful and honorable settlement was in sight. . . . He acted as a follower—not a leader."[46]

In fact, the problem McKinley confronted had less to do with Spain than with Cubans, who, in refusing to observe the cease-fire and suspend military operations, seemed poised to overrun Spanish positions. In-deed, intervention was as much against the expanding Cuban claim of sovereignty as the declining Spanish claim. McKinley could not have ac-cepted Spanish acquiescence to the March 27 ultimatum without Cuban participation, and Cuban participation was predicated entirely on the proposition of independence.

Thus, the war arrived in the early spring of 1898 and its origins have continued to be debated in terms established one hundred years ago. The *Maine* propelled the nation to war, a denouement that was inexora-ble in the face of an aroused public and timid public officials. In the process, an "unnecessary" war became known an "inevitable" one.

Constructing the Cuban Absence

Less assistance than expected was obtained from the Cubans. . . . In the campaign in Cuba we had so little aid from the Cubans. It must be allowed that they made very weak allies.
—Andrew S. Draper, *The Rescue of Cuba* (1899)

It becomes necessary to speak of the men's opinions of the Cubans. To put it shortly, both officers and privates have the most lively contempt for the Cubans. They despise them. They came down here expecting to fight side by side with an ally, but this ally has done little but stay in the rear . . . manifesting an indifference to the cause of Cuban liberty which could not be exceeded by some one who had never heard of it.
—Stephen Crane (July 14, 1898)

The [June 20] meeting between General Shafter and General Garcia was very cordial, and they immediately repaired to General Rabi's tent, around which a guard was placed. . . . In General Rabi's tent were gathered Admiral Sampson, General Shafter, General Garcia, General Rabi, and a few members of their respective staffs. The object of General Shafter's visit was to learn from General Garcia and his officers what they knew concerning the strength of the enemy in and around Santiago, to question them concerning the nature of the country, and to ascertain what assistance could be expected of them.
—Lieutenant Colonel John D. Miley, *In Cuba with Shafter* (1899)

General García . . . received numerous visits at his headquarters. American commanders and officers, marines and naval officers, newspaper reporters and representatives of foreign governments consulted with him. American troops conducted frequent movements, while their officers were completely disoriented. They besieged us with questions and heaped attention upon us. They needed us: they knew that without our cooperation, their failure was imminent.
—Mariano Corona Ferrer, *De la manigua (Ecos de la epopeya)* (1900)

The Americans waited for the support of the *insurrectos* in order to be able to land at Daiquirí, given that without Cuban assistance, they would not have been able to land their troops. This seemed strange to us, that such a powerful nation needed the help of our forces, given that during three years of war they could not help us, with us needing help far more than they did.
—Rodolfo Bergés, *Cuba y Santo Domingo: Apuntes de la guerra de Cuba de mi diario de campaña, 1895–1898* (1905)

I search in vain in the history books of my country for proper appreciation and recognition of the role which Cuban patriots played in the liberation of this country. It would seem that the Spanish-American War was fought only by American soldiers. Not that I would in any way discredit the patriotic service which my countrymen lent your country in 1898. . . . However, I wish to take this occasion to assure you that patriots throughout the world appreciate the valor and unselfishness of the valiant Cuban patriots who, long before their American brothers arrived here, had fought and died for the liberation of their country.
—Senator Dennis Chavez (D-N.M.), Havana: On the occasion of the 50th anniversary of the *Maine* (February 15, 1948)

Senator Chavez turned over the text of his speech to the Public Affairs Officer of the Embassy one day prior to the ceremony, but declined to make any changes when it was pointed out that Americans do appreciate the efforts of the Cubans to achieve independence and that his remarks might be used to our disadvantage by the Communists.
—U.S. Ambassador R. Henry Norweb (February 17, 1948)

The war ended in August 1898, but not entirely the way the Cubans had envisioned it would. Spain had been defeated, to be sure, and at least that part of the Cuban purpose had been achieved. However, the pursuit of independence had provided the occasion for U.S. intervention, whereupon everything changed, as it was meant to. From the outset the State Department had crafted the "neutral intervention," precisely, Assistant Secretary of State Alvey A. Adee explained, for the purpose of operating "in territory transiently ours by conquest." Even before the formal armistice of August 12, General William Shafter proclaimed Santiago de Cuba conquered territory. "The soil occupied by the army of the United States was part of the Union," Shafter said, "and would remain so until the Union through its proper offices should declare otherwise." Attorney General John Griggs informed the Cuban provisional vice president, Domingo Méndez Capote, that the U.S. army in Cuba was an "invading army that would carry with it American sovereignty wherever it went." Admiral William T. Sampson gave explicit meaning to the U.S. presence. "It does not make any difference whether the Cubans prove amenable to the sovereignty of the Government or not," he asserted.

"We are there. We intend to rule and that is all there is to it." Secretary of War Elihu Root was brief and blunt. The United States had the "right to protect Cuba," Root affirmed after the Treaty of Paris, "by virtue of our occupation of Cuba and the terms under which sovereignty was yielded to by Spain."[1]

The war became known as the "Spanish-American War," a construct that in purpose and point of view denied the Cuban presence and participation. Cubans seemed to have disappeared, denied a role in the very outcome to which they had contributed so significantly. They had been displaced from the front lines. They were excluded from the negotiations for the surrender of Santiago de Cuba. They did not take part in the deliberations on the armistice. They were not signatories to the Treaty of Paris. On January 1, 1899, during the official ceremonies in Havana signaling the end of four hundred years of Spanish rule, Cubans formed an audience of mere onlookers as sovereignty of the island passed from Spain to the United States.

It did indeed appear that the sixty-day conflict in Cuba was a Spanish and American war. Appearances mattered. Observers were not slow to draw portentous inferences. The scale of public opinion in the United States turned against the Cubans. In press dispatches and army field reports, Cubans were portrayed as unworthy allies, undeserving of the sacrifices made in their behalf, whereupon it became easy to disparage, dismiss, or deny altogether their contribution in the final months of their war for independence.

Cubans had contributed nothing to the victory over Spain, the Americans proclaimed. "They are the most worthless . . . lot of bushwackers extant," Captain Frank R. McCoy informed his parents. Major James Bell was brief and to the point: "What they want is to see us do the work and themselves reap the fruits." The *New York Times* war correspondent agreed: "The Cubans did little or no fighting. The insurgent army, therefore, has borne no testimony to its desire for a free Cuba. If it wants it, it was not willing, in the presence of a magnificent opportunity to fight for it, or make any sacrifice for it." One Missouri volunteer recalled Cubans contemptuously: "We did not expect much help from them, so were not disappointed when they failed to come into the battle when we needed them badly. They disappeared almost immediately into the jungle." When later asked to evaluate the contribution of Cuban troops during the war, General Samuel B. M. Young responded categorically: "They were of no use to me whatever." General Shafter expressed his views with his usual parsimony of language: "They were of no earthly service to me." In one of the most complete contemporary accounts of the Santiago campaign, Herbert H. Sargent, himself an infantry officer during the war, pronounced the definitive judgment on Cubans:

> Since the Americans were in the island fighting to make Cuba free, one would naturally suppose that the Cuban soldiers would have fought with desperate determination and courage, and that they would have been ready and anxious to take the initiative and lead the way in every battle, in order to show their allies and the world that they were worthy of freedom, in that they knew at least how to fight and how to die. The truth is that the insurgents did little or no hard fighting at this time or afterwards. . . . They could not be depended upon to close with the enemy and fight till one or the other was defeated or crushed. Nor could they be depended upon to prosecute in a systematic manner any particular military operation that required severe fighting or great sacrifice.

Sargent could reach only one conclusion: "While the freedom of Cuba was being decided under their very eyes, they stood by inefficiently, inactive. The rewards were theirs, but the Americans made the sacrifice. By the blood of the Americans the victories were won."[2]

These pronouncements had far-reaching implications, of course, for if it could be demonstrated that Cubans had actually declined to play a part in their own liberation, their claim to independence could hardly warrant serious consideration. War correspondent Stephen Crane understood the significance, if not the source, of these developments. If the Cuban "stupidly, drowsily remains out of these fights," Crane pondered, "what weight is his voice to have later in the final adjustments? The officers and men of the [U.S.] army, if their feeling remains the same, will not be happy to see him have any at all. . . . It is the worst thing for the cause of an independent Cuba that could possibly exist."[3]

This sentiment gained currency immediately after the surrender of Santiago de Cuba. "The assistance [Cubans] were to give to our men," affirmed John Ward of the Second Division Hospital Corps, "has turned out to be an absolute delusion. . . . In fact, the Cuban insurgents are looked upon by all our men who have seen them in their native land as a huge fake. The idea of giving them controlling power in the government of the island is farcical." The *New York Times* correspondent agreed: "The Cubans who have made a pretense of fighting with us have proved worthless in the field. . . . It would be a tragedy, a crime, to deliver the island into their hands."[4]

In the weeks and months that followed, hostility against the Cubans increased. They were not, as the American public had been led to believe, inspired by love of liberty but by the lure of looting. "From the highest officer to the lowliest 'soldier,' " Rough Rider Burr MacIntosh wrote scornfully, "they were there for personal gain."[5] Perhaps the United States was the victim of an elaborate hoax, duped into an unnecessary war to assist an unworthy cause in behalf of an undeserving people. "We are not unmindful of this Nation's pledge concerning 'Cuba for Cubans,' " the *New York Tribune* assured its readers. "But why was it made? Because Cuban leaders declared, and their friends here declared, that the people of the island were ready for self-government. . . . Have our troops found such to be the case? The answer is an unhesitating and emphatic No. . . . If thus the basis and foundation of our pledge be found false and unsubstantial, with what grace can it be demanded that the pledge itself stand?" Reports from the island made the same point. "Poll the United States troops in the province of Santiago de Cuba," the *New York Evening Post* war correspondent suggested five days after the surrender of Santiago de Cuba, "and 99 out of 100 will say in almost so many words: 'We have bought a gold brick in *Cuba Libre.*' "[6]

These propositions seemed possessed of an internal logic of their own, from which a number of conclusions seemed irresistible. There was no Cuban army or Cuban republic; there was no such thing as Cuba. "The Cuban soldier is a myth," proclaimed General H. W. Lawton, "an evanescent dream." *New York Times* correspondent Stanhope Sams, who was attached to General Shafter's staff, reflected official thinking after the fall of Santiago de Cuba. "We came to conquer for another people," he wrote on July 29, "vainly imagining that a new nation had been born. But there is no Cuba. There are no Cuban people. There are not freemen here to whom we could deliver this marvelous island. We have fought for a spectral republic. . . . If we are to save Cuba, we must hold it. If we leave it to the Cubans, we give it over to a reign of terror—to the machete and the torch, to insurrection and assassination." A week later Sams returned to this theme more forcefully: "There is . . . no Cuban aspiration, no Cuban sentiment. Indeed, there could be discovered no 'Cuban people' where the United States sent its fleets and armies to find them, and to aid in establishing another free republic among the nations of the world."[7]

• • •

The absence of Cubans from frontline U.S. military operations was the result of decisions made at the highest official levels in Washington precisely as a means to reduce, if not preclude altogether, Cuban demands to participate in the negotiations of postwar settlements. U.S. officials scrupulously avoided any contact or communication that might be construed as official recognition of the authority of the provisional government and insurgent army command. Control over the conduct of the war guaranteed mastery over the arrangements of peace. Adjutant General H. C. Corbin specifically warned General Shafter against "putting too much confidence in any persons outside of your own troops." Lieutenant Colonel John D. Miley recalled the meeting at which Cuban General Calixto García offered to place his troops under U.S. command, an offer that Shafter deftly declined, responding that he "could not exercise any authority over him, but would, however, be very glad to accept his voluntary services." Colonel Arthur L. Wagner, a cavalry officer at Santiago de Cuba, subsequently disclosed that he was "enjoined to be extremely careful to avoid in every way anything that might be construed as a recognition by my superiors of the Cuban forces as the army of an independent power or belligerent nation." The *Nation* was direct: "It is our war and we must depend upon ourselves to conduct it."[8]

In fact, Cubans played a decisive if largely unacknowledged role in the U.S. victory. They served as scouts, guides, and interpreters; they provided vital intelligence and information.[9] But most of all, they engaged in military operations at critical moments of the campaign. Cubans secured the beaches and facilitated the landing of U.S. forces. A division under the command of General Demetrio Castillo Duany secured the designated landing site at Daiquirí, east of Santiago de Cuba. U.S. forces under General Shafter arrived there on June 22, and within twenty-four hours, 15,000 soldiers had safely reached shore without a single hostile shot being fired. "Landing at Daiquiri unopposed," Shafter cabled Washington triumphantly.[10] At exactly the same moment, seven miles away, another U.S. division waded ashore at Siboney, also unopposed. Simultaneous with the U.S. landing Cuban General Jesús Rabí led 500 troops in a diversionary attack against Spanish positions at Cabañas west of Santiago de Cuba to distract local Spanish forces. At no point did the United States encounter Spanish resistance upon landing. Indeed, one reason the United States selected southeastern Cuba as a disembarkation site was the control Cubans exercised over vast expanses of the province, the interior as well as the coastline, thereby guaranteeing U.S. forces a safe landing.[11] The U.S. march from the landing site at Daiquirí inland toward Las Guásimas was aided by a Cuban vanguard column commanded by Colonel Carlos González Clavell, with Cuban soldiers serving as flankers and skirmishers.

In the days and weeks that followed, Cuban army units took up positions across southeastern Cuba to contain and check the movement of Spanish military forces. An estimated 3,000 Cuban officers and men under General Luis de Feria were deployed at Holguín and prevented 12,000 Spanish soldiers from relieving the garrison at Santiago de Cuba. An estimated 3,000 Cuban soldiers under the command of General Pedro A. Pérez contained 6,000 Spanish troops inside the city of Guantánamo in the east, while another 1,000 insurgents soldiers commanded by General Salvador Ríos were deployed to contain 6,000 Spaniards in Manzanillo on the west. General Francisco Estrada's forces were deployed south of Bayamo. Over 1,000 Cuban soldiers under the command of General García subsequently participated alongside U.S. forces in the battle of El Caney. After El Caney and San Juan, several thousand Cuban troops under the command of Generals García and Agustín Cebreco occupied positions along an extensive perimeter west and northwest of Santiago de Cuba along mountain passes leading in and out of the eastern capital.

At several points during the campaign, the Cuban role was decisive. On June 22, the day U.S. forces landed at Daiquirí and Siboney, a Spanish relief convoy of 3,750 officers and men under the command of Colonel Federico Escario set out from Manzanillo to reinforce the Spanish garrison at Santiago de Cuba. Much depended on the timely arrival of this column. "If your excellency can hold out until the arrival of Escario . . . ," Spanish governor general Ramón Blanco in Havana cabled the Spanish army commander in Santiago de Cuba, "the situation will be much improved."[12]

For ten days, throughout the course of the 160-mile march eastward, a smaller Cuban force of some 600 troops under the command of General Francisco Estrada attacked, ambushed, and harassed the relief column daily, engaging Spanish troops in frequent if intermittent day-long skirmishes. "The column has been harassed all day . . . ," Colonel Escario recorded in his operations diary on June 23; "all day . . . a steady lively fire"; in an entry two days later, he noted: "The same as yesterday, the column was harassed all day." Near Palma Soriano, Escario wrote of having "to fight the enemy all along the road, on both sides of which the latter occupied good positions and endeavored to detain the column at any price." The next day the Cubans mounted a fierce attack, to which Escario conceded grudging respect, remarking "there were moments during that battle when the tenacity of the enemy and the order with which they fought gave the impression that they might belong to our own column." He added: "To do the enemy justice it must be stated that they defended these well-chosen positions with persistency and in good order, and that they rose to unusual heights that day, making this the fiercest battle which we sustained on the march from Manzanillo to Santiago and one of the most remarkable ones of the present campaign."[13]

Escario reached Santiago de Cuba on July 3, but at considerable cost. The column had been engaged in no less than thirty combats, suffering a total of twenty-seven dead and more than seventy officers and soldiers wounded. It had expended more than 30,000 rounds of Mauser cartridges and consumed vital supplies originally destined for the relief of the defenders of Santiago de Cuba. In fact, the column arrived so depleted and its resources so spent as to be of no use in the defense of the city. On the contrary, the arrival of Escario's force made a bad situation worse. "Provisions and ammunition, already scarce," Spanish lieutenant José Müeller y Tejeiro remembered, "became still more so, because there were twice the number of mouths to be fed and twice the number of muskets to be supplied." J. Rodríguez Martínez was also in Santiago de Cuba the evening that Escario arrived and remembered the occasion well: "Such timely reinforcement could not but have been received with rejoicement, but at the same time it was depressing to think about the lack of provisions, for if supplies were extremely scarce for those who were already there defending the city, what was going to happen as a result of the increased consumption produced by the new arrivals?"[14]

Escario's arrival in Santiago de Cuba had been expected on or about June 28. The Manzanillo–Santiago de Cuba march was normally completed in six days, but on this occasion, as a result of Cuban harassment, the march took ten days. The delay was decisive. Had Escario arrived as planned, G. J. A. O'Toole speculated, the Spanish fleet might not have had to sail out of the harbor to face certain destruction. During the four-day delay, moreover, U.S. forces had overrun Spanish positions at El Caney and San Juan. Captain Alfred Mahan, later musing on small events with big outcomes, reflected on the delay of the Escario column—without, however, mentioning the reason for it. The column reached Santiago de Cuba on July 3, "too late, to take part in the defence of San Juan and El Caney," Mahan wrote, "upon holding which the city depended for food and water," observing that "it gives a shivering suggestion how much more arduous would have been the task of our troops had Escario come up in time." Mahan concluded: "The incident but adds another to history's long list of instances where desperate energy and economy of time have wrested safety out of the jaws of imminent disaster."[15]

In the larger view, the Cuban insurrection had already brought the Spanish army to the brink of defeat. During three years of relentless war, the Cubans had destroyed railroad lines, bridges, and roads and paralyzed telegraph communications, making it all but impossible for the Spanish army to move across the island and between provinces. That Cubans had, moreover, inflicted countless thousands of casualties on Spanish soldiers and effectively driven Spanish units into beleaguered defensive concentrations in the cities, there to suffer further the debilitating effects of illness and hunger, in no small fashion contributed to the final ease with which Spain was defeated.[16]

The part played by Cubans in the outcome of the war passed largely unrecognized and unacknowledged in the United States. What was remarkable about contemporary accounts was the degree to which U.S. victories were attributed either to American valor or Spanish blunders, or a combination of the two, but rarely to the contribution of Cubans. Afterward, Admiral William Sampson was at a loss to explain Spanish ineffectiveness. "What motive induced the Spaniards to leaving [the] landing-places without a defense remains a mystery," Sampson pondered. "Had [Spain] been prepared to resist," he suggested, "it would have greatly increased the danger in landing our men and the time required in landing. The very irregular character of the ground would have furnished good protection for its defenders." John J. Pershing also took measure of conditions and arrived at the same conclusion: "One thousand determined men could have made this disembarkation difficult if not impossible." That they seemed to have failed to do so obliged Pershing to improvise some plausible explanation: "Spain, realizing the ultimate outcome, waged it much as an inferior swordsman who had been challenged by a master of the art; she accepted the engagement and let the adversary shed a certain amount of her blood. In other words, she saved her honor." Correspondent George Kennan concluded that the United States was the beneficiary of Spanish ineptitude. If the landing sites had been held by a more determined enemy, he speculated, "it would have been extremely difficult, if not absolutely impossible, to get the troops ashore." He explained:

"In order to drive them out it would have been necessary to land in the surf under fire, and storm the heights by scaling the precipitous terraces in front of the rampart on the sea side. This might, perhaps, have been done, but it would have involved a great sacrifice of life. Fortunately for General Shafter and his troops, the Spaniards did not attempt to oppose the landing. The Spanish officers in Cuba . . . were not skillful tacticians. Instead of anticipating General Shafter's movements and occupying, with an adequate force, the only two places in the vicinity of Santiago where he could possibly land, they overlooked or neglected the splendid defensive positions that nature herself had provided for them, and allowed the army of invasion to come ashore without firing a shot. It was great luck for us, but it was not war."[17]

Some years later General Shafter recalled his apprehensions as he steamed toward Santiago de Cuba, mindful of the presence of tens of thousands of Spanish troops in the surrounding provincial towns, fearful that they "would any day be upon us." But they never appeared, and Shafter confessed complete bafflement: "Why they did not come is something no military man can appreciate or understand." Theodore Roosevelt was similarly puzzled: "Five hundred resolute men could have prevented the disembarkation at very little cost to themselves."[18]

• • •

In light of the subsequent conduct of U.S. military operations, it is not difficult to envision a different outcome of the Santiago campaign without Cuban participation. The U.S. command fully understood the hazards of military operations in Cuba. From the outset army leaders grasped the importance of a quick war, concerned that U.S. troops could not survive a long midsummer campaign in the tropics. "I estimated that the troops would have immunity for two or three weeks," General Shafter later acknowledged, "and to be successful with my force it was to be a dash or nothing." On another occasion he was more specific: "I knew . . . well before I landed . . . that within three or four or perhaps five weeks (it came sooner), that army would be prostrated with disease. And I determined I would make it a question of brawn and strength of the American Army, against disease and death which lurked in the jungles of that island."[19]

In fact, the American military campaign began in chaos and nearly ended in calamity. Preparations for war suffered from a combination of inexperience, incompetence, and inefficiency. The tens of thousands of men who rushed to volunteer for military service overwhelmed the capacity of the quartermaster department. Chronic shortages of almost everything, including the most essential military equipment, medical supplies, clothing, and food, beset the swollen ranks of the army. U.S. military historians have provided sobering accounts of the woeful inadequacies that attended preparations for war in 1898. Army historian Major William Addleman Ganoe wrote of the "sad state of uselessness" of the newly augmented army, which "proved to be as much of a menace to friend as foe." Major C. Joseph Bernardo and Eugene H. Bacon concluded that "our incompetent conduct of the Spanish-American War was unbecoming a nation on the eve of becoming a major world power." *American Military History* (1969), the official text of the Office of the Chief of Military History of the U.S. Army, provided a chilling chronicle of preparations for war, including "a steady diet of badly prepared food, unbelievably poor sanitary conditions, inadequate medical facilities, and a lack of up-to-date weapons." The "nation went to war without any kind of over-all military plans of operations or even adequate intelligence about the enemy. . . . [T]he War Department bureaus and the Army high command found themselves almost totally unprepared." W. E. Woodward cited a long list of shortcomings, including a "military management" that was "more than inefficient; it was downright stupid," the lack of a "general staff to co-ordinate military operations," an army "wholly unprepared for war," and "sanitary and medical arrangements [that] . . . were shockingly inadequate." In *An Army for Empire: The United States Army in the Spanish-American War* (1971), Graham A. Cosmas provided a virtual catalog of follies and failures. Cosmas wrote of the "failure of the War Department to relate command assignments to the military tasks that had to be performed"; of a "system of administration in the field" that "suffered a near breakdown in the first weeks of the Spanish War"; of "a critical shortage of trained staff officers" that "prevented efficient management"; of ineffective administrators, incompetent commanders, inadequate supplies, inappropriate clothing. "The War Department," he concluded, "had neither the time nor the planning agency to work out in detail the strategy of the campaign, to study the terrain of the area, and to determine the transportation requirements of an army that was to fight under those conditions for the objective set."[20]

U.S. military operations in Cuba nearly resulted in a debacle for a host of reasons. Interservice rivalries between the army and the navy almost paralyzed the Cuban campaign.[21] The U.S. army command lacked accurate maps of the zones of operations. The landings at Daiquirí and Siboney were chaotic and disorganized. Communications broke down. Transportation problems nearly crippled the movement of soldiers and supplies. Lieutenant Colonel John Miley recalled the grim details of the campaign, of "transportation [that] was not ready for use"; of roads between the front lines and the supply lines "blocked by wagons stalled in the mud or breaking down, delaying the entire train into the night and sometimes so as to interfere with the next day's trip"; of the daily summer rains that not only made "the roads practically impassable for wagons . . . but [produced] streams so swollen that at times they were unfordable by pack-trains." Sick teamsters were replaced by inexperienced drivers. The condition of the animals was deplorable: "The mules, as well as the horses, were affected very much like the men. Day by day these animals sickened and became unserviceable, but often kept going until they dropped in their tracks."[22]

And there was more. The oppressive summer heat and daily tropical rains demoralized and disabled. Within days, senior U.S. commanders, including Generals Shafter, Joseph Wheeler, Samuel B. M. Young, and Hamilton Hawkins, themselves succumbed to disease and illness. Conditions among the troops were worse. Days within landing, U.S. forces confronted the prospect of a military disaster. Shortages of supplies, food, and medicine reached desperate proportions. Without sufficient food and medicine, soldiers succumbed to malaria, typhoid, and dysentery. Inadequate hospital facilities compounded the crisis. On July 6, only three days after General Shafter commenced negotiations with the Spanish command for the surrender of Santiago de Cuba, the dreaded quarantine flag was raised ominously behind U.S. lines: yellow fever had struck. The longer the Spanish army command refused to surrender, the greater the likelihood that a yellow fever epidemic would ravage U.S. military forces. Operations had already lasted longer than Shafter had planned. Conditions became desperate. The army seemed unable to hold its position, and Shafter was reluctantly forced to contemplate withdrawal. Theodore Roosevelt urgently appealed to Washington for help. "We are within measurable distance of a terrible military disaster," he cabled only two days after celebrating the victory at San Juan Hill; "we *must* have help—thousands of men, batteries and *food* and ammunition." Roosevelt's despair deepened as the days passed. "The mismanagement has been beyond belief," he wrote on July 7. "The lack of transportation, food and artillery has brought us to the very verge of disaster."[23]

The enemy was no longer Spain but rather time and the elements. By midsummer, the war outside Santiago de Cuba had come to a grim standstill: a contest of wills pitting the determination of the besieging army against the durability of the besieged. The scales quivered in the balance, each army weighed down with a sense of impending disaster. Within three weeks of arriving in Cuba, after having landed unopposed to face an army weakened by three years of war, the United States was on the verge of a humiliating withdrawal.

Shafter's request to pull back produced consternation in Washington. "All realized," Secretary Alger recalled, "that it would be exceedingly unfortunate if Shafter were compelled to abandon his position, for, besides loss of prestige abroad, in the United States the effect would be most keenly felt, and the Spanish government would, without doubt, be greatly encouraged to further resistance." General E. J. McClernand recorded his thoughts at the time:

> Our distinguished Surgeon General . . . has told us this evening that disease had driven its fangs into our men. . . . We know its progress was rapid, and beyond question a delay followed by a demand to retake positions that had once been captured only to be surrendered would have been fatal. While we waited the physical strength of officers and men would have lessened, and never again would our gallant little Army have been equal to the burst of speed and conquering energy that enabled it to capture El Caney and carried it to the heights of San Juan on July 1. It would have been necessary to have sent another Army to accomplish its mission.[24]

A pall settled over U.S. forces. An army that had landed unopposed and enjoyed a protective buffer on its flanks provided by thousands of Cuban soldiers now faced failure. It remained for the Spanish army commander in Santiago de Cuba to acknowledge the Cuban role in the final outcome. Conditions behind Spanish lines in Santiago de Cuba were at least as desperate as they were behind U.S. lines. Spanish troops also lacked adequate medicine and food supplies and were simultaneously wracked by sickness and disease. Many hundreds of soldiers lay ill, in varying degrees of incapacitation, from malnutrition, illness, and battle wounds. They had been abandoned to their fate, as tens of thousands of civilians hurriedly evacuated the city in anticipation of the dreaded U.S. bombardment. "Santiago is not Gerona," General Arsenio Linares explained to Madrid in asking for authorization to surrender, seeking to disabuse his superiors that Santiago de Cuba had anything in common with the heroic eight-month Spanish defense against Napoleon in 1809. Gerona was in Spain, Linares explained, "defended inch by inch by her own sons, by old men, women, and children without distinction, who encouraged and assisted the combatants and exposed their lives, impelled by the sacred idea of independence." In contrast, the defenders of Santiago de Cuba had been abandoned by Cubans as well as Spaniards, by public officials and church authorities. "The ideal is lacking," Linares noted. Spanish troops were "defending the property of people who have abandoned it in their very presence, and of their own foes, the allies of the American forces." But most important, Linares stressed, was the condition of the thousands of officers and soldiers under his command: "The defenders are not just beginning a campaign, full of enthusiasm and energy; they have been fighting for three years with the climate, privations and fatigue; and now that the most critical time has arrived their courage and physical strength are exhausted, and there are no means for building them up again."[25]

Spanish officers were in a unique position to assess the impact and implications of the Cuban insurgency. General Valeriano Weyler was unequivocal in identifying General Calixto García as "the principal person (*el alma principal*) in the subsequent military operations," adding that without Cuban aid "the Americans would not have been able to effect their landing, attack the city of Santiago de Cuba with success, and secure its surrender."[26] Another Spanish officer took similar measure of Spain's defeat, detailing the vital role Cubans played in the operations against Spanish forces. Captain Víctor M. Concas y Palau wrote:

> Despite the unwillingness of the Americans to acknowledge the aid received from the *insurrectos*, in fact, this assistance was so decisive that without the Cubans they would not have achieved their objectives in so short a period of time. In effect, on the very day of their landing, Santiago de Cuba was cut off from all supplies it received from the countryside, producing widespread hunger; all communications were cut off; forests, roads, and foothills: all were covered by Cubans, and even the west coast of the harbor itself was unsafe, as the American army was relieved of this arduous service.[27]

What is noteworthy about accounts of the Santiago campaign is the discrepancy between U.S. and Cuban first-person narratives of military operations. In American diaries and memoirs Cubans are conspicuous by their absence; if they appear at all, it is usually as objects of scorn. What makes these silences all the more striking is that, by contrast, Cuban memoirs are filled with details of joint U.S-Cuban operations throughout the campaign.[28]

The reasons for the discrepancies are not altogether clear. Some of this, certainly, was due simply to the conduct of Cuban operations beyond the direct field of vision of U.S. observers. Then, too, it may have been impossible for Americans to fully appreciate the cumulative effect of more than three years of war on the Spanish forces. But the situation was more complicated. Nothing had prepared American soldiers for their encounter with Cuban troops, many of whom were men of color, weary and worn, wary of the North American presence; all of this was further compounded by language differences. These were not the allies the Americans had imagined Cubans to be. "They were the dirtiest, most slovenly looking lot of men I had ever seen," wrote Rough Rider Thomas Hall. The Cubans were "almost all blacks and mulattos and were clothed in rags," was what Theodore Roosevelt remembered. "I think that 80 percent of them are the worst specimens of humanity I ever saw," one appalled army medic anguished; "a majority of them are ignorant and very filthy." George Kennan, previously sympathetic to Cubans, could not conceal his disillusionment. "The Cubans disappointed me," Kennan confessed. "I suppose, because I had pictured them to myself as a better dressed and better disciplined body of men, and had not made allowance enough for the hardships and privations of an insurgent's life."[29]

The Americans had arrived as liberators, a point of view that allowed them easily enough to take charge, with a task to perform, to seek to organize around short-term needs and long-range objectives, which may or may not have been consistent with the goals of Cubans, who in any case had their own ideas about how to do things. Originally the U.S. command sought to use Cuban troops as porters, orderlies, messengers, and day laborers, working for rations behind U.S. lines. The Cubans balked. "My men are soldiers, not laborers," General Calixto García protested.[30]

Displaced at the front lines and declining to perform menial tasks behind the lines, it soon appeared as if the Cubans had retired from the war. "You observe the intense pride of this Cuban libre," complained one U.S. officer. "It is manifested the very first time you suggest anything manual labor—even for such purpose as camp sanitation, carrying rations, or for any other purpose. His manly chest swells with pride and exclaims in accents of wounded dignity, 'Yo soy soldado!' Still his pride does not get him knowingly under fire."[31] War correspondents quickly acquired—and added to—prevailing antipathies. "The suggestion that [Cubans] help build roads was received with haughtiest scorn," the New York Tribune correspondent cabled. "Soldiers of Cuba Libre felling trees, shoveling earth and moving stones! The idea was not to be entertained."[32]

In view of the fundamental cross-purposes at which Cubans and Americans found themselves in 1898, it was perhaps inevitable that misunderstandings would arise. The North American army unexpectedly had entered a difficult campaign. However "splendid" the war may have seemed from afar, then and now, it was in fact a difficult campaign for most of the men who fought it, a war, too, whose outcome at the time seemed far from a foregone conclusion. The U.S. advance on Santiago de Cuba had stalled in the face of reversals, any one of which could have resulted in a retreat, a possibility that General Shafter indeed was contemplating. American difficulties could easily be attributed to the Cubans. That the Escario column succeeded reaching Santiago de Cuba led to widespread anger against Cubans and disdain of their focus and force. Escario had reached Santiago de Cuba, an irate General E. J. McClernand claimed, "through the inefficiency of the Cubans." Theodore Roosevelt was exasperated with the Cubans, who seemed "quite unable to prevent the Spanish regulars from marching wherever they wished."[33] The *Washington Post* correspondent similarly reported that Spanish troops had entered Santiago "through the cowardice or the indifference of Gen. Garcia, who refused to attempt to intercept them, and whose action was the subject of very unfavorable comment."[34]

At that instant—it seemed as if it happened all at once, but actually it had been building up for weeks—U.S. resentment, racial animosity, and arrogance found an outlet: demonstrable evidence to confirm what the Americans had previously suspected about their allies. At once there was proof and pretext: Cubans *were* incompetent and derelict, worthless as allies, useless as soldiers, who could not be relied on for anything; now, the Americans concluded, they would have to defeat Spain without the Cubans—indeed, despite the Cubans. "We should have been better off if there had not been a single Cuban with the army," Theodore Roosevelt grumbled. "They accomplished literally nothing, while they were a source of trouble and embarrassment, and consumed much provisions."[35]

Cubans were thus transformed into objects of the U.S. mission, a purpose necessary to fulfill, for it was at the heart of how Americans saw themselves; not even the Cubans, in whose behalf the Americans professed to act, could be permitted to prevent the U.S. forces from completing the task they had come to do. From this perspective, the Cubans' only roles in the war were instrumental, supporting and subordinate, assigned by their deliverers, parts they were expected to play unquestioningly and unhesitatingly. Anything less would impede the Americans' mission. War correspondent Stephen Bonsal understood the source of mounting tensions. "At this stage of the siege," he wrote on July 10, "our Cuban allies are certainly not generally popular with either the rank or the file of the army." He continued: "The reason for this unhappy state of affairs is not far to seek. Matters are not going entirely to our liking, and it is convenient and very human to place the responsibility for our short-comings and our mishaps upon the Cubans."[36]

American troops arrived in Cuba on a self-proclaimed mission of liberation, in the self-conscious role of liberators, to rescue the downtrodden Cubans from Spanish oppression. It is not unreasonable to appreciate their desire to be received the way they saw themselves. Instead, they were greeted with doubt and distrust. Anticipating enthusiasm, they encountered indifference; expecting appreciation, they met with suspicion. Wary of the American purpose, Cuban soldiers conveyed little of the gratitude that their would-be deliverers expected. One war correspondent wrote of the "sour and sullen" mood of *insurrectos*; another described Cubans as "vain and jealous"; another reporter said they were "conceited."[37] "Do they admire us?" asked Thomas R. Dawley Jr. "Are their hearts full of gratitude? To answer these questions one had only to draw near and overhear their usual discussions. You would expect them to be filled with gratitude towards us who are about to redress their wrongs. But that is not so."[38]

"One must not suppose that there was any cheering enthusiasm at the landing of our army here," Stephen Crane cabled from Cuba. On the contrary, the Cubans acted "stolidly, almost indifferently." The results were immediate, perhaps predictable. Disappointment soon turned into disillusionment and eventually into disaffection. "The American soldier," Crane observed, "thinks of himself as a disinterested benefactor, and he would like the Cubans to play up to the ideal every now and then. . . . He does not really want to be thanked, and yet the total absence of anything like gratitude makes him furious." General O. O. Howard attributed "the prejudice against the Cubans" principally to "a feeling that these patriots have not properly appreciated the sacrifices of life and health that have been made to give them a free country." These circumstances were similar, Howard suggested, to the "dislike of black men in 1863" in the United States, "because so many of them did not seem to understand, or be grateful for, what had been done for them."[39]

Cubans not only seemed to have vanished from the war; they were even excluded from the peace. Left out of the negotiations for the surrender of Santiago, Cubans were also prohibited from entering the city. By the terms of the surrender, the Cuban Liberation Army was denied entrance to the eastern capital. On July 14 General Calixto García learned to his horror that not only were his soldiers forbidden from entering Santiago de Cuba, but also Spanish officials were to be retained in office pending a permanent peace settlement. The implications were clear. "This war . . . ," General Shafter informed García, "is between the United States of America and the Kingdom of Spain and . . . the surrender . . . was made solely to the American Army."[40]

To have been excluded from the negotiations leading to the formal surrender of Santiago offended Cubans; that Santiago was proclaimed "part of the Union" alarmed them. "I will never accept that our country be considered as conquered territory," General García vowed.[41] A final insult was added to the original injury, gratuitously it seemed, but an official explanation seemed necessary and one was therefore improvised. Shafter proceeded to justify the decision to bar Cuban soldiers from Santiago de Cuba on the grounds that they could not be restrained from plunder and pillage, from looting stores and ransacking homes. War correspondent Bonsal recalled that Shafter had publicly expressed fear that the Cubans "would fall upon the Spaniards and massacre them" and could not be "restrained from murdering Spanish women and children."[42]

Indignation swept across Cuban army camps. García denounced Shafter and openly broke with the United States. It was inconceivable, García protested, that the Americans retained Spaniards in office, "the very same Spanish authorities against whom I have struggled these three years as enemies of Cuban independence." He denounced as "absurd" the reasons Shafter cited for denying Cubans entrance to Santiago de Cuba. "Allow me to protest against even a shadow of such an idea," García responded. "We are not savages who ignore the principles of civilized warfare. . . . We respect our cause too much to stain it with barbarity and cowardice."[43] García immediately forwarded a copy of his protest along with his resignation from the Cuban army to General Máximo Gómez. Shafter's actions, García explained, made continued cooperation with the United States impossible. "I am no longer disposed to continue obeying orders and cooperating with the plans of the American Army, and I do not want it said that I disobey the orders of my government. I have no other form to protest the attitude of the American government other than to offer my resignation."[44]

• • •

The circumstances of the war soon receded from memory as Americans basked in the afterglow of victory. "It has been a splendid little war," John Hay proclaimed cheerfully only days after the fall of Santiago de Cuba. Henry Cabot Lodge was euphoric. "What a wonderful war it has been," he exulted a week after the armistice. General Shafter agreed. "It was over quickly," he later boasted to an audience of Los Angeles businessmen; "it was simply a walk-over. It was a foregone conclusion that they would not make a stand. They knew it and did not try it."[45]

The war was thus then and thereafter rendered as victory swiftly and uneventfully obtained: "A short and glorious war," proclaimed Louis M. Hacker and Benjamin B. K. Kendrick; "A succession of unbroken victories," H. Addington Bruce wrote; and "a series of unchecked successes," according to Harold Underwood Faulkner. "Rarely has glory been won at so low a price," marveled Henry Bamford Parkes, adding that "the conflict in Cuba seemed like a holiday jaunt to most participants." Foster Rhea Dulles chose to characterize the war as a "casual skirmish." James Truslow Adams offered a more colorful description: "Victories seemed to come as easily as picking ripe strawberries."[46]

That Cubans seemed to have disappeared from the view of contemporary observers was in large measure the doing of U.S. policy. That they also vanished from U.S. historical accounts suggested in still one more fashion the ways that the policy paradigms of 1898 continued to shape the historiographical representations of 1898. Admittedly, narrative is a difficult structure in which to cast the events of Santiago de Cuba. Many things, diverse and dispersed, unconnected and unrelated, were going on at the same time, from many different vantage points, so as to make narrative something of a forced form.

This point of view developed early in the dominant narrative device. North American historiography routinely incorporated as a matter of course and a matter of fact the hostile judgments rendered by U.S. authorities as the basis from which to form explanations of subsequent events. The Cubans "soon became a nuisance," proclaimed Richard J. Walton in terms that could just as easily have been uttered by Theodore Roosevelt. "The glamour had passed," wrote William A. Robinson in his biography of Speaker of the House of Representatives Thomas Reed. "The noble army of Cuban martyrs had become an armed rabble as unchivalrous as it was unsanitary." Charles Morris made a definitive judgment in 1899, affirming that the Cubans' "evident disinclination to exert themselves in any useful way excited a scorn in the Americans which they took little pains to conceal." Harry Peck, who in his otherwise detailed account of military operations neglected to make a single mention of Cuban participation, proceeded to characterize insurgent forces as "worthless allies," appearing "more like a swarm of enervated mendicants than a host of heroes struggling to be free." Peck's account was virtually indistinguishable from official U.S. dispatches. "A Cuban republic had been proclaimed," he wrote, "but it had no capital and had organized no government. It had not even an army, in the proper sense of the word; and its prowling bands of ill-armed peasants appeared and disappeared like phantoms." And to the obvious point: "There was little enthusiasm in the United States in response to the cry of 'Cuba for the Cubans.' " Ellis Paxson Oberholtzer concluded that "little could be done" with Cubans, "who were so suspicious of our motives and so jealous of their own glory as to deny us the opportunity to render them useful aid." Oberholtzer was further critical of Cubans "after we had entered upon the war for their liberation," whose "few, ill clothed, meagerly accoutered, undisciplined men" had "failed to meet or to check the advance of Spanish reinforcements from the north."[47]

Walter Millis's classic account, *The Martial Spirit: A Study of Our War with Spain* (1931), gave enduring historiographical form to the official accounts. His depiction of the Escario incident was entirely from the point of view behind the U.S. lines. On July 3, 1898, Millis wrote, "while our people were rejoicing over the naval victory, Colonel Escario's column . . . slipped into the city." The Cubans "posted to intercept them had failed in their mission, and the [Spanish] strong lines were now heavily reinforced." Millis maintained that the "failure of García's insurgents to prevent the entrance of Escario's relieving column into Santiago" created "a most unfavorable impression" and led to "a really remarkable reversal of opinion." He gave full credence to the U.S. official view: "We, too, began to discover that the insurgents, after all, composed only one element of the Cuban population. We, too, began to entertain serious doubts as to the Cubans' capacity for self-government. We perceived that it was necessary to go slowly. We faced the possibility that our military effort might be of long duration; and at all events, we saw clearly that we should have to assume for the present fully and undivided responsibility for government in Cuba."[48]

Contemporary accounts early shaped the dominant historiographical discourses and served as the texts around which 1898 passed into the North American familiar. In the historical literature of the "Spanish-American War," Cubans all but vanished, a disappearance that began with the very name by which the war became known. Thus, Richard Collin could characterize 1898 as a "war between two untested powers," without a mention of Cubans: place and people disappeared altogether. "The Cuban troops . . . ," William Wood and Ralph Henry Gabriel asserted flatly, "played no decisive part in determining the outcome of the war."[49]

The disappearance also transformed Cubans from active to passive, from subjects to objects, from agents of their own liberation to recipients of U.S. largess, circumstances that, in turn, set up the premises from which many of the central historiographical formulations of 1898 were subsequently derived. "With the surrender of Santiago . . . ," Barbara Tuchman proclaimed confidently, "Spanish rule came to an end, defeated, not by the Cuban insurgents, but by the United States." Henceforth, too, the proposition that the United States "gave" Cubans their independence assumed a position of prominence in U.S. historical narratives. Cuba, James Truslow Adams affirmed, "would appear to have been given its independence by us on rather anomalous terms."[50]

The proposition of the Cuban absence in 1898, proclaimed at the time and reiterated thereafter, worked its way to the center of U.S. historiography, from where it proceeded to influence in decisive ways explanations of the war. North American historical narratives of 1898, fashioned without acknowledgment of the Cuban role and without consultation of Cuban sources, were thus obliged to improvise and invent plausible explanations for the dispatch with which Spain was defeated in the face of the unremarkable performance of U.S. operations. These accounts have depended largely on inference and implication, drawn and developed by way of speculation and supposition. Explanations thus summoned were often as forced as they were fanciful: possible certainly, persuasive on occasion, but rarely more than assumptions passing as facts.

One explanation of military success, especially among early accounts, tended to idealize the conduct of the U.S. campaign. Mismanagement and malfeasance were hardly noted, except perhaps as one more obstacle U.S. soldiers were obliged to overcome en route to victory. The source of success was inferred from the outcome. "Whatever deficiencies the Americans may have had in organization, training, and military education," observed Carl Russell Fish, "they undoubtedly possessed fighting spirit, courage, and personal ingenuity." Fish acknowledged ineptitude "so marked that . . . the whole campaign on land appears as an amateur undertaking," but he nevertheless insisted that "the individual character of both volunteers and regulars was high. The American victory was fundamentally due to the fighting spirit of the men and to the individual initiative of the line and field officers." Charles Morris declared that "no finer work [had] ever been done," adding: "The work of the American soldier in this desperate conflict was of the most admirable character. . . . With a vim and valor which foreign observers designated as superb, they rushed upon the works of the foe, pushing forward with grim determination. . . . It was truly a remarkable instance of American courage and self-reliance, and the battle of Santiago must take its place in history among the most glorious of those in which American soldiers have fought." Frederick Merk was downright exultant: "Fighting in the war was marked by brilliant victories on the American side. . . . Spanish resistance crumbled. Within a little more than three months Spain was asking for peace." John R. Musick insisted that "all honor should be given to U.S. soldiers," attesting: "To them we owe our splendid victories, unequaled in other wars or time. The sunny-haired Anglo-Saxon soldier of the North proved equally as energetic in the tropics as at home." William Harding Carter heaped praise on the regular army for "the splendid achievements of the brief campaign in Cuba," soldiers who "disembarked on the surf of a tropical shore, without dependable reserves of men and supplies . . . moved to the assault of an entrenched enemy, and . . . wrested victory from astonished opponents, received the surrender of an enemy larger in numbers, and materially hastened the downfall of Spanish power in the West Indies."[51]

Most accounts, however, acknowledged the woeful mismanagement of the U.S. campaign and, obliged to explain the American victory, found the answer in the condition of the Spanish army, not the collaboration of the Cuban army. Incompetence may have characterized the U.S. war effort, and indeed brought the campaign within measurable distance of disaster, but the Spanish were even more inept. The inference is inescapable: it was the lesser ineptitude or greater good fortune that explained the U.S. victory. Frank Freidel's *The Splendid Little War* (1958), long one of the standard accounts of 1898, combined elements of both to explain the U.S. success. Freidel referred to the good fortune that smiled on the U.S. purpose. "It was a little war," he wrote, "but only the incredible ineptitude of the Spaniards and the phenomenal luck of the Americans kept it from stretching into a struggle as long and full of disasters as the Boer War became for the British." Allan Nevins and Henry Steele Commager agreed: "Our victories were attributable in part to dash and courage, but in still larger part to Spanish weakness."[52]

These views situated themselves at the center of U.S. historical narratives. "Spanish forces were no match for even the ill-prepared Americans," Robert Beisner proclaimed. Julius Pratt wrote of a "strange war," a "one-sided war," and reduced the conflict to two contending parties: "Both [*sic*] contestants were unprepared, but Spain's lack of preparation was much worse than ours." Pendleton Herring made the same point: the "Spanish-American War found us in a position of unexampled unpreparedness," but "fortunately, our enemy in this war . . . was even less prepared than we were." T. Harry Williams wrote that "the United States fought the war in a dream, but Spain, fortunately, was in a trance," and Oscar Handlin concluded that the "enemy was sufficiently weak to compensate for the failure of American military leadership, lack of preparation, and endless inefficiency." Walter Nugent marveled at U.S. successes. "The war was brief," he wrote, "and, for Spain, disastrous. Despite shocking disorganization and some outright corruption in the American army, the Spanish forces in Cuba rapidly capitulated." W. E. Woodward also acknowledged mismanagement, but, he asserted, the shortcomings of the U.S. army paled in comparison with those of the Spanish military. Without mentioning Cuban participation in the campaign, Woodward attributed the U.S. victory to the condition of the Spanish army:

> If the Spanish army had been up to the level, in morale and training, of contemporary European armies, we would have had a hard time in taking Santiago. But the Spanish army was composed of poor little peasants in overalls who had been dragged from their Andalusian farms to fight in a distant land, and for a cause which meant nothing to them. They did not want to fight; they wanted to go home. Their officers consisted chiefly of nervous, nail-biting young men, sallow-faced and uneasy. They were inadequately trained, and had long been bored by chasing rebels through tropical jungles.

In Charles M. Dollar et al.'s version, the inability of Spain to move its troops across the island was due to "inefficient . . . Spanish communication and transportation networks." An ill-prepared U.S. army thus obtained "its quick victory" as a result of a Spanish army being "even more incompetent and ill-equipped, with its officers riddled with corruption and its troops often indifferent."[53]

William Miller insisted that the "defending Spaniards . . . were even more spent than the Americans," and according to Winthrop Jordan and Leon Litwack, after two days of battle the "American attack petered out," but "luckily for Shafter the Spaniards were in even worse shape." In *The National Experience* (1963), at one time one of the most widely used U.S. history textbooks, John Morton Blum et al. developed this argument: "The fact was that blundering inefficiency brought the army to the brink of disaster. The Spaniards blundered badly too, but with an unstable government, a tradition-bound leadership, and a backward economy, they had even more excuse for inefficiency than the Americans, who had none of these handicaps. . . . As it turned out, the real explanation of the quick American military success lay in the even more incredible inefficiency and blundering of the Spaniards." However ill-prepared the United States may have been, in the view of Foster Rhea Dulles, Spain "was even less prepared and more bungling"; Roderick Nash suggested that "a badly disorganized American force . . . managed to defeat an even more mismanaged Spanish army." Edwin C. Rozwenc made the case explicitly: "The [U.S.] expeditionary force was badly led and badly coordinated; only the greater incompetence of the Spanish army prevented military disasters for the Americans that might have rivaled those endured by the federal government in the opening months of the Civil War." Thomas Bailey wrote that the United States was "grossly unprepared for fighting in the tropics," exhibiting "confusion, mismanagement, and bungling that . . . almost defy belief," but "fortunately for the invader, Spanish ineptitude far eclipsed that of the attacker." In his account, John K. Mahon wholly dismissed the Cubans and attributed the U.S. victory entirely to Spanish ineptitude. "Shafter's army, at first poorly organized and supplied," Mahon stated, "was very vulnerable; it was saved by the enemy's incompetence." He concluded: "The failings of the Spanish commanders contributed as much as any factor to ensure U.S. success in Cuba. If they had handled their military resources with even moderate skill, they might have repelled Shafter's advance and greatly prolonged the entire war. As it was, they did nothing to oppose the landing of the U.S. expeditionary force, even though the place chosen to go ashore favored the defense. . . . Spanish blunders gave the McKinley administration the quick military and political victory that it needed."[54]

The treatment of the disembarkation at Daiquirí persisted in the historical literature with the same bafflement that it did in 1898, and virtually nowhere was the Cuban role in securing the beaches acknowledged. Frank Freidel dwelled at length on Daiquirí: "If the Spanish army had displayed even moderate initiative, it could have turned the landing at Daiquiri into one of the most costly and painful military disasters in United States history." And: "Had General Linares chosen to leave only a thin line of interior defense . . . along the ridges behind Daiquiri, Siboney, and the beaches of Santiago, he scarcely could have failed to hurl back the American invaders with disastrous results." Freidel continued to marvel how the disorganized landing succeeded: "It seemed almost miraculous that they were able to do so without a single Spanish shot being fired against them." Hermann Hagedorn was no less confounded. "The Spaniards," he wrote, "for some reason which no one seemed able to fathom, did not contest the landing of the American army at Daiquiri." In Irving Werstein's account of Daiquirí, good fortune was identified as the principal determinant of the outcome, for how else to explain that by even "the lowest military standards it was a miserable exhibition of ineptitude, poor

planning and outright stupidity"? Werstein drew the inescapable inference: "Had the Spaniards put up even mild resistance the Americans
either would have been driven into the sea or else annihilated on the
sands." Allan Keller pointed out that a "more determined army could
have easily mustered between three and four thousand men who were
within a half day's marching time of Daiquirí and sent them to turn the
landing into a catastrophe for the Americans." Robert Leckie speculated
that if Spanish army commander Arsenio Linares had ordered his troops
"to oppose the American landing, he might have dealt the *Yanquis* one of
the bloodiest defeats in their history. Even 300 men fighting from the
fortified stone bluffs above the Daiquirí beaches could have raked and
ripped the go-as-you-please amphibious assault launched on that spark-
ling, sunlit morning." Maurice Matloff affirmed simply that the Spanish
"did nothing to prevent Shafter's men from getting ashore."[55]

Donald Barr Chidsey fashioned still another explanation to account
for the apparent failure of Spain to respond effectively to U.S. landings,
in which the Cuban absence persisted: "Spanish soldiers . . . were scattered over a large number of small posts, as was natural with what after
all amounted to an army of occupation, and these places could not
readily reinforce one another or even communicate with one another, so
poor were the roads, so rugged the mountains." George Tindall similarly
characterized U.S. preparations for war as "spotty," as a result of which
American armed forces "suffered badly from both inexperience and
maladministration," but he added: "The United States' salvation was
that Spanish forces were even worse off, their morale infinitely so."[56]

The state of Spanish morale was, in fact, often invoked as one of the
chief reasons for the U.S. victory. Walter Millis described how Spanish
commanders "forfeited the opportunity" to defeat the United States due
to "the profound hopelessness, the moral inertia, with which they regarded the whole issue. They were beaten before they began." James
Henretta et al. suggested that the "half-trained and ill-equipped" U.S.
troops "might have been checked by a determined opponent; but the
Spaniards lacked the heart for battle." Richard Current, T. Harry Williams, and Frank Freidel made a similar point: "The Spanish army numbered almost 130,000 troops. . . . Despite its imposing size, it was not an
efficient force; its commanders seemed to be paralyzed by a conviction
of certain defeat." The United States, Keith Ian Polakoff et al. argued,
was "remarkably unprepared for war and conducted it with staggering
inefficiency"; however, "the primary American advantage was psycho-
logical: the Spanish expected to be beaten; Americans thought only of
victory."[57]

A final, catch-all explanation is that the United States simply enjoyed good fortune. Paul Carlson, General Shafter's biographer, explained the "quick and decisive victory" as much by "good luck and Spanish misfortune and ineptitude . . . as by Shafter's leadership." The war could have been "far bloodier and more prolonged had it not been for considerable luck and Spanish incompetence," Jerald A. Combs suggested, noting, too, that U.S. forces "were equally lucky in their invasion of Cuba." Combs concluded: "Fortunately, the invasion force landed unopposed on Cuban beaches because the Spanish foolishly abandoned their coastal defenses for inland positions." Based on the U.S. victory in Cuba, Jack Cameron Dierks also reasoned that "luck and providence do play a part in war." Shafter's "tactical errors," Dierks insisted, "which were serious and could have been very costly had the Spaniards taken advantage of them," no less than "inconsistent" leadership and "inarticulate, unimaginative generalship," indicated that "someone, somewhere, was looking out for the fledgling American military expedition."[58]

• • •

Recent U.S. scholarship on 1898, which is more attentive to the historiography on Cuba, has advanced a much more balanced treatment of the war, particularly the impact of Cuban participation. "U.S. historians," John Scott Reed acknowledged in 1994, "have long ignored the relationship between the Cuban War of Independence of the 1890s and the Spanish-Cuba/American War of 1898." Reed continued: "The military consequences of the earlier struggle were profound: by the time U.S. forces landed near Santiago, Cuban forces had inflicted thousands of casualties on Spain's occupation army and driven it into a pattern of dispersed static local garrisons unable to cooperate against an invasion and effectively isolated from the island's major food-producing centers. By July 1898, near-starvation, combined with a range of endemic tropical diseases, had reduced the Spanish army in Cuba to a state of offensive impotence." David Healy accorded greater prominence to the participation of Cuban military forces at the Daiquirí landing, indicating that "the Americans found fifteen hundred Cuban troops holding the landing beach when they reached it." David Trask recognized the importance of Cuban participation in the final outcome of the war, writing that the U.S. decision to land near Santiago de Cuba was "logical" because "Cuban insurgents could support American operations most effectively in eastern Cuba," circumstances that "contributed a great deal to the ultimate success at Santiago de Cuba." Thomas Paterson, J. Garry Clifford, and Kenneth Hagan similarly assigned greater significance to the role of "experienced Cuban rebels" in the victory of Spain, whereas Jules Benjamin described in meticulous detail the racial and political factors that produced the redefinition of "the U.S. aim in Cuba from independence to control."[59]

Historiographical redress is thus under way, albeit slow and tentative. The degree to which these propositions enter the mainstream historical literature and obtain parity with the more traditional views remains to be seen, of course. But the signs are hopeful. A review of some textbooks on U.S. history published during the 1990s suggests that these perspectives have indeed taken hold.[60] That these propositions have been advanced by some of the more important historians of their generation certainly adds to their credibility; in the process, such historians have provided entrée to some of the central formulations of nearly one hundred years of Cuban historiography.

1898 to 1998: *From Memory to Consciousness*

When the American intervention was effected, the people of Cuba under arms believed that Providence, taking the American nation as an instrument, was coming to their help. When during the first days we saw ourselves treated as allies and our help asked for and appreciated, treating with the General in Chief of the American Army as to the form, manner, and number of men with which we should assist, we believed ourselves to be free in fact by our own efforts, not by foreign aid. . . . Peace came and with it our incapacity was declared by the allies, who in time of danger found us competent and treated with us, disposing of our forces and our blood. We now see ourselves relegated to an inferior condition, our banner lowered, our treasury occupied, our men ostracized as useless, our people despised, our army condemned to misery and to live on the charity which the new and victorious master throws to the gutter.
—Enrique Collazo to Leonard Wood (December 28, 1899)

I received a message . . . informing me that the Spanish fleet had been destroyed in the waters outside Santiago de Cuba. My troops, to whom I read the message, erupted into *"Vivas"* to *Cuba Libre* and to the United States, whereas in me, I must confess, the news did not produce a similar exhilaration. I have always been devoted to my ancestry, and at that instant I felt the blood of my ancestors—Spanish blood—stir in my veins. That victory of the men of the North over those of my origins wounded my pride. At the same time, I was not satisfied with the imprecise and arbitrary form in which the United States had intervened in our fight. It is true that the Joint Resolution of Congress specified that "the people of Cuba are and of right ought to be free and independent," but it seemed to me that the act of that government, of sending its soldiers to Cuba without prior recognition of our belligerency, without a treaty of alliance or a military pact with the Cuban Army, was not an act of good faith. Suspicious of their intentions, for all these reasons, I experienced horror by acting in cooperation with the destruction of a sovereign authority derived from historic, ethnic, linguistic, and religious sources, not to substitute it with our own, but with the domination of another people without any authority to rule except force.
—Manuel Piedra Martel, *Mis primeros treinta años: Memorias* (1944)

There was no necessity for the Americans to get involved in the war, for the war was practically won by the Cubans.
—José B. Fernández, *Los abuelos: Historia oral cubana* (1987)

PROCLAMATION TO THE PEOPLE OF SANTIAGO
You are not free yet. . . . The war has not ended because the murderers remain armed. The military men who organized the coup insist that the rebels cannot enter Santiago de Cuba; we have been prohibited from entering a city that we could take with the valor and courage that our fighters have taken other cities. They want to prohibit the entrance into Santiago de Cuba to those who have liberated the *patria*. The history of 1895 will not be repeated; this time the liberators (*mambises*) will enter Santiago de Cuba.
—Fidel Castro (January 1, 1959)

Consensus and continuity have served as hallmarks of U.S. historiography on 1898. A vast body of scholarship has been distinguished principally by the persistence of formulations developed at the turn of the century, to which have been added few new insights or significant new information. With some notable exceptions, the accumulated historical knowledge has been noteworthy for the absence of historiographical advances. The literature has flourished primarily as the reworking and refining of old themes, mostly from old sources, reformulating old conclusions, restating old arguments. Advances have been more in the form of style than substance; new explanations have been more derivative than innovative.

The historical literature has generally commemorated the success of the U.S. purpose, typically presented as an achievement of altruism, which makes the commemoration all the more celebratory. The North Americans seized the past in part because historians conceded preeminence to the self-proclaimed victors, but particularly because historians themselves have shared the normative foundations and ideological assumptions on which that success was constructed and because winners have a special way of generating a vast and varied body of records that are irresistible to scholars. That a comparably large and rich body of records was available in Cuba seems to have hardly mattered. These materials, if considered at all, were routinely dismissed as irrelevant. The assumptions that have driven and defined research on 1898 have made alternative historiographical frameworks all but impossible to imagine. It is not simply that the historiography has failed to represent the presence of Cubans as relevant to outcomes; it has not even noticed their absence.

In fact, the presumption of the Cubans' absence has had to do with larger assumptions of their irrelevance. The publication of Ernest May's landmark study, *Imperial Democracy: The Emergence of America as a Great Power* (1961), provides a suggestive case study in which the Cuban absence raised important methodological issues, all of which passed undetected and unrecognized. *Imperial Democracy* was widely reviewed and uniformly acclaimed as a triumph of historical inquiry based on research broadly conceived and diligently pursued. Indeed, it was precisely the breadth of the research that earned *Imperial Democracy* critical acclaim, including the praise of many of the most prominent scholars in the field. In addition to U.S. archival records, May examined materials from England, France, Austria, Spain, Russia, and Japan. Conspicuously absent, however, were Cuban archival and manuscript sources. Moreover, with the exception of scattered references to six published titles, May did not consult Cuban published sources either, an omission made all the more remarkable in a study dedicated mainly to the island's war with Spain. In truth, these omissions were totally consistent with the traditions of U.S. historiography on 1898.

What was noteworthy, however, was the failure of reviewers, almost all of whom commended the breadth of the research, to notice the absence of Cuban archival sources. Frank Freidel praised *Imperial Democracy* as "brilliantly researched . . . diplomatic history of a perspective and vividness seldom encountered."[1] Charles Campbell agreed, commenting that the "great merit of this . . . book, in fact, is its unusually solid foundation of multi-archival research," out of which emerged an "excellent book, particularly because of its attention to the international setting of American foreign relations at a decisive time."[2] Carl Degler heaped lavish praise on *Imperial Democracy*, congratulating May for his exhaustive archival research that included "the archives of the major powers of Europe, including Russia's, as well as reading widely in the press of Europe and America." The result, Degler concluded, was "a much more rounded picture . . . than has ever been presented before in a single study." The absence of Cuban archival and manuscript sources escaped Degler's attention, even after he had complimented May for "properly" placing "the impact of the Cuban revolution at the center of his story." This omission notwithstanding, Degler proclaimed that "[w]e see the crisis from all [*sic*] sides and with many eyes."[3]

• • •

The historiography of 1898 has long served as a source and a symbol of some of the most enduring narratives of self-definition. It has provided plausible explanations derived from and supportive of dominant ideals of self-representation. The historiography turned in on itself, properly self-contained and self-validating, inferring larger meanings often by way of metaphysical musings. "Forces" were invoked through which to render reality comprehensible. Robert Endicott Osgood has chided historians for attributing outcomes in 1898 to "an Unseen Hand or some great impersonal force." The literature is indeed rich with such allusions. The war, insisted H. H. Powers as early as 1898, was "scarcely even voluntary," but rather "the natural outcome of forces constantly at work in . . . the American people." Brooks Adams made note of the necessity of empire as a "great movement," one "not determined by argument, but . . . determined by forces which override the volition of man." Howard Jones depicted President McKinley as "a gentle man caught up in uncontrollable forces." "Things got out of hand," was the way Solomon Bulkey Griffin explained the coming of the war.[4]

"Destiny" has also served as a popular explanatory device. President McKinley often alluded to duty and destiny, divine and defined, manifest and mandated. "The war with Spain was undertaken," McKinley insisted, "not that the United States should increase its territory, but that oppression at our very doors should be stopped." In his view, "Duty determines destiny. Destiny . . . results from duty performed. . . . Almighty God has his plans and methods for human progress, and not infrequently they are shrouded for the time being in impenetrable mystery."[5] Yale law professor Theodore Salisbury Woolsey early pondered what he characterized as "a divinely ordered responsibility," observing: "Whether we wish it or not, the civilization and Christianization of these populous islands have been suddenly laid upon our shoulders. Let us not prove unworthy of the trust." McKinley biographer Charles S. Olcott referred to "the hand of Destiny" that transformed the United States "from the position of an isolated nation to one of vastly greater influence among the powers of the world." Robert F. Riegel and David F. Long hedged slightly: "Call it destiny, call it luck, the results of the Spanish-American War . . . impelled the United States into world politics." Jack Cameron Dierks speculated that the "whole thing might have been predestined" and further suggested: "Just as the young must supplant the aged, so had the United States been ordained by a far-seeing Almighty to don the surcoat and tilting helm and enter the lists against the Old World and what it stood for." John Dobson affirmed that "the emergence of the United States was preordained—or to use a popular phrase of the period, it was the nation's 'manifest destiny' to become great."[6]

Chance has also assumed a prominent place in the explanations of 1898. Chance transcends choice; no one is held accountable or responsible for war. These are merely circumstances that happen, a matter of random events. Obviously these developments could not implicate human agency and certainly, under the circumstances, could hardly imply a larger purpose. President McKinley himself was fond of this explanation and invoked it often. "The march of events rules and overrules human actions," the president suggested. "The Philippines, like Cuba and Porto Rico, were intrusted to our hands by the war, and to that great trust, under the providence of God and in the name of human progress and civilization, we are committed. It is not a trust we sought; it is a trust from which we will not flinch."[7]

The proposition of chance entered into the historiography early and has long enjoyed a position of importance. Ernest May argued that President McKinley "found himself overtaken by events." Richard Leopold referred to "events largely beyond McKinley's control," and John Dobson likened McKinley's situation to "a man trying to rein in a runaway team." James Henretta et al. contended that "McKinley had no choice." McKinley biographers in particular have traditionally stressed choicelessness. Margaret Leech insisted that the president "was forced to make war," and H. Wayne Morgan said that McKinley "had lost freedom of action." It is difficult to disagree with Walter Karp's observation that in "no major episode of American history has so little been attributed to the intentions of political leaders and so much to forces beyond their control."[8]

The dominant explanation of 1898 has subscribed to the proposition of war as accident, a conflict into which the United States unwittingly stumbled, with wholly unforeseen and unanticipated outcomes. The war in its most common representation has appeared as an improvised and involuntary response to an unpredictable circumstance. William James pondered the larger meaning of the war and could come to only one conclusion. "[I]t beautifully corroborates the 'chance' theory of history," he stated in June 1898, "to find that the critical turning-points in these great movements are purely accidental. A victory often depends on the weather." And it was to the *Maine* that James pointed: "Without the *Maine* explosion we should still very likely be at peace,—that was the last item in the summation of the stimuli, and that explosion was possibly due to the free-will of one of the molecules in the dynamite magazine!" The United States "stumbled headlong into war," affirmed William Leuchtenburg. G. J. A. O'Toole offered a slightly different version but with similar effect: The war "happened because history is sometimes the plaything of chance."[9]

The absence of context reduced the war to episode and incident, isolated and unconnected to anything else, with far-reaching consequences, to be sure, but outcomes related to happenstance and circumstance, more to opportunity than opportunism, more as response than initiative. There was no malice of forethought in 1898, no larger meaning to be inferred, only innocent intentions honestly expressed and nobly pursued. The proposition of empire—that is, the process of acquiring and administering colonial possessions, which was an irrefutable outcome of the war—thus appeared as entirely unforeseen and unanticipated. "We did not go there to conquer the Philippines," McKinley insisted in 1899, ". . . but in the providence of God, who works in mysterious ways, this great archipelago was put into our lap." A. Lawrence Lowell insisted as early as 1899 that "the acquisition of the Spanish colonies was an accident, in the sense that the war was not waged with any deliberate intention of expansion." Several years later a similar view was expressed by Henry William Elson, who maintained that "we have taken pride in the fact that we had not and did not wish to have colonial possessions." Elson continued: "But suddenly, unexpectedly, our policy has been changed, and we have expanded into a world power. No man planned or foresaw the change. It came probably because it was time for it to come." This belief was shared by Samuel Flagg Bemis, who characterized these developments as a "great national aberration," with "astonishing and partially unexpected results." James Henretta et al. rejected out of hand the proposition that war had been deliberately undertaken for territorial expansion. "Was this really a war of aggression, secretly motivated by a desire to seize strategic territory from Spain?" he asked rhetorically. "In a strict sense, almost certainly not. It was not *because* of expansionist ambitions that McKinley pressed Spain into a corner. On the other hand, once war came he saw it as an opportunity." No doubt S. E. Forman best captured the essence of one of the enduring historiographical formulations of 1898: "Doubtfully, almost unwillingly, the nation fronted its fate, stooped to take up 'the White Man's burden,' and undertook to govern strange people."[10]

There have been creative variations on these themes. The notion of "accident" has often been employed. "The acquisition of the Philippines," Tony Smith contended, "was something of an accidental conquest." Carl Degler insisted that the decisions from which war resulted "were taken with no grand purpose in mind"; empire was "not by design but by accident." Some have suggested subliminal forces. "Almost unconsciously the United States had taken the road to empire," G. J. A.

O'Toole noted. John Richard Alden asserted that "neither McKinley nor the American people quite knew what they were doing in April 1898," but it was "to their credit that their motives, so far as they knew, were not sordid." Robert Endicott Osgood paraphrased Macaulay to describe the U.S. experience, whereby the Americans acquired "an empire in a fit of absent-mindedness." Some have employed the notion of surprise. Gilman M. Ostrander wrote that "the nation went to war with Spain to free Cubans from oppression and emerged, to nearly everybody's surprise, as one of the great powers of the world." H. W. Brands stated that "the Spanish-American War brought surprises, including possession of an American overseas empire."[11]

It is precisely within the realm of chance that the *Maine* has held such enduring appeal. An unforeseen development, unexpected and beyond control, was thus fashioned into the circumstance that denied choice and diminished options. The historical literature has recorded and repeated as privileged narrative the proposition of accident, the role of unintended consequences, and the haphazard flow of daily random events. In this order of things, the *Maine* served a vital corroborative function in explanations of the war as chance, from which the larger discursive framework of 1898 was derived. That the war was attributed to such improbable and wholly fortuitous origins as the destruction of the *Maine* set the tone and determined the structure of historical accounts. The *Maine*-as-cause construct fit well into a larger idealized view of a political universe. It lent itself easily to the service of validating normative democratic theory. It added credence to commonly shared values of the national purpose. Most important, it served a larger epistemological function: plausible denial of the proposition of war as an instrument of policy for the purpose of territorial expansion. In conjunction with other elements in the historiography, the *Maine* provided the critical explanatory element for the rendering of the war as a mission inspired by noble intentions, a selfless undertaking to liberate an oppressed people from iniquitous colonial rule, and only after the ship was destroyed. The *Maine* was refractory, a useful means through which to create a usable past that served at once to reflect and reinforce generally shared assumptions about the character of the U.S. purpose. The war was thus transformed into the final chance element in a series of random events, one in which the United States was overtaken by events it could not control.

Historians who otherwise advanced explanations that favored complex and long-term processes of political, economic, and cultural developments, who ordinarily eschewed such problematical formulations as the contingent, the unexpected, and the accidental as factors of transcendental importance, employed the explosion of the *Maine* as the central element in a war that reshaped the configuration of global power relations. As early as 1900 Charles Conant gave this construct its most compelling form: "Apparently as the result of an accident in Havana Harbor, the path of destiny has been opened for us in the East."[12]

A war that happened to serve as a means of territorial expansion was thus represented as an accident, and newly acquired territories, subsequently administered as colonial possessions, appeared as an incidental and wholly unforeseen outcome of this accident—not a product of policy calculations, and certainly not the continuation of political relations carried out by other means. There is no place for Clausewitz here.

Efforts to replace the "accident" thesis of 1898 with more conceptually coherent explanations have encountered resistance, and predictably the *Maine* has been invoked as rebuttal. First among the "common failings" of the new historiography, argued James Field, was that the "approach is too rational." Field continued: "Chance (or the unexpected), which plays so important a part in the life of the individual, seems unacceptable in the life of the nation: these authors simply will not remember the *Maine*."[13]

The disavowal of war as a means of calculated policy for empire, another way to reject the proposition of territorial aggrandizement, has been conveyed by the tone of the historical literature. One tradition of the historiography has been to treat the war dismissively, perhaps even disparagingly. A war not taken seriously surely could not possess serious purpose. This literature has acquired a distinctive tone, suggesting something between farce and folly, lending itself to characterization as parody and mockery. The "splendid little war" motif has indeed served this purpose well.

Whimsy has developed as one of the principal literary modes through which to represent the war and has reinforced the proposition of chance and the absence of choice: a "remote and picturesque conflict," affirmed George Kennan; possessed of "comic opera overtones," Daniel Smith commented cheerfully; it "smacked of a Gilbert and Sullivan operetta," Richard Leopold wrote. William H. Nelson and Frank E. Vandiver characterized the war "more as a joke than anything else. It was an *opera bouffe*." "It had all been a little like a comedy of errors or the children's game of pin the tail on the donkey," Allan Keller observed, "which must be played while blindfolded." An "exhilarating experience, sensational, not dangerous," Robert Ferrell insisted. "Almost everyone but the Span-iards had a wonderful time," Robert Riegel and David Long could jest, adding that the disembarkation of U.S. forces "took place near such fascinating Cuban villages as tuneful Siboney and the rather alcoholic-sounding Daiquirí."[14] The descriptions are rich and plentiful: "it was all very thrilling"; "a colorful war" and "glorious adventure"; "a grand, disorganized coup"; a "dazzling venture"; "a comic-opera kind of war"; "though short, [the war] provided more than its quota of thrills."[15] The war, Joseph Wisan remarked, "would prove little more than a picnic." It was "chivalrous and gallant," wrote G. J. A. O'Toole, "short, glorious, and easily understood," whereas Frank Thistlethwaite described the conflict as an "exuberant little adventure." "[S]mall, glamorous," was the way H. Wayne Morgan chose to characterize the war, "a thing of charg-ing rough-riders and flashing sabers to many." "In essence the Spanish-American War was a kind of gigantic coming-out party," Thomas Bailey and David Kennedy proclaimed in their U.S. history textbook. "The whole affair was a picnic," pronounced James Truslow Adams.[16]

• • •

The proposition of empire as the purpose of war has not fit easily into the historiography of 1898. Imperialism and colonialism as facets of the American experience, that is, territories acquired by military force and administered without the consent of the governed, have not been com-patible with the ideals of constitutional democracy and civil liberties. It was a proposition that even at the time—and especially at the time—was not easy to reconcile with long-held notions of the nation and could not be readily accommodated within the normative hierarchies by which Americans chose to arrange the terms of self-definition. Constructs of the acquisition of distant places and peoples were obliged to conform to larger national ideals. Professor Theodore Salisbury Woolsey, only weeks after the Joint Resolution, anticipated outcomes and prepared the expla-nations. "We declare that our motives are pure," Woolsey proclaimed. "But can we part with our prospective conquests?" he asked and an-swered: "Too weak to stand alone as they are, we could not add them to the number of bastard republics. Nor could we give them or sell them to this power and to that. . . . Yet to hand them back to Spain, no matter on what condition, would be a deliberate surrender of their peoples to the grinding tyranny from which, at great cost, we have rescued the Cuban brothers. Are we not, then, by process of exclusion, forced to accept as our own what the future of war may give us, even if it be a white elephant?"[17]

The same anomalies and ambivalences loom large in the historiography. A good deal of creative energy has been dedicated to efforts to reconcile imperialism with the commitment to democratic institutions through which Americans articulate their principles of conduct in world affairs.[18] H. Wayne Morgan grappled with these issues throughout *America's Road to Empire: The War with Spain and Overseas Expansion* (1965) and found imaginative ways to finesse the distasteful implications of imperialism. "The war's results," he argued, "usually labeled 'imperialism' with no real definition of the term, flowed logically from the conflict." Morgan flinched from the word "imperialism," insisting that the U.S. purpose instead "involved altruism toward native peoples considered unready for self-rule"; he added that "since this complex policy did not really involve mere exploitation, I call it 'expansionism.'" At another point Morgan stated that "altruism and the needs of a long-term policy of American participation in world affairs dictated the process of expansion overseas." Richard Collin similarly attempted to fend off sordid associations of U.S. policy with imperialism through clever phrasing and artful prose. "[W]hat we thought to be imperialism," Collin suggested of 1898, "is instead a quickening of the spirit in general, and a new sense of identity shared by many Americans." In this scheme of things, imperialism was considered more as "a literary or journalistic slogan than an authentic historical phenomenon"; regardless, "Americans were careful to avoid any taint of a European phenomenon they held in contempt." Collin could describe the "alleged American imperialism" as Americans coming to terms with "the dictates of their own better natures." Richard Leopold also insisted that the "clash with Spain was humanitarian in origin, not imperialistic." Although in his next passage he suggested a momentary lucidity—"In retrospect, to be sure, it seems incredible that the administration did not foresee the territorial temptation a successful war would bring"—Leopold nevertheless concluded: "[McKinley] was swept along by the logic of events, by a vague sense of duty and destiny, and by the belated realization that it was simpler to retain, at least temporarily, the lands that fell to American arms than to give them up immediately."[19]

That the war did not result in a vast empire, moreover, somehow mitigated the charge of imperialism. When compared to the African territories seized by European powers, Jack Cameron Dierks argued, the new U.S. possessions "made no great splash on the map"—although Dierks did acknowledge that the "prizes were nevertheless rich and colorful and the subject peoples exotic enough to satisfy the most romantic of the imperialists." However, he hastened to add, "the United States showed a good deal of restraint in subsequent years in the matter of exercising the prerogatives of an expansionist power."[20]

In the end, when imperialism could be neither denied nor disregarded, it could be defended: as different, as high-minded, something akin to a unique expression of American "exceptionalism." Lloyd C. Gardner was absolutely correct in his observation that it "was very important to Americans, as the Teller Amendment demonstrated, that they continually reassure themselves that they were not adopting an imperial policy but were expanding the Empire of Liberty, not repeating European mistakes but forging ahead along a new path."[21]

McKinley increasingly addressed the issue of imperialism after the war, especially as Filipino resistance to U.S. rule found the country drawn into a full-scale colonial war. "Our concern was not for territory or trade or empire," the president insisted, "but for the people whose interest and destiny, without our willing it, had been put into our hands." Hence, under the circumstances, concern for consent of the governed could not be allowed to influence U.S. decisions:

> Did we need their consent to perform a great act for humanity? We had it in every aspiration of their minds, in every hope of their hearts. Was it necessary to ask their consent to capture Manila, the capital of their islands? Did we ask their consent to liberate them from Spanish sovereignty . . . ? We did not ask these things; we were obeying a higher moral obligation, which rested on us and which did not require anybody's consent. We were doing our duty by them, as God gave us the light to see our duty, with the consent of our own consciences and with the approval of civilization. . . . [W]hile the war that destroyed [Spanish sovereignty] was in progress we could not ask their views. Nor can we now ask their consent. . . . It is not a good time for the liberator to submit important questions concerning liberty and government to the liberated while they are engaged in shooting down their rescuers.

The United States, McKinley vowed, would not "alienate a single foot of territory which we have honestly acquired, or give up sovereignty over it to any other peoples." The "shedding of the blood of misguided Filipinos" was a "matter of sorrow" to Americans, he lamented; however, "our flag is there—rightfully there, . . . not as the flag of tyranny or as the symbol of slavery," not as "the banner of imperialism," but as "what it is here and for what it is everywhere—justice and liberty and right and civilization."[22]

These formulations passed directly and wholly into mainstream historiography. Louis B. Wright et al. proclaimed flatly that "American imperialism was the most enlightened of any in the world." Julius Pratt adopted a different tack. " 'Imperialism' has often been used as a term of reproach," Pratt wrote in 1950. "Today it has become a stock expression in the Marxist vocabulary connoting, to the leftist mind, both the wickedness and the decay of capitalism." He continued:

> There is no reason why Americans should feel ashamed of their experiment in imperialism. . . . Only the naive assume that a relationship of ruled and rulers is necessarily and always bad. Peoples of primitive or retarded cultures, thrust into the currents of advanced international politics and economics, may need guardians to guide and direct their development and to give them government and protection while they learn to care for themselves in the modern world. Those who have fallen under the guardianship of the United States have fared well in the main. . . . American imperialism has, on the whole, been benevolent.

Allan Nevins and Henry Steele Commager similarly suggested that "at heart the nation remained nonimperialistic," choosing instead to become "consciously . . . one of the tutors of backward peoples." Tony Smith explained the U.S. purpose in 1898 as an impulse to democratize. The American commitment to democracy conferred "a moral purpose to [U.S.] imperialism," Smith noted; "the nature of its own internal economic and political structure made democratization and the presumption of eventual self-government the only possible point of consensus on which to establish American rule." For Dexter Perkins and Glyndon G. Van Deusen, "American imperialism was, from the beginning, not despotism, but preparation for self-government." They wrote with conviction that Americans created "values that would not have existed at all were it not for the energy and technical 'know-how' they brought to national development" and promoted education and health improvements. "American imperialism was, from the beginning, imperialism with an uneasy conscience."[23]

• • •

The way to war in 1898 had far-reaching implications. Political leaders had obtained public support for the defense of national interests through appeals to a higher moral purpose. It is not at all clear that a war launched explicitly in defense of strategic interests and economic spheres of influence could have easily summoned or long retained popular support. Such objectives seemed somehow to resonate as too cynical, too European, too Old World. War in behalf of a moral purpose, however, in the name of principle and out of a sense of right, precisely the terms by which Americans professed their secular faith, a war more as an expression of self-respect than the expansion of self-interests, was an undertaking perfectly consistent with the creed to which the nation had been consecrated. Popular representations assumed a logic of their own. The war, Talcott Williams exulted with a newfound sense of purpose in 1899, forged a "common conception of moral responsibility" and "a new conception of national duty." Specifically, "that the American lands to the south of us shall never by our will be left in any inhuman oppression and wrong we can right. We have fought a war to vindicate our duty." This was the same point made by Senator Joseph Foraker, but with far more portentous implications. "We were justified . . . in intervening," he insisted; "and it was our duty, when we did intervene . . . to make it clear to all concerned that our voice must be attended to and our wishes carried out."[24]

The defense of U.S. interests in the Western Hemisphere was henceforth embedded in discourses of beneficence and formulated in narratives of lofty purpose. Congressman Townsend Scudder outlined the rationale of 1898 in terms that would endure for nearly one hundred years: "[I]t devolved upon us as the guardian of human liberty and free political institutions in the Western Hemisphere to correct the intolerable evils and set up in their place the institutions of enlightened government."[25]

It is difficult, indeed, to assess fully the impact and the implications of 1898 across the twentieth century or to determine with any precision the full extent of its reach. The historical literature is rich with meditations on the meaning of 1898, portentous musings, reflections on the nation on the eve of the twentieth century. The sequence by which the trajectory of 1898 has been chartered in U.S. historiography seems so self-evident as to be almost irresistible. Possessions both in the Pacific and the Caribbean heightened the importance of an isthmian canal, whereupon the circum-Caribbean was transformed into a region of vital North American strategic interests. The Philippines projected a U.S. presence in Asia, directly on a collision course with first Japan, later China, then Korea, and eventually Vietnam. "Never again, after the war with Spain," Roger Burlingame wrote in 1957, "were we capable of complacency in our isolation. From now on we must engage in world politics." The U.S. presence in Asia "prepared the way for the war with Japan," and henceforth and thereafter the United States was obliged to develop "from a national to an international conscience."[26]

These issues became clearer as the twentieth century wore on, as each new development served as an occasion to contemplate 1898 anew as the decisive moment in which the nation crossed the threshold into what was soon to be proclaimed as "the American century." Meanings of 1898 appeared as a series of continual revelations. The relationships seemed manifest and insinuated themselves fully into the principal historiographical discourses of the twentieth century. The United States was represented as emerging from the war as an ascendant world power, rendering 1898 as something of a profoundly transformative experience. The process assumed transcendental proportions, in which the role of the United States in the world was henceforth assigned and fixed. "For the United States it was metamorphosis," G. J. A. O'Toole reflected; "the shell of isolation was broken and a new American dominion suddenly stretched from the Caribbean to the Far East." At another point, he observed: "It was a national rite of passage, transforming a former colony into a world power." The full impact of 1898 was in the realm of consciousness, Robert Endicott Osgood asserted with breathtaking implications. The "dramatic events of the Spanish-American War," Osgood wrote, brought "the American people to the full consciousness of their power in the world"; he added: "[B]y the end of that war the United States had become a world power. . . . The important transformation that did take place was the sudden awareness among many Americans, and Europeans as well, that the United States was in fact a world-wide power, not simply a hemispheric power, which was bound to exert a mighty influence upon the destinies of all peoples and play a major role in the calculations of every other great nation."[27]

This may have been what Charles M. Thompson meant when he wrote in 1922 that the war "gave the people a higher regard for their own fighting ability and made them consider more seriously the probability of future wars." Richard Collin depicted 1898 as the experience that "plunged America from a state of innocence into the role of superpower and conqueror." For J. Rogers Hollingsworth, the war launched the nation on its path to greatness in still another way: "The Spanish-American War created an infectious feeling of optimism in American society. The war stimulated new industries and drove prices upward. The demand for more railroads and new buildings set off a boom in the iron and steel industries. As the economy underwent a frantic period of expansion and speculation, the nation gained confidence in the future. . . . Everywhere men talked about success, progress, and prosperity."[28] According to David Trask, the war "thrust the United States into the maelstrom of world politics." In the opinion of H. Wayne Morgan, it "had profound diplomatic, economic, and political repercussions around the world" and "dated America's entry into the arena of world affairs." After the war, wrote Benson Lossing, the United States assumed its "place as one of the great powers of the world, not encumbered by old traditions, not hampered with the accumulated burdens of centuries, but in all the vigor of youth, with youthful hopes and ideas, ready to proclaim the doctrine of true liberty in 'a government of the people, by the people, and for the people.' " "It was then," Irving Werstein reflected, "that [the United States] reached the turning point and came of age. Grown to reluctant maturity, she became a nation responsible not only to herself but to the entire world." Robert D. Schulzinger advanced another view in 1994, no less far-reaching: "Modern American diplomacy dates from the war with Spain in 1898."[29]

• • •

The reach of 1898 spanned the twentieth century, with impacts and implications of other kinds. The North American rendering of 1898 was at the heart of the terms by which the United States defined its relationship with Cuba through the first half of the century. Something special linked Cuba to the United States, Americans proclaimed. Destinies were joined in 1898, when the United States sacrificed life and treasure in behalf of Cuban independence and in the process consecrated a relationship that was both primary and permanent. Cuba was always to have been bound to the United States, obligated to North Americans for having obtained its independence, something akin to moral memory, as a condition of appreciation in permanent requital. This is the future that President McKinley envisioned in his address to Congress in 1899, when he spoke of a Cuba "bound to us by ties of singular intimacy."[30]

These propositions were central to the resilience of U.S. hegemony, for they served as the basis on which the United States arranged the terms of its moral authority over Cuba. The U.S. appropriation of victory in 1898 worked powerfully to weaken the Cuban claim to sovereignty. Cubans seemed to have played no part in their own liberation. Rather, as the story was told and recorded, the United States had obtained the island's independence through the expenditure of U.S. life and treasure. Cuban efforts were represented as insignificant if not altogether inconsequential, and only the U.S. intervention rescued the flagging independence cause and finished the task Cubans had started but were themselves unable to complete. Cubans were thus encouraged to believe that they owed their independence to the United States, a point of view that the United States maintained through much of the twentieth century.

The year 1898 was henceforth the point at which the North Americans subsequently defined their relationship to Cuba and always as benefactor, as protector—as progenitor of sorts. Cuban independence acquired as a result of the "Spanish-American War," that is Cuba, sovereign and independent, as an accomplishment of North American beneficence, was a proposition that took hold early and persisted for a long time. Narratives of 1898 were at the heart of the official discourse of U.S. policy constructs, the point at which North American officials dated the origins of the "special" relationship, always with an unambiguous if unstated moral, a reminder to Cubans of what had been done for them as a way to insinuate what was expected of them. "American intervention gave to Cuba its independence," asserted U.S. ambassador Harry Guggenheim. "The United States helped the Cuban people win their independence as a free people," Assistant Secretary of State Sumner Welles proclaimed in 1934; "American blood was shed upon the soil of Cuba . . . to obtain Cuban liberty." Fifteen years later, on the fiftieth anniversary of the war with Spain, President Harry S. Truman pointed to the Joint Resolution as "the foundation upon which our relations with the Cuban Republic are based." This act of Congress, Truman could maintain in 1948, "expressed our determination that once the Cuban people were liberated, they, and they alone, should govern the Island of Cuba." On the same occasion, the *Washington Post* was unabashedly celebratory: "It was just 50 years ago . . . that Cuba with American help attained her independence . . . and respect, and the two countries have perhaps a closer bond than most because of the circumstances of Cuba's deliverance." Ambassador Earl E. T. Smith referred to 1898 as the foundation of "special" U.S.-Cuban ties. "The close relationship between our two countries goes back many years," Smith wrote in 1962. "The United States and Cuba fought side by side in the Spanish-American War of 1898."[31]

The claim that the United States had obtained independence for Cuba led to other claims, most of which had to do with the proposition that because of the debt they had incurred in 1898, Cubans were obliged to accommodate U.S. interests. It was the least they could do. More than half a century of Cuban-U.S. relations was driven by North American paradigms of 1898. The insistence on concessions as acts of gratitude could not but induce dependence and produce a condition of indebtedness and inevitably an obligation that could be discharged only by reciprocating U.S. beneficence in forms demanded by the United States. Repeatedly, North American officials claimed a moral right to dictate the terms of transactions of gratitude. This was the point made by the *New York Times* on July 19, 1898, only days after the fall of Santiago de Cuba: "The self-government which we are called upon to establish is self-government guided by equity and common sense. The sacrifices of treasure and life that we have made clearly entitle us to fix the conditions under which the observance of these principles shall be secure, and to retain whatever power is requisite to enforce these conditions."[32] Congressman Townsend Scudder agreed. "After spending millions of dollars in money and sacrificing many lives," he proclaimed, "we are in a position to make demands upon the island much more severe than any we will make, and still the Cubans would have no cause to complain." When Cubans initially balked at the Platt Amendment in January 1901, an irate Secretary of War Elihu Root countered with an explicit threat: "If the American people get the impression that Cuba is ungrateful and unreasonable they will not be quite so altruistic and sentimental the next time they have to deal with Cuban affairs as they were in April, 1898." Two months later, Root again admonished the recalcitrant Cubans, this time threatening to withhold trade concessions. "If they continue to exhibit ingratitude and an entire lack of appreciation of the expenditure of blood and treasure of the United States to secure their freedom from Spain," Root warned, "the public sentiment of this country will be more unfavorable to them and less disposed to favorable trade relations than it is towards any of their competitors."[33]

Congressman Scudder also responded impatiently to Cuban resistance to the Platt Amendment. "In view of the cost of Cuba's freedom to this country in treasure and in blood," he pronounced, "gratitude should impel her to lean upon America as her best friend and protector.... A bit of gratitude and friendly feeling on the part of the people whom we brought out of bondage would be a pleasant thing to contemplate just now." Senator Orville Platt could hardly contain his indignation at the failure of Cubans to display proper appreciation for U.S. beneficence. Platt denounced the "false pride" among Cubans, expressing dismay that there was "no recognition of the United States, no expression of gratitude or friendliness." The display of ingratitude itself seemed sufficient to suggest that perhaps Cubans did indeed lack the capacity for self-government. The "fact that so many of their leaders seem devoid of all gratitude to the United States for the many millions of dollars we have spent in their behalf," proclaimed Congressman Henry Gibson, "makes me suspicious of what Cuba may be when wholly committed to their hands."[34]

• • •

The events of 1898 had different meanings in Cuba. Long after the United States had turned its attention away from the island, satisfied that it had discharged its self-proclaimed mission of liberation, Cubans were left to contemplate what had transpired in 1898, what had become of the independence project for which a generation of men and women had struggled and sacrificed. The significance of 1898 became a Cuban preoccupation; there was a brooding sense that history seemed to have gone awry in 1898, and everyone was implicated. "In more than one respect," Roberto Fernández Retamar reflected one hundred years later, "we are the sons and daughters of the violent turning point in 1898."[35]

Memories were difficult to reconcile. Americans expected gratitude; Cubans harbored grievances. Americans remembered 1898 as something done for Cubans; Cubans remembered 1898 as something done to them. For Cubans, the Joint Resolution of 1898 was a cruel hoax. The Americans had arrived as allies but remained to rule. Worse still, many Cubans could not escape the sense that they themselves had served as unwitting accomplices to their own undoing. The turn of events was more than disappointment; it was deception. This was a profoundly disillusioning denouement to decades of heroic mobilizations; there was something very wrong about the way things ended.

These circumstances had direct implications for the ways that Cubans recalled and recorded their past. U.S. hegemony insinuated itself into all facets of their daily lives and nowhere perhaps with more discernible effects than in notions of the past. Cubans understood the implications of the term "Spanish-American War," as well as the larger meaning of the Cuban absence. Moreover, they came to comprehend the degree to which historical transactions were contingent and contextual, in a continuous state of contention. North American claims over Cuban sovereignty derived particular resonance from formulations fashioned in 1898, first as policy constructs and subsequently as historical truths.

Through the first half of the twentieth century, the first-born republican generation of Cuban historians engaged the dominant historiographical paradigms of the North. Beginning in the late 1930s and early 1940s, the Sociedad Cubana de Estudios Históricos e Internacionales served as the forum by which historians reworked the historiography of 1898. One change occurred in 1945, when the Cuban national congress decreed that thereafter all references to the conflict of 1895–98 were to be known officially as the "Spanish-Cuban-American War." The scholarship of Herminio Portell Vilá, Fernando Portuondo, Emilio Roig de Leuchsenring, and Enrique Gay Calbó, among others, was dedicated to the task of breaking the grip of what might easily be called hegemonic historiography. They sought the recognition of one truth with far-reaching political implications: Cuba was not, after all, indebted to the United States for its independence. The conclusion of Roig de Leuchsenring's small monograph, *Cuba no debe su independencia a los Estados Unidos* (1950), gave definitive form to the principal tenets of revisionist historiography: "Cuba does not owe its independence to the United States of North America, but to the efforts of its own people, through their firm and indomitable will to end the injustices, abuses, discriminations, and exploitation suffered under the despotic colonial regime."[36]

• • •

The issues of 1898 were not confined to historiographical disputation, however. On the contrary, this tension affected the very narratives of nationality and served as a means by which Cubans took stock of their relationship with the United States. Long after the Americans had forgotten that they had denied General Calixto García and his army entrance to Santiago de Cuba in July 1898, or excluded Cubans from the peace negotiations, at a time when most Americans probably could not have identified the Platt Amendment, when representations of the "Spanish-American War" had assumed something of a whimsical tone in U.S. history textbooks, Cubans continued to contemplate the meaning of 1898. Almost sixty years later, as the victorious rebel army under Fidel Castro converged on Santiago de Cuba and as the regime of Fulgencio Batista crumbled, the parallels were simply too powerful to let pass without comment. Memory lingered in places of unsuspected profundity. On this occasion of unmediated victory and celebration of unencumbered liberation, the nation found itself immersed in a discourse on 1898. Its resonance was demonstrated in its capacity to imply meaning by way of metaphor. This was an exquisite existential moment, when the past and present collapsed in on one another and at that instant revealed the power of the past to give purpose to the present. This was history as an analogue for the present, a way to validate the authenticity of what was about to happen. In the euphoria and exaltation of the early hours and days of the triumph of the Cuban revolution in 1959, fresh and flushed with victory, Fidel Castro chose that moment to remember. "This time the revolution will not be thwarted," he thundered on January 2, 1959, in Santiago de Cuba. "This time, fortunately for Cuba, the revolution will be consummated. It will not be like the war of 1895, when the Americans arrived and made themselves masters of the country; they intervened at the last minute and later did not even allow Calixto García, who had been fighting for thirty years, to enter Santiago de Cuba."[37]

Certainly Cubans knew exactly what Castro referred to, but they also sensed that he was saying something more, that the message was greater than the sum of its parts. These were allusions with portentous implications, for they reached deeply into a place of unsettled memories, of dormant sensitivities, that would not be aroused without a larger purpose. It was left to César Leante to capture the moment in his short story "El día inicial," as the narrator in Havana listens to Fidel Castro speak for the first time in a radio broadcast from Santiago de Cuba and contemplates the allusion to 1898:

> Finally, at dawn, . . . the voice of Fidel Castro. It's not a deep voice, not as full as many have expected, but thin, tense, a little forced, that does not construct brilliant paragraphs, that speaks in everyday language, that gets entangled in clauses that remain incomplete, and that, most of all, already, from this early moment, sounds troubling. . . . "This time the revolution will not be thwarted"—predicts the distant orator. "This time, fortunately, for Cuba, the revolution will be consummated." And in continuation, a warning, the sounding of an alarm that should have made the contented well-to-do slightly uneasy—only slightly, for the time being. "It will not be like the war of 1895, when the Americans arrived and made themselves masters of the country; they intervened at the last minute and later did not even allow Calixto García, who had been fighting for thirty years, to enter Santiago de Cuba." That allusion to the United States. . . . that allusion. . . .[38]

Larger meanings were not long in revealing themselves. A historical project had been completed, belatedly, and at the expense of history but also in the name of history. Fidel Castro was situated into 1898 as leader of the *mambises* marching into Santiago de Cuba, or perhaps it was the other way around, that the *mambises* had returned in 1959. It really did not matter. The ambiguity was useful, for either way the meaning was the same and could be deciphered without difficulty. "Today," affirmed *Revolución*, the newspaper of the 26 of July Movement, "when we saw the troops of Calixto García led by Fidel Castro enter Santiago on January 1, we have to think that we live in different times. And if Santiago de Cuba of yesterday was the tomb of the Spanish empire in the New World, Cuba of today . . . could well be the . . . site where the now obsolete imperialism is shattered."[39]

That these allusions "worked" as a means of mass mobilization—indeed, that they could be imagined at all and employed explicitly as political discourse—corroborated the resonance of 1898 in the realm of popular sensibilities. Cubans carried knowledge of 1898 in the form of received wisdom. It was, so to speak, "common knowledge," the way a people know something with such certainty and conviction that they lose awareness that it is apprehended at all. This was history as popular memory, accessible to all. Moreover, that scores of *mambises* were still alive in 1959 to tell their stories, to recount an injustice done a long time ago, gave authenticity and authority to the conventional wisdom. One such *testimonio* appeared as the published oral history of Esteban Montejo, *The Autobiography of a Runaway Slave* (1966). Montejo recalled 1898: "The truth is that Calixto García won the day at Santiago. . . . Then the Americans ran up their flag to show that they had taken the city. What a farce! . . . The worst thing was that the American commanding officer ordered that no Cuban should enter the city. That was what made everyone's blood boil. When the Cubans found they weren't allowed in, they began to resent the Americans, and Calixto García said some hard things to them."[40]

These themes reverberated across the island in early 1959. What had happened sixty years earlier now mattered in new ways and with far-reaching implications. Enrique Gay Calbó reminded his readers in January 1959 that the U.S. victories at El Caney and Santiago de Cuba were "possible only as a result of the cooperation of General Calixto García, with the veteran Cuban forces of liberation" and added: "The intervention by the United States came when the Liberation Army had already won the war. . . . But Cubans were not even permitted to take part in the peace negotiations nor in the transfer of control of towns. The United States arrived as if to a conquered country."[41] Teresa Casuso, who broke with Fidel Castro in 1959, was still able to summon indignation about 1898. The revisionist counternarrative had indeed taken hold among Cubans of all political persuasions. Casuso scoffed at the oft-cited U.S. contention that Americans had sacrificed life and treasure in behalf of Cuban independence. "No American lives at all need have been lost," she wrote in 1961, "if instead of intervening in our war the United States had limited itself to sending war materials to the Cubans for their final drive. It is not Cuban ingratitude to say this. We know why the United States wished to participate directly. It was in order to retain rights, and to try to exercise control over our independence and our national life." After the Cuban army had provided the decisive contribution to the defeat of Spain, Casuso argued, "it was at once prohibited from entering Santiago de Cuba, and was not allowed to participate in the surrender conference. Cuba was then militarily occupied by U.S. troops." Casuso brooded about the past, almost as if to suggest that what the Americans had done in 1898 was somehow responsible for creating the conditions that allowed Castro to rise to power. "[O]ur irrepressible island had grown tired of fearing the bogey of American intervention," she reflected, "and rose up clamoring once again for freedom, for the independence it had fought for, and won, but had never obtained."[42]

Again and again throughout early 1959, the events of 1898 were recounted as an injustice done to the nation, the point after which Cuba was opened to decades of U.S. military intervention and political meddling. The moral was not difficult to divine. The invocation of the past was not simply an incantation of woeful lament. On the contrary, remembrance of 1898 served as a way to rectify history and reclaim the past on Cuban terms, to resume history from the time before Cubans were left out, before they were diverted from consummating the independence project. The meaning was clear: the independence denied in 1898 had been attained in 1959. Connections were drawn early and repeatedly. "The Republic was not free in 1895," Fidel Castro recalled on January 3, "and the dream of the liberators (*mambises*) was frustrated at the last minute." He declared "that those men who had fought for thirty years and not seen their dreams realized" would have rejoiced in 1959 at the realization of the "revolution that they had dreamed of, the *patria* that they had imagined."[43] In a speech at the Lions Club of Havana, Castro denounced the Platt Amendment as "an injustice . . . imposed on a generation which fought for independence, a law that served purposefully to deny them that independence." When the U.S. State Department criticized the new Cuban government for the trials and execution of *batistianos*, Castro retorted: "We are not living in 1901 . . . when they intervened here and imposed upon us an Amendment that was truly a disgrace and humiliation for the nation." On the commemoration of the *Grito de Baire* (February 24) in 1959, Fidel Castro returned to this theme. "At the end of the war for independence," he recounted, "when the Spanish army was virtually defeated, for I can assure you that had the war continued the Cubans would have totally defeated the Spanish army, the American intervention took place. . . . If the Cubans would have won the war alone, how different everything would have been."[44] On February 23 Castro proclaimed outright that "the *mambises* initiated the war for independence that we have completed."[45]

These themes loomed large in the political pronouncements of early 1959. Minister of Education Armando Hart insisted that the revolutionaries "were more committed, more obligated than were the Cubans of 1898 . . . not to permit the frustration of the revolution." Novelist Guillermo Cabrera Infante similarly defended Cuban sovereignty against those who would be the "new Rough Riders who would disembark against Cuba." Writer Bernardo Díaz asserted that "the intervention of the United States in all our revolutionary and political processes since 1898 was undeniable." However, in 1959, Díaz added: "In this ostensibly friendly game of checkers which is the politics of the Continent, the people of Cuba have recovered a king that they had lost in 1898 with the intervention: the [liberation] soldiers have finally entered the cities." *Revolución* often alluded to 1898 editorially. "Independence," it affirmed on January 15, "was frustrated by the foreign intervention." A day later the newspaper provided its readers with a history lesson: "We are going to talk about a little history. Once upon a time, some of our grandfathers, after nearly a century of conspiracy and war, at the point of obtaining their victory as a result of the exhaustion of Spain, and its impending financial collapse, due to the futility of its arms and the fever of its sons, suddenly received the intervention of their neighbors, who until then had remained indifferent to their years of suffering. The war ended but . . . the liberators all but starved to death."[46]

These evocations must have appeared incomprehensible to most Americans, many of whom no doubt had little if any idea of what the Cubans were referring to. Frank Freidel was more than slightly defensive about the Cuban charges and took the occasion of his review of Ernest May's *Imperial Democracy* in 1961 to respond: "Today, when Fidel Castro and his claque are screaming epithets at the United States and charging that the Spanish-American War was fought only for imperialistic reasons, it is heartening to be reminded of the fundamentally humanitarian motives that took Americans into the war." The "history of this island since its liberation from Spain," *New York Times* correspondent Ruby Hart Phillips smarted, "does not record many examples of Cuban gratitude for contributions made by the United States in lives, blood and dollars." In Washington, bafflement was as commonplace as it was highly placed. "What do you suppose, sir, is eating [Fidel Castro]?" President Dwight D. Eisenhower was asked at a press conference on October 28. Eisenhower was at a loss:

I have no idea of discussing possible motivation of such a man, what he is really doing, and certainly I am not qualified to go into such abstruse and difficult subjects as that. I do feel this: here is a country that you would believe, on the basis of our history, would be one of our real friends. The whole history—first our intervention in 1898, our making and helping set up Cuban independence . . . and the very close relationships that have existed most of the time with them— would seem to make it a puzzling matter to figure just exactly why the Cubans and the Cuban Government would be so unhappy. . . . I don't know exactly what the difficulty is.[47]

• • •

There are, perhaps, many truths about 1898. Amid shifting boundaries and fluctuating perspectives, the assorted chronicles of Cuba suggest a persistent historical elusiveness. For North American historians writing between World War I and the end of World War II, the years of U.S. ascendancy, 1898 was celebrated as the point of debut on the global stage, an affirmation of a place of importance in world affairs. Scholars writing between the late 1940s and the 1960s, a time in which Cold War paradigms acted powerfully to divide the world into Manichaean dichotomies of good and evil, the American purpose in 1898 assumed the form of narratives about the beneficence of the United States, about the virtues of exporting liberal democratic capitalist forms to such far-flung areas of the world as the Philippines, Guam, Cuba, and Puerto Rico. After the 1970s U.S. historiography reflected the onset of disillusionment of U.S. involvement abroad. The road to Vietnam passed directly through the Philippines.

The importance of 1898 in Cuba was heightened by the triumph of the Cuban revolution in 1959. It is difficult to imagine that these issues would have assumed such salience had it not been for Fidel Castro. The revolution challenged the foundations of U.S. hegemony in Cuba, in all its forms, at all its moments. It just so happened that historiography was one of them. The year 1898, Cubans understood, was the point of preemption; 1959, they believed, was the moment of redemption. One of the objectives of the revolution was to make Cuba for Cubans, and this necessarily had to begin with history, to recover a usable past in which the Cuban presence mattered. In reconfiguring the way they saw themselves, Cubans also redefined the ways others saw them. After 1959 it was not uncommon for U.S. histories to view the war as the "Spanish-Cuban-American War." Cubans had regained their past.[48]

The historiography of 1898 has traditionally divided sharply along national lines. Scholarship in the United States has largely ignored the participation of Cubans; in Cuba, the historical literature has minimized if not often denied the contribution of the United States. The division underscores the ways that contested historiographies often have to do with representations of power and manifestations of resistance. In the end, however, the central issue is not whether the United States had interests to pursue. It did—and, indeed, the inquiry rightfully should focus on how precisely those interests were broadly conceived and, in particular circumstances, defended, no less than on the assumptions on which they rested and the implications they suggested. Rather, the point is that the Cubans had interests to pursue as well, and these interests were no less meaningful to the way they envisioned the requirements of their daily well-being. It is clear now—and probably was at the time— that these two sets of interests were intrinsically incompatible. The United States prevailed simply by negating Cubans interests through force of arms. At this point matters got complicated, for it was not enough merely to subordinate Cuban interests to North American ones. It also became necessary for Americans to represent the deed then and thereafter as an act of beneficence, one undertaken in the best interests of Cuba.

In a manner that was both representative and recurring, Sumner Welles seemed to have persuaded himself, or sought to persuade others, that U.S. policy was designed for the good of "the Cuban people," who "entered their independence without the benefits of honest, efficiency, and democratic government." Welles concluded: "For the protection of the Cuban people themselves, therefore, a treaty was consequently entered into between the United States and Cuba which contained provisions, also incorporated into the Cuban Constitution, commonly known as the Platt Amendment."[49] Puzzled observers have contemplated the source and significance of such pronouncements, articulated first as policy rationale and repeated later as historical truths, uncertain whether these representations suggest hypocrisy, dissimulation, self-deception, or some combination of all three.

At this point it would seem hardly necessary to make a further case for a historiography of 1898 that would embrace the proposition of a "Spanish-Cuban-American War." Similarly, it is unnecessary to deny the contribution of the United States in the Cuban struggle for independence. The U.S. intervention surely hastened the end of the war and no doubt saved countless Cuban lives. Nor should the authenticity of the zeal of the American people in behalf of Cuba Libre in 1898 be questioned, irrespective of the fact that this sentiment may have been manipulated by policymakers in pursuit of larger objectives.

The understanding of meaning involves an explicit invocation of the past, predicated on the proposition that the past is never really resolved: things do not simply happen and end. There is always uncertainty and debate about whether the past is really over and done with, or whether it continues, albeit in different forms, in our midst, shaping and determining the future, precisely as suggested by the Jack Nicholson character in the motion picture "The Two Jakes" (1990): "the past never goes away."

It may be useful to contemplate the proposition that a more balanced view of the past might well provide the basis for a more balanced sense of the future. In fact, these elements underscore, one hundred years later, the bases by which to contemplate ties between peoples possessed of similar ideals with shared sources in the nineteenth century. The generosity of people in both countries, rooted in respect and goodwill, do indeed have common sources traceable to 1898.

NOTES

CHAPTER ONE

1. Frank Freidel, *The Splendid Little War* (Boston, 1958), p. 5; Richard Hofstadter, "Manifest Destiny and the Philippines," in Theodore P. Greene, ed., *American Imperialism in 1898* (Boston, 1955), pp. 68–69; Robert L. Beisner, *From the Old Diplomacy to the New, 1865–1900*, 2d ed. (Arlington Heights, Ill., 1986), p. 76; David Healy, *U.S. Expansionism: The Imperialist Urge in the 1890s* (Madison, 1970), p. 109; Gerald F. Linderman, *The Mirror of War: American Society and the Spanish-American War* (Ann Arbor, 1974), p. 5; Daniel M. Smith, *The American Diplomatic Experience* (Boston, 1972), p. 209; Mary Beth Norton, David M. Katzman, Paul D. Escott, Howard P. Chudacoff, Thomas G. Paterson, and William M. Tuttle Jr., *A People and a Nation: A History of the United States*, 5th ed. (Boston, 1998), p. 632.

2. John Quincy Adams to Hugh Nelson, April 28, 1823, in Worthington Chauncey Ford, ed., *The Writings of John Quincy Adams*, 7 vols. (New York, 1913–17), 7:372.

3. Ibid., pp. 372–73; James Buchanan to Romulus M. Saunders, June 17, 1848 (11:62), William L. Marcy to Pierre Soulé, November 13, 1854 (11:197), and Marcy to Augustus C. Dodge, May 1, 1855 (11:210), all in William R. Manning, ed., *Diplomatic Correspondence of the United States: Inter-American Affairs*, 12 vols. (Washington, D.C., 1932–39); *Congressional Globe*, 35th Cong., 2d sess., 1858–59, pt. 1:540 (Toombs), 543 (Bayard).

4. Thomas Jefferson to James Monroe, June 23, 1823, in H. A. Washington, ed., *The Works of Thomas Jefferson*, 9 vols. (New York, 1884), 7:300; James Buchanan to Romulus M. Saunders, June 17, 1848, in Manning, *Diplomatic Correspondence*, 11:57; Daniel Webster, Speech, April 1826, in Daniel Webster, *Speeches and Forensic Arguments*, 2 vols. (Boston, 1838), 1:344; "The Ostend Manifesto," October 18, 1854, House Executive Document 93, 33d Cong., 2d sess. (Washington, D.C., 1855), pp. 127–32.

5. Thomas Jefferson to James Monroe, June 11, 1823, in Washington, *Works of Thomas Jefferson*, 7:288.

6. Edward Livingston to William Shaler, September 1, 1832 (11:6–7), John H. Eaton to the Count of Ofalia, February 22, 1838 (11:312–13), and Daniel M. Barringer to John M. Clayton, June 19, 1850 (11:506), all in Manning, *Diplomatic Correspondence*.

7. Thomas Jefferson to James Monroe, October 24, 1823, in Washington, *Works of Thomas Jefferson*, 7:37; Washington Irving to Abel P. Upshur, March 2, 1854 (11:335), John Forsyth to Aaron Vail, July 15, 1840 (11:23–24), and John M. Clayton to Daniel M. Barringer, August 2, 1847 (11:70), all in Manning, *Diplomatic Correspondence*.

8. Richard B. Olney to Grover Cleveland, September 25, 1895, Grover Cleveland Papers, Manuscript Division, Library of Congress, Washington, D.C.; Olney to Enrique Dupuy de Lôme, April 4, 1896, in U.S. Department of State, *Papers Relating to Foreign*

Relations of the United States, 1897 (Washington, D.C., 1898) (hereafter cited as *FRUS: 1897*), p. 541.

9. Máximo Gómez to John R. Caldwell, December 5, 1897, *New York Herald*, December 29, 1897, p. 3; *New York World*, February 10, 1898, pp. 1–2; Tomás Estrada Palma to John Sherman, December 1, 1897, Notes from the Cuban Legation in the United States to the U.S. Department of State, General Records, 1844–1906, Record Group 59, National Archives, Washington, D.C.

10. *New York Journal*, February 24, 1898, p. 12 (Masó); Calixto García to Editor, December 28, 1897, *New York Journal*, January 5, 1898, p. 7; Walter B. Barker to William R. Day, October 18, 1897, Dispatches from U.S. Consuls in Sagua la Grande, U.S. Department of State, General Records, 1878–1900, Record Group 59, National Archives, Washington, D.C.

11. José Conangla Fontanilles, *Cuba y Pi y Margall* (Havana, 1947), pp. 422–23; *New York Times*, March 22, 1898, p. 1; *El Nuevo Régimen*, December 25, 1897; *La Epoca*, January 8, 1898.

12. *New York World*, January 2, 1898, p. 3; Presidente de la República, "Manifiesto al pueblo de Cuba," October 27, 1897.

13. Máximo Gómez to Tomás Estrada Palma, July 30, 1897, *Boletín del Archivo Nacional* 30 (January–December 1931): 74; Alexander Gollan to Foreign Office, August 6, 1897, Foreign Office Records, Embassy and Consular Archives, Cuba, 1870 Onwards, Group 277, No. 57, British Public Records Office, Kew, London.

14. Máximo Gómez to Tomás Estrada Palma, January 1898, *Boletín del Archivo Nacional* 31 (January–December 1932): 90; Gómez to Ernesto Fonts Sterling, March 1, 1898, in Máximo Gómez, *Algunos documentos políticos de Máximo Gómez*, ed. Amalia Rodríguez (Havana, 1962), p. 20; Gómez to Gonzalo de Quesada, March 10, 1898, *New York Tribune*, April 10, 1898, p. 3.

15. Máximo Gómez to Gonzalo de Quesada, March 10, 1898, *New York Tribune*, April 10, 1898, p. 3; Luis Miranda y de la Rúa, *Con Martí y con Calixto García (recuerdos de un mambí del 95)* (Havana, 1943), p. 77; Eduardo Lores y Llorens, *Relatos históricos de la guerra del 95* (Havana, 1955), pp. 41–51; Rafael Gutíerrez, *Oriente heroico* (Santiago de Cuba, 1915), p. 62.

16. Hannis Taylor, "A Review of the Cuban Question in Its Economic, Political, and Diplomatic Aspects," *North American Review* 492 (November 1897): 610; *New York World*, August 7, 1897, p. 2; William R. Day to Stewart L. Woodford, March 28, 1898, in U.S. Department of State, *Papers Relating to the Foreign Relations of the United States, 1898* (Washington, D.C., 1899) (hereafter cited as *FRUS:1898*), p. 704; Day, "Recognition of Independence," n.d., William R. Day Papers, Manuscript Division, Library of Congress, Washington, D.C.

17. Fitzhugh Lee to William R. Day, August 25, 1897, Personal Correspondence, General Lee to the Secretary of State, 1897–98, John Bassett Moore Papers, Manuscript Division, Library of Congress, Washington, D.C.; *The State* (Columbia, S.C.), April 16, 1898, p. 4; Henry Cabot Lodge, *The War with Spain* (Boston, 1899), p. 34; George L. Dyer to Susan Dyer, April 1, 1898, George Leland Dyer Papers, Special Collections, Joyner Library, East Carolina University, Greenville, N.C.

18. John Quincy Adams to Hugh Nelson, April 28, 1823, in Ford, *Writings of John Quincy Adams*, 7:374–75; Henry Clay to Alexander H. Everett, April 27, 1825, in James F. Hopkins and Mary W. M. Hargreaves, eds., *The Papers of Henry Clay*, 8 vols. (Lex-

ington, Ky., 1959–92), 4:298; Hamilton Fish Diary, April 1869, Box 314, Hamilton Fish Papers, Manuscript Division, Library of Congress, Washington, D.C.

19. Richard B. Olney to Enrique Dupuy de Lôme, April 4, 1896, *FRUS: 1897*, p. 543.

20. Grover Cleveland to Richard B. Olney, July 16, 1896, in Allan Nevins, ed., *Letters of Grover Cleveland* (Boston, 1933), p. 448.

21. Stewart L. Woodford to William McKinley, March 9, 1898, Dispatches from U.S. Consuls to Spain, U.S. Department of State, General Records, 1792–1906, Record Group 59, National Archives, Washington, D.C. (hereafter cited as Dispatches/Spain); Woodford to William McKinley, March 17 and 18, 1898, Private Correspondence, General Woodford to the President, August 1897 to May 1898, Moore Papers.

22. U.S. Congress, Senate, *Affairs in Cuba*, ser. 4053 (Washington, D.C., 1896), p. 73.

23. Grover Cleveland, "Third Annual Message to Congress," December 2, 1895, in James D. Richardson, ed., *A Compilation of the Messages and Papers of the Presidents, 1789–1902*, 10 vols. (Washington, D.C., 1896–1902), 9:636.

24. Lyman J. Gage, "Work of the Treasury Department," *The American-Spanish War: A History by the War Leaders* (Norwich, Conn., 1899), p. 369; French Ensor Chadwick, *The Relations of the United States and Spain: Diplomacy* (New York, 1909), p. 490.

25. Tomás Estrada Palma to Antonio Maceo, October 17, 1895, in Maceo, *Antonio Maceo: Documentos para su vida*, ed. Julián Martínez Castells (Havana, 1945), p. 152; Estrada Palma to Emeterio Betances, November 27, 1896, in Joaquín Llaverías y Martínez, ed., *Correspondencia de la delegación cubana en Nueva York durante la guerra de 1895 a 1898*, 5 vols. (Havana, 1943–46), 1:95; Samuel Flagg Bemis, ed., *The American Secretaries of State and Their Diplomacy*, 18 vols. (New York, 1958–70), 8:286; Elbert J. Benton, *International Law and Diplomacy of the Spanish-American War* (Baltimore, 1908), p. 42.

26. Stewart L. Woodford to William McKinley, March 9, 1898, Dispatches/Spain.

27. Stewart L. Woodford to William McKinley, March 17, April 1, 1898, Private Correspondence, General Woodford to the President, August 1897 to May 1898, Moore Papers (Woodford's emphasis).

28. Stewart L. Woodford to William McKinley, March 18, 1898, ibid.

29. William R. Day to Stewart L. Woodford, March 27, 1898, *FRUS:1898*, p. 712; Woodford to William McKinley, April 5, 1898, Private Correspondence, General Woodford to the President, August 1897 to May 1898, Moore Papers.

30. Luis Polo de Bernabé to John Sherman, April 10, 1898, in Spain, Ministerio de Estado, *Spanish Diplomatic Correspondence and Documents, 1896–1900, Presented to the Parliament by the Minister of State* (Washington, D.C., 1905), p. 12.

31. Horatio Rubens, *Liberty: The Story of Cuba* (New York, 1932), pp. 326–27. Tomás Estrada Palma, the head of the New York Junta, later wrote of the "enormous pressure . . . brought to bear on the Delegation to persuade the Cubans to accept the armistice." See Tomás Estrada Palma, "The Work of the Cuban Delegation," in *The American Spanish War: A History by the War Leaders* (Norwich, Conn., 1899), pp. 419–20.

32. Bartolomé Masó, "Manifiesto," April 24, 1898, in Cuba, Secretaria de Gobernación, *Documentos históricos* (Havana, 1912), pp. 165–66; Calixto García to Mario G. Menocal, April 18, 1898, in Calixto García, *Palabras de tres guerras* (Havana, 1942), pp. 143–44; Juan J. E. Casasús, *Calixto García (el estratega)*, 2d ed. (Havana, 1962), p. 251; Máximo Gómez, "Orden General del día 20 para el Ejército," in Máximo Gómez, *Cartas a Francisco Carrillo*, ed. Hortensia Pichardo (Havana, 1986), p. 212.

33. Máximo Gómez, *Diario de campaña del mayor general Máximo Gómez* (Havana, 1940), p. 354.

34. Richardson, *Messages and Papers of the Presidents*, 10:63–64.
35. Alvey A. Adee to William R. Day, April 7, 1898, Day Papers; *New York Tribune*, April 7, 1898, p. 6; Charles G. Dawes, *A Journal of the McKinley Years* (Chicago, 1950), p. 154; *Washington Evening Star*, April 14, 1898, p. 1.
36. José Martí to Gonzalo de Quesada, December 14, 1889 (3:197), October 19, 1889 (vol. 1, pt. 2:656), in José Martí, *Obras completas*, ed. Jorge Quintana, 5 vols. (Caracas, 1964); Antonio Maceo to Federico Carbó, July 14, 1896, in Antonio Maceo, *Pensamiento vivo de Antonio Maceo*, ed. José Antonio Portuondo (Havana, 1962), p. 94; Bernabé Boza, *Mi diario de guerra*, 2 vols. (Havana, 1924), 1:270–71; Emilio Roig de Leuchsenring, *Máximo Gómez: El libertador de Cuba y el primer ciudadano de la república* (Havana, 1959), pp. 42–44.
37. "Borrador relacionado con la Resolución Conjunta," April 1898, Gonzalo de Quesada, *Documentos históricos* (Havana, 1965), p. 409; *Washington Evening Star*, April 6, 1898, p. 1.
38. See William R. Day, "Memorandum," March 24, 1898, Day Papers.
39. Paul S. Holbo, "Presidential Leadership in Foreign Affairs: William McKinley and the Turpie-Foraker Amendment," *American Historical Review* 72 (1967): 1321–35.
40. *Congressional Record*, 55th Cong., 2d sess., 1898, 31:3988.
41. Calixto García to Tomás Estrada Palma, April 26, 1898, in Felipe Martínez Arango, *Cronología de la guerra hispano-cubano-americana* (Santiago de Cuba, 1960), p. 44.

CHAPTER TWO

1. James Henry Brownlee, ed., *War-Time Echoes: Patriotic Poems, Heroic and Pathetic, Humorous and Dialectic, of the Spanish-American War* (Akron, 1898), p. ix; "The War Spirit of the People," *Harper's Weekly*, April 16, 1898, p. 363.
2. Alonzo Stone, *Cuba Must Be Free* (Philadelphia, 1898).
3. Edward Thurston Wood and Nanna Branham Wood, *We Are Coming with Old Glory* (Chicago, 1898).
4. S. H. Byers, *Cuban Battle Song* (Des Moines, Iowa, 1898); Harry Holliday, *The Song of Our Nation* (New York, 1898).
5. L. J. Gillham, "Freedom for Cuba," in Sidney A. Witherbee, ed., *Spanish-American War Songs: A Complete Collection of Newspaper Verse during the Recent War with Spain* (Detroit, 1898), p. 400.
6. "War," in Brownlee, *War-Time Echoes*, p. 32.
7. Thomas Sullivan, "Hail Our Glorious Banner," in ibid., p. 86.
8. George E. Woodberry, "The Islands of the Sea," in ibid., p. 108.
9. Charles Henry Butler, *Cuba Must Be Free* (New York, 1898); Harry H. Ross to Editor, *The Freeman*, September 30, 1898, in Willard B. Gatewood Jr., *"Smoked Yankees" and the Struggle for Empire: Letters from Negro Soldiers, 1898–1902* (Urbana, Ill., 1971), p. 197; Joseph H. McDermott to Magdalene McDermott, June 25, 1898, Joseph H. McDermott Letters, Manuscript Department, New-York Historical Society, New York, N.Y.; Carl Sandburg, *Always the Young Strangers* (New York, 1953), pp. 376–77, 404; Oswald Garrison Villard, *Fighting Years: Memoirs of a Liberal Editor* (New York, 1939), p. 134.
10. Gertrude Franklin Horn Atherton, *Senator North* (New York, 1900), p. 267; Edward Stratemeyer, *A Young Volunteer in Cuba* (Boston, 1898), pp. 15, 59, 66; Alvan Elmar Clarendon, *Shackles Cast* (Omaha, 1912), p. 62; John Fox Jr., *Crittenden: A Kentucky*

Story of Love and War (New York, 1911), p. 20; Joseph Hergesheimer, *The Bright Shawl* (New York, 1922), p. 48. For an excellent treatment of the war as a theme in U.S. literature, see Woodruff Christian Thomson, "The Spanish-American War in American Literature" (Ph.D. dissertation, University of Utah, 1962).

11. For a discussion of the pro-independence press, see Joseph E. Wisan, *The Cuban Crisis as Reflected in the New York Press, 1895–1898* (New York, 1934), pp. 400–21.

12. Whitelaw Reid to James H. Wilson, September 11, 1900, James Harrison Wilson Papers, Manuscript Division, Library of Congress, Washington, D.C.

13. Richard Olney, "The Growth of Our Foreign Policy," *Atlantic Monthly*, March 1900, p. 291; Albert J. Beveridge, "Cuba and Congress," *North American Review* 172 (April 1901): 549–50; Orville H. Platt to Edwin Atkins, June 11, 1901, Orville H. Platt Papers, Connecticut State Library, Hartford (the author wishes to thank Lars Schoultz for bringing this document to his attention); James H. Wilson to Theodore Roosevelt, July 5, 1899, Theodore Roosevelt Papers, Manuscript Division, Library of Congress, Washington, D.C.

14. *New York Times*, December 19, 1898, p. 2, in Walter Millis, *The Martial Spirit: A Study of Our War with Spain* (Boston, 1931), p. 362; *New York Times*, July 22, 1898, p. 2; William Ludlow to Chief of Staff, Division of Cuba, October 4, 1898, File 287874, Adjutant General's Office, Records, 1780s–1917, Record Group 94, National Archives, Washington, D.C.

15. *New York Times*, July 23, 1898, p. 1; Leonard Wood, "The Future of Cuba," *Independent* 54 (January 23, 1902): 193.

16. *Philadelphia Inquirer*, August 6, 1898, p. 6; *New York Times*, August 12, 1898, p. 6; *New York Tribune*, August 17, 1898, p. 6; Dawes, *Journal of the McKinley Years*, p. 165.

17. Louis A. Coolidge, *An Old-fashioned Senator: Orville H. Platt of Connecticut* (New York, 1910), p. 331 (first quotation); Orville H. Platt, "The Pacification of Cuba," *Independent* 53 (June 27, 1901): 1466; *New York Tribune*, August 7, 1898, p. 6.

18. Joseph Benson Foraker, "Our War with Spain: Its Justice and Necessity," *Forum* 25 (June 1898): 391–92; Foraker, *Notes of a Busy Life*, 2 vols., 3d ed. (Cincinnati, 1917), 2:39.

19. Beveridge, "Cuba and Congress," p. 545; Herbert P. Williams, "The Outlook in Cuba," *Atlantic Monthly*, June 1899, pp. 835–36; *Congressional Record*, 1901, 34, app., pt. 4:357.

20. Leonard Wood to Elihu Root, January 13, 1900, Leonard Wood Papers, Manuscript Division, Library of Congress, Washington, D.C.; Wood to William McKinley, February 6, 1900, Special Correspondence, Elihu Root Papers, Manuscript Division, Library of Congress, Washington, D.C.

21. Philip C. Jessup, "Conversation with Mr. Root at 998 Fifth Avenue," November 19, 1929, Philip C. Jessup Papers, Manuscript Division, Library of Congress, Washington, D.C.; Orville H. Platt to Edwin Atkins, June 11, 1901, Platt Papers; Platt, "The Pacification of Cuba," pp. 1465–66. See *La Lucha*, April 14, 1899, p. 1.

22. *The Statutes at Large of the United States*, 50 vols. (Washington, D.C., 1937–), 31:897.

23. Leopoldo Figueroa to William McKinley, March 8, 1901, File 568-29, Bureau of Insular Affairs, Record Group 350, National Archives, Washington, D.C. (hereafter cited as BIA/RG 350); Council of Veterans to Leonard Wood, March 9, 1909, File 3051, Letters Received, Records of the Military Government of Cuba, Record Group 140, National Archives, Washington, D.C.; Municipal Council, Regla, to War Depart-

ment, March 7, 1901, File 568-28, BIA/RG 350; Pelayo García to William McKinley, March 4, 1901, File 568-64, BIA/RG 350.

24. Leonard Wood to Elihu Root, March 20, 1901, Root Papers.

25. *Congressional Record*, March 1, 1901, 34, pt. 4:358; Elihu Root to Leonard Wood, March 2, 1901, File 331-71, BIA/RG 350.

26. Octavio Ramón Costa y Blanco, *Manuel Sanguily* (Havana, 1950), p. 91; José Manuel Cortina, *Manuel Sanguily en la evolución de Cuba* (Havana, 1929), pp. 24–25; Albert G. Robinson, *Cuba and the Intervention* (London, 1905), p. 270.

27. Leonard Wood to Theodore Roosevelt, October 28, 1901, Wood Papers.

28. Máximo Gómez to Sotero Figueroa, May 8, 1901, in Máximo Gómez, *Papeles dominicanos de Máximo Gómez*, ed. Emilio Rodríguez (Ciudad Trujilllo, 1954), pp. 396–97.

29. *Congressional Record*, 1901, 34, pt. 4:3340–41.

30. Theodore Roosevelt, *Autobiography* (1913; New York, 1946), p. 504.

31. For some of the better discussions of the constraints of the Platt Amendment, see David F. Healy, *The United States in Cuba, 1898–1902: Generals, Politicians, and the Search for Policy* (Madison, 1963); Philip S. Foner, *The Spanish-Cuban-American War and the Birth of American Imperialism*, 2 vols. (New York, 1972); and Jules R. Benjamin, *The United States and the Origins of the Cuban Revolution* (Princeton, 1990).

32. R. D. W. Connor, *The Story of the United States* (Raleigh, N.C., 1916), p. 366; Mabel B. Casner and Ralph Henry Gabriel, *The Rise of the American Democracy* (New York, 1938), p. 531; John Holladay Latané and David W. Wainhouse, *A History of American Foreign Policy*, 2d ed. (New York, 1940), p. 511; James Ford Rhodes, *The McKinley and Roosevelt Administrations, 1897–1909* (New York, 1922), p. 177; Gary B. Nash, John R. Howe, Allen F. Davis, Julie Roy Jeffrey, Peter J. Frederick, and Allan M. Winkler, *The American People: Creating a Nation and a Society*, 2 vols., 2d ed. (New York, 1990), 2:696; William Wood and Ralph Henry Gabriel, *In Defense of Liberty* (New Haven, 1928), p. 202; Randolph Greenfield Adams, *A History of the Foreign Policy of the United States* (New York, 1933), p. 227; Ralph Henry Gabriel, *Main Currents in American History* (New York, 1942), p. 160; H. Wayne Morgan, *America's Road to Empire: The War with Spain and Overseas Expansion* (New York, 1965), p. 112; Robert E. Welch Jr., "William McKinley: Reluctant Warrior, Cautious Imperialist," in Norman A. Graebner, ed., *Traditions and Values: American Diplomacy, 1865–1945* (Lanham, Md., 1985), pp. 37, 39; John A. S. Grenville and George Berkeley Young, *Politics, Strategy, and American Diplomacy: Studies in Foreign Policy, 1873–1917* (New Haven, 1966), pp. 263, 266.

33. John A. Garraty, *The American Nation* (New York, 1983), p. 555; Richard H. Collin, *Theodore Roosevelt: Culture, Diplomacy, and Expansion* (Baton Rouge, 1985), pp. 136–37; Frederic L. Paxson, *Recent History of the United States, 1865 to the Present* (Boston, 1937), pp. 326–27; Paul L. Haworth, *The United States in Our Own Times, 1865–1920* (New York, 1920), p. 254.

34. Julius W. Pratt, *A History of United States Foreign Policy*, 3d ed. (Englewood Cliffs, N.J., 1972), p. 199; David F. Trask, *The War with Spain in 1898* (New York, 1981), p. 58; John M. Dobson, "Spanish-Cuban/American War," in Benjamin R. Beede, ed., *The War of 1898 and U.S. Interventions, 1898–1934: An Encyclopedia* (New York, 1994), p. 521; J. Rogers Hollingsworth, *The Whirligig of Politics* (Chicago, 1963), p. 138.

35. Walter T. K. Nugent, *Modern America* (Boston, 1973), p. 153; Foster Rhea Dulles, *Prelude to World Power: American Diplomatic History, 1860–1900* (New York, 1965), pp. 178–79; Wayne S. Cole, *An Interpretative History of American Foreign Relations*, rev. ed.

(Homewood, Ill., 1974), p. 212; Daniel M. Smith, *The American Diplomatic Experience* (Boston, 1972), p. 209; John A. Garraty, *A Short History of the American Nation*, 6th ed. (New York, 1993), p. 363; Maldwyn A. Jones, *The Limits of Liberty: American History, 1607–1992*, 2d ed. (New York, 1995), p. 400; Trask, *The War with Spain*, p. 483.

36. Russell A. Alger, *The Spanish-American War* (New York, 1901), p. 4; Charles G. Dawes, *A Journal of the McKinley Years* (Chicago, 1950), p. 149; John Hay to Theodore Roosevelt, May 8, 1898, in William Roscoe Thayer, ed., *The Life and Letters of John Hay*, 2 vols. (Boston, 1915), 2:167; Champ Clark, *My Quarter Century of American Politics*, 2 vols. (New York, 1920), 1:401; Carl Schurz, "Thoughts on American Imperialism," *Century Magazine*, September 1898, p. 783; *Congressional Record*, 55th Cong., 2d sess., 1898, 31, app.:293, 300.

37. William McKinley, "Special Message to the Congress of the United States," April 11, 1898, *Messages and Papers of the Presidents*, 5 vols. (Washington, D.C., 1789–1902), 13:6284, "Instructions to the Peace Commissioners," September 16, 1898, in U.S. Department of State, *Papers Relating to the Foreign Relations of the United States: 1898* (Washington, D.C., 1901), pp. 906–7, and *Speeches and Addresses of William McKinley from March 1, 1897 to May 30, 1900* (New York, 1900), pp. 114, 127–28, 317.

38. Alexander K. McClure and Charles Morris, *The Authentic Life of William McKinley* (Philadelphia, 1901), p. 229; Woodrow Wilson, *A History of the American People*, 5 vols. (New York, 1902), 5:274.

39. A. D. Hall, *Cuba: Its Past, Present, and Future* (New York, 1898), pp. 170, 174–75.

40. William James to Thomas Fournoy, June 17, 1898, in Ralph Barton Perry, *The Thought and Character of William James*, 2 vols. (Boston, 1935), 2:307; Jack London to Edward Applegarth, September 13, 1898, in Earle Labor, Robert C. Leitz III, and I. Milos Shepard, eds., *The Letters of Jack London*, 3 vols. (Stanford, Calif., 1988), 1:12.

41. Daniel M. Smith, *The American Diplomatic Experience* (Boston, 1972), p. 208; Randolf Greenfield Adams, *Foreign Policy of the United States*, p. 274; H. Addington Bruce, *The Romance of American Expansion* (New York, 1909), p. 188; Harold Sprout and Margaret Sprout, *The Rise of American Naval Power, 1776–1918* (Princeton, 1939), p. 230; Albert Shaw, *International Bearings of American Policy* (Baltimore, 1943), p. 251; Howard Jones, *The Course of American Diplomacy*, 2 vols., 2d ed. (Chicago, 1988), 2:55–259; Arthur Hendrick Vandenburg, *The Trail of a Tradition* (New York, 1926), p. 321; Frank Freidel, *The Splendid Little War* (New York, 1958), pp. 3, 6, 10.

42. Ruhl Bartlett, *Policy and Power: Two Centuries of American Foreign Relations* (New York, 1963), pp. 126–27; A. F. Pollard, *Factors in American History* (New York, 1925), p. 215; Robert Endicott Osgood, *Ideals and Self-Interest in America's Foreign Relations* (Chicago, 1953), p. 42.

43. Morgan, *America's Road to Empire*, pp. 8–9, 61, 113.

44. Allan Keller, *The Spanish-American War: A Compact History* (New York, 1969), p. 43; Sam Acheson, "Joseph W. Bailey and the Spanish War," *Southwest Review* 17 (January 1932): 142.

45. Tony Smith, *America's Mission* (Princeton, 1994), pp. xiii, 5.

46. John Truslow Adams, *The March of Democracy: A History of the American People*, 6 vols. (New York, 1941–45), 4:76–77, 96; John Schutz, *The Promise of America* (Belmont, Calif., 1970), p. 227; Robert H. Ferrell, *American Diplomacy: A History* (New York, 1975), p. 398; John S. Bassett, *A Short History of the United States, 1492–1938*, 3d ed. (New York, 1939), p. 797.

47. George F. Kennan, *American Diplomacy, 1900–1950* (Chicago, 1951), p. 8; Norman A. Graebner, "The Year of Transition: 1898," in Norman A. Graebner, ed., *An Uncertain Tradition: American Secretaries of State in the Twentieth Century* (New York, 1961), p. 16; Bartlett, *Policy and Power*, p. 125; Bernard Bailyn, David Brion Davis, David Herbert Donald, John L. Thomas, Robert H. Wiebe, and Gordon S. Wood, *The Great Republic: A History of the American People*, 2 vols., 2d ed. (Lexington, Mass., 1981), 2:709; William E. Leuchtenburg, "The Needless War with Spain," *American Heritage*, February 1957, p. 95; James C. Bradford, Introduction to James C. Bradford, ed., *Crucible of Empire: The Spanish-American War and Its Aftermath* (Annapolis, 1993), p. xiv.
48. Hans J. Morgenthau, *In Defense of the National Interest* (New York, 1951), pp. 4, 23.
49. Welch, "William McKinley," p. 49; James M. McCormick, *American Foreign Policy and Process*, 2d ed. (Ithaca, 1992), pp. 27–28; Osgood, *Ideals and Self-Interest*, pp. 17, 19, 27, 43–44.
50. Graebner, "Year of Transition," pp. 1, 6, 12, 16.
51. Elihu Root to Albert Shaw, February 23, 1901, File 331-71, BIA/RG 350; Root to Leonard Wood, February 9, 1901, Elihu Root Papers.
52. Theodore Salisbury Woolsey, *America's Foreign Policy* (New York, 1898), p. 108.
53. *Congressional Record*, 57th Cong., 1st sess., 1902, 35:7639–40.
54. Roosevelt, *Autobiography*, p. 209; Alfred Thayer Mahan, *Lessons of the War with Spain and Other Articles* (Boston, 1899), p. 26; Henry Cabot Lodge, "Our Blundering Foreign Policy," *Forum* 19 (March 1895): 17; *Congressional Record*, 54th Cong., 1st sess., February 1896, 28:1972; Henry Cabot Lodge, *The War with Spain* (New York, 1899), p. 14. Mahan's views on "national interests" are most explicitly outlined in his book, *The Interest of America in Sea Power, Present and Future* (Boston, 1898). In "The 'Large Policy' of 1898," *Mississippi Valley Historical Review* 19 (September 1932): 219–42, Julius Pratt argued persuasively that empire was indeed a driving force behind the war with Spain as advocated primarily by Roosevelt, Lodge, and Mahan.
55. Trumbull White, *United States in War with Spain and the History of Cuba* (Chicago, 1898), p. 583.
56. Herbert H. Sargent, *The Campaign of Santiago de Cuba*, 3 vols. (Chicago, 1907), 2:43.
57. John D. Hicks and Gorge F. Mowry, *A Short History of American Democracy*, 2d ed. (Boston, 1956), p. 558; David Saville Muzzey, *The American Adventure*, 2 vols. (New York, 1927), 2:294; Kennan, *American Diplomacy*, p. 7; John L. Offner, *An Unwanted War: The Diplomacy of the United States and Spain over Cuba, 1895–1898* (Chapel Hill, 1992), pp. 6, 144; Harry T. Peck, *Twenty Years of the Republic, 1885–1905* (New York, 1907), p. 531; David Gawronski, *Out of the Past* (Beverly Hills, 1969), p. 56; Ellis Paxson Oberholtzer, *A History of the United States since the Civil War*, 5 vols. (New York, 1937), 5:522, 578; Joseph Smith, "Military Cooperation of the United States with the Cuban Revolutionaries (1898)," in Beede, *The War of 1898*, p. 329.
58. John W. Chambers, *The Tyranny of Change: America in the Progressive Era, 1890–1920*, 2d ed. (New York, 1992), p. 46; Freidel, *Splendid Little War*, p. 11; Walter Karp, *The Politics of War: The Story of Two Wars Which Altered Forever the Political Life of the American Republic, 1890–1920* (New York, 1979), p. 77; Sidney Lens, *The Forging of the American Empire* (New York, 1971), p. 169; Charles S. Campbell, *The Transformation of American Foreign Relations, 1865–1900* (New York, 1976), p. 271; Foster Rhea Dulles, *Prelude to World Power: American Diplomatic History, 1860–1900* (New York, 1965), p. 176; Albert Shaw, *International Bearings of American Policy* (Baltimore, 1943), p. 250; H. Wayne

Morgan, *William McKinley and His America* (Syracuse, 1963), p. 341; Lately Thomas, *A Pride of Lions* (New York, 1971), p. 242; Alan Brinkley, Richard N. Current, T. Harry Williams, and Frank Freidel, *American History: A Survey*, 2 vols., 8th ed. (New York, 1991), 2:600; Collin, *Theodore Roosevelt*, p. 136.

59. Norman A. Graebner, *Foundations of American Foreign Policy: A Realist Appraisal from Franklin to McKinley* (Wilmington, Del., 1985), p. 327; John Schutz, *The Promise of America* (New York, 1990), p. 224; Robert H. Ferrell, Introduction to Curtis V. Hard, *Banners in the Air: The Eighth Ohio Volunteers and the Spanish-American War* (Kent, Ohio, 1988), p. xii; Karp, *The Politics of War*, pp. 28–29; William Miller, *A New History of the United States* (New York, 1958), p. 330; Harry J. Carman, William G. Kimmel, and Mabel Walker, *Historic Currents in Changing America* (Chicago, 1938), p. 480; Dumas Malone and Basil Rauch, *Empire for Liberty*, 2 vols. (New York, 1960), 2:200–201; Walter LaFeber, *The American Age*, 2 vols., 2d ed. (New York, 1994), 2:197; Thomas A. Bailey, *The American Pageant: A History of the Republic*, 4th ed. (Lexington, Mass., 1971), p. 658; Morgan, *America's Road to Empire*, p. 9; Daniel J. Boorstin and Brooks Mather Kelley, *A History of the United States* (Needham, Mass., 1996), p. 512; Leuchtenburg, "Needless War with Spain," February 1957, p. 41.

60. Ferrell, *American Diplomacy*, p. 354; John Richard Alden, *Rise of the American Republic* (New York, 1963), p. 577; Bailey, *American Pageant*, p. 658; Harold Underwood Faulkner, *American Political and Social History*, 7th ed. (New York, 1957), p. 645; John Holladay Latané, *America as a World Power, 1897–1907* (New York, 1907), p. 19; Arthur S. Link and Stanley Coben, *The Democratic Heritage: A History of the United States* (Waltham, Mass., 1971), p. 359; Gerald R. Baydo, *A Topical History of the United States* (Arlington Heights, Ill., 1974), p. 123; Cole, *An Interpretative History*, p. 217.

61. Morgan, *America's Road to Empire*, p. 61; Samuel Flagg Bemis, *A Diplomatic History of the United States* (New York, 1936), pp. 438, 442; Nelson Manfred Blake and Oscar Theodore Barck Jr., *The United States in Its World Relations* (New York, 1960), p. 377; Lester D. Langley, *The Cuban Policy of the United States* (New York, 1961), p. 99; Offner, *An Unwanted War*, pp. 226–27.

CHAPTER THREE

1. Theodore Roosevelt to Benjamin Harrison Diblee, February 16, 1898, in Elting E. Morison, ed., *The Letters of Theodore Roosevelt*, 8 vols. (Cambridge, Mass., 1951–54), 1:775.

2. "Message from the President of the United States Transmitting the Report of the Naval Court of Inquiry Upon the Destruction of the United States Battleship *Maine* in Havana Harbor, February 15, 1898, Together with the Testimony Taken before the Court," 55th Cong., 2d sess., 1898, S. Doc. 207, p. 281.

3. An investigation in 1976 directed by Admiral Hyman G. Rickover, under the auspices of the Naval History Division of the U.S. Department of the Navy, concluded that, "in all probability, the *Maine* was destroyed by an accident which occurred inside the ship," and that a fire in a coal bunker was "the primary source of the explosion . . . [and] caused partial detonation of the other forward magazines." The study concluded: "There is no evidence that a mine destroyed the *Maine*." See Hyman G. Rickover, *How the Battleship "Maine" Was Destroyed* (Washington, D.C., 1976), pp. 91, 104.

4. G. J. A. O'Toole, *The Spanish War: An American Epic—1898* (New York, 1984), p. 400; Peggy Samuels and Harold Samuels, *Remembering the "Maine"* (Washington, D.C., 1995), pp. 3–4.

5. Theodore Roosevelt, *Autobiography* (1913; New York, 1946), p. 212; Shelby M. Cullom, *Fifty Years of Public Service* (Chicago, 1911), pp. 283–84; Champ Clark, *My Quarter Century of American Politics*, 2 vols. (New York, 1920), 1:401; Russell A. Alger, *The Spanish-American War* (New York, 1901), p. 4; Nelson A. Miles, "America's War for Humanity," *Cosmopolitan Magazine*, October 1911, p. 637.

6. Richard H. Titherington, *A History of the Spanish-American War of 1898* (New York, 1900), p. 70; John R. Musick, *Cuba Libre: A Story of the Hispano-American War* (New York, 1900), p. vi; Horace Edgar Flack, *Spanish-American Diplomatic Relations Preceding the War of 1898* (Baltimore, 1906), pp. 46, 83; Theodore E. Burton, *John Sherman* (Boston, 1906), p. 412; Trumbull White, *United States in War with Spain and the History of Cuba* (Chicago, 1898), p. 36. See also James Rankin Young, *History of Our War with Spain* (n.p., 1898), p. 66, and F. W. Holman George, "The Destruction of the *Maine*," in *The American-Spanish War: A History by the War Leaders* (Norwich, Conn., 1899), p. 92.

7. William A. Robinson, *Thomas B. Reed: Parliamentarian* (New York, 1930), p. 360; David Burner, Robert D. Marcus, and Emily S. Rosenberg, *America: A Portrait in History*, 2d ed. (Englewood Cliffs, N.J., 1978), p. 431; William E. Leuchtenburg, "The Needless War with Spain," *American Heritage*, February 1957, p. 38; A. E. Campbell, *Great Britain and the United States, 1895–1903* (Westport, Conn., 1960), p. 132; Elmer Plischke, *Conduct of American Diplomacy*, 3d ed. (Princeton, 1967), p. 116; Charles S. Campbell, *The Transformation of American Foreign Relations, 1865–1900* (New York, 1976), p. 256; White, *United States in War with Spain*, p. 37; Herman Reichard Esteves, "The United States, Spain, and the *Maine*, or the Diplomacy of Frustration," *Revista/Review Interamericana* 2 (1973): 555; Allan Nevins and Henry Steele Commager, *A Short History of United States*, 5th ed. (New York, 1966), p. 413; Thomas A. Bailey, *A Diplomatic History of the American People*, 7th ed. (New York, 1964), p. 458. These views are variously shared by Robert H. Ferrell, *American Diplomacy: A History*, 2d ed. (New York, 1969), p. 389; Richard Hofstadter, "Cuba, the Philippines, and Manifest Destiny," in Richard Hofstadter, *The Paranoid Style in American Politics and Other Essays* (New York, 1967), p. 156; Elbert J. Benton, *International Law and Diplomacy of the Spanish-American War* (Baltimore, 1908), p. 76; Matthew Josephson, *The President Makers*, 2d ed. (New York, 1964), p. 80; Arthur Wallace Dunn, *From Harrison to Harding*, 2 vols. (New York, 1922), 1:236; John Edward Weems, *The Fate of the "Maine"* (New York, 1958), p. 167; Foster Rhea Dulles, *The Imperial Years* (New York, 1956), p. 122; and Frank Freidel, *The Splendid Little War* (New York, 1958), p. 12.

8. Notable exceptions include Julius W. Pratt, *The Expansionists of 1898* (Baltimore, 1936), Walter LaFeber, *The New Empire: An Interpretation of American Expansion, 1860–1898* (Ithaca, 1963), and H. Wayne Morgan, *America's Road to Empire: The War with Spain and Overseas Expansion* (New York, 1965), who, in otherwise detailed explanations of the circumstances leading to the Spanish-American War, accorded only passing attention to the destruction of the *Maine*.

9. Marrion Wilcox, *A Short History of the War with Spain* (New York, 1898), pp. 72–73; James Morton Callahan, *Cuba and International Relations* (Baltimore, 1899), p. 485; Willis Fletcher Johnson, *America's Foreign Relations*, 2 vols. (New York, 1916), 2:251; Robert L. Jones, *History of the Foreign Policy of the United States* (New York, 1933), p. 322; Nelson Manfred Blake and Oscar Theodore Barck Jr., *The United States in Its World Relations* (New York, 1960), p. 386; Charles S. Campbell, *Transformation of American Foreign Relations*, p. 257. Similar arguments are suggested by Julius W. Pratt, *A History*

of United States Foreign Policy, 2d ed. (Englewood Cliffs, N.J., 1972), p. 200; Armin Rappaport, *A History of American Diplomacy* (New York, 1975), p. 194; Alexander DeConde, *A History of American Foreign Policy*, 2 vols., 3d ed. (New York, 1978), 1:313–14; Walter Karp, *The Politics of War: The Story of Two Wars Which Altered Forever the Political Life of the American Republic, 1890–1920* (New York, 1979), p. 88; and A. E. Campbell, *Great Britain and the United States*, p. 32. This line of reasoning was also adopted by key public officials in 1898. See Alger, *Spanish-American War*, pp. 4–5; Joseph Benson Foraker, *Notes of a Busy Life*, 2 vols., 3d ed. (Cincinnati, 1917), 2:19; Henry Cabot Lodge, *The War with Spain* (New York, 1899), p. 32.

10. White, *United States in War with Spain*, p. 37; Bailey, *Diplomatic History*, p. 458; David F. Trask, *The War with Spain in 1898* (New York, 1981), p. 474.

11. J. Rogers Hollingsworth, *The Whirligig of Politics* (Chicago, 1963), p. 138; Paul H. Buck, *The Road to Reunion, 1868–1900* (Boston, 1947), p. 306; Weems, *Fate of the "Maine,"* p. 168; Benton, *International Law and Diplomacy*, p. 76; Jack Cameron Dierks, *A Leap to Arms: The Cuban Campaign of 1898* (Philadelphia, 1970), p. 25.

12. For a general discussion of public opinion and foreign policy, see Bernard C. Cohen, *The Public's Impact on Foreign Policy* (Boston, 1973); Thomas A. Bailey, *The Man in the Street: The Impact of American Public Opinion on Foreign Policy* (New York, 1948); Gabriel A. Almond, *The American People and Foreign Policy*, 2d ed. (New York, 1960); John E. Mueller, *War, Presidents, and Public Opinion* (New York, 1973); and Barry B. Hughes, *The Domestic Context of American Foreign Policy* (San Francisco, 1978). For a dated but still useful discussion of public opinion and the "Spanish-American War," with particular emphasis on the press, see Marcus M. Wilkerson, *Public Opinion and the Spanish-American War* (Baton Rouge, 1932).

13. Charles Morris, *The War with Spain: A Complete History of the War of 1898 between the United States and Spain* (Philadelphia, 1899), p. 124; Russell H. Fitzgibbon, *Cuba and the United States, 1900–1935* (Menasha, Wis., 1935), p. 22; Bailey, *The Man in the Street*, p. 79; George F. Kennan, *American Diplomacy, 1900–1950* (Chicago, 1951), p. 9; Daniel M. Smith, *The American Diplomatic Experience* (Boston, 1972), p. 206.

14. David F. Healy, "McKinley as Commander-in-Chief," in Paolo E. Coletta, ed., *Threshold to American Internationalism: Essays on the Foreign Policy of William McKinley* (New York, 1970), p. 81; Kennan, *American Diplomacy*, p. 10; Dorothy Burne Goebel, *American Foreign Policy: A Documentary Survey, 1776–1960* (New York, 1961), p. 134; Dexter Perkins, *The Evolution of American Foreign Policy*, 2d ed. (New York, 1966), p. 41.

15. Trask, *The War with Spain*, pp. 474 (first quotation), 59 (last quotation); T. Harry Williams, Richard N. Current, and Frank Freidel, *A History of the United States* (New York, 1965), p. 255; Fitzgibbon, *Cuba and the United States*, p. 22; Bailey, *Diplomatic History*, p. 457; Donald Barr Chidsey, *The Spanish-American War* (New York, 1971), p. 62; Robert Endicott Osgood, *Ideals and Self-Interest in American Foreign Relations* (Chicago, 1953), p. 43; John Richard Alden, *Rise of the American Republic* (New York, 1963), p. 577; Dulles, *Imperial Years*, p. 113; Nathaniel Wright Stephenson, *Nelson W. Aldrich: A Leader in American Politics* (New York, 1930), p. 155; Ernest R. May, *Imperial Democracy: The Emergence of America as a Great Power* (New York, 1961), p. 142. Similar characterizations are found in Dexter Perkins and Glyndon G. Van Deusen, *The United States of America: A History* (New York, 1968), p. 250; Sheldon Appleton, *United States Foreign Policy: An Introduction with Cases* (Boston, 1968), p. 64; and Foster Rhea Dulles, *America's Rise to World Power, 1898–1954* (New York, 1954), p. 41.

16. Alexander K. McClure and Charles Morris, *The Authentic Life of William McKinley* (Philadelphia, 1901), p. 229; Morris, *The War with Spain*, p. 120; Oscar Doane Lambert, *Stephen Benton Elkins* (Pittsburgh, 1955), p. 235; Charles E. Chapman, *A History of the Cuban Republic* (New York, 1927), p. 87; John A. S. Grenville and George Berkeley Young, *Politics, Strategy, and American Diplomacy: Studies in Foreign Policy, 1873–1917* (New Haven, 1966), p. 255; James A. Henretta, W. Elliot Brownlee, David Brody, and Susan Ware, *America's History* (Chicago, 1987), p. 638; E. Berkeley Tompkins, *Anti-Imperialism in the United States: The Great Debate, 1890–1920* (Philadelphia, 1970), p. 89; John M. Dobson, *America's Ascent: The United States Becomes a Great Power, 1880–1914* (De Kalb, Ill., 1978), p. 105. See also Irwin Unger and Debi Unger, *The Vulnerable Years: The United States, 1896–1917* (New York, 1978), p. 50, and Arthur Link et al., *The American People: A History*, 2d ed. (Arlington Heights, Ill., 1987), p. 501.

17. Foster Rhea Dulles, *Prelude to World Power: American Diplomatic History, 1869–1900* (New York, 1965), p. 171.

18. Hollis W. Barber, *Foreign Policies of the United States* (New York, 1953), pp. 259–60; Samuel W. McCall, *The Life of Thomas Brackett* (Boston, 1914), pp. 232–33; William Roscoe Thayer, *Theodore Roosevelt: An Intimate Biography* (Boston, 1919), p. 117; Donald Barr Chidsey, *The Spanish-American War* (New York, 1971), p. 62; Millis, *The Martial Spirit*, p. 78; Morris, *The War with Spain*, p. 119. Others who subscribe to this view include Roger D. Masters, *The Nation Is Burdened: American Foreign Policy in a Changing World* (New York, 1967), pp. 298–99; John A. Garraty, *Henry Cabot Lodge: A Biography* (New York, 1953), p. 185; and Alden, *Rise of the American Republic*, p. 577.

19. Henry Watterson, *History of the Spanish-American War, Embracing a Complete Review of Our Relations with Spain* (Boston, 1898), p. 42; Harry T. Peck, *Twenty Years of the Republic, 1885–1905* (New York, 1907), p. 542; Roscoe Lewis Ashley, *American History* (New York, 1916), p. 496; Bailey, *Diplomatic History*, pp. 456, 460; John Holladay Latané, *History of American Foreign Policy*, rev. ed. (Garden City, N.Y., 1934), p. 506.

20. Margaret Leech, *In the Days of McKinley* (New York, 1959), p. 168; James MacGregor Burns, *The Workshop of Democracy* (New York, 1985), p. 237; Alfred L. Dennis, *Adventures in American Diplomacy, 1896–1906* (New York, 1928), p. 69; William Appleman Williams, *Americans in a Changing World* (New York, 1978), p. 42; Lewis A. Harding, *The Preliminary Diplomacy of the Spanish-American War* (Indianapolis, 1912), p. 14. Similar accounts are found in McClure and Morris, *Authentic Life of William McKinley*, p. 229; Louis Martin Sears, *A History of American Foreign Relations* (New York, 1927), p. 438; Everett Walters, *Joseph Benson Foraker: An Uncompromising Republican* (Columbus, Ohio, 1948), p. 149; Jerald A. Combs, *American Diplomatic History: Two Centuries of Changing Interpretations* (Berkeley, 1983), p. 78; James Morton Callahan, *Cuba and International Relations* (Baltimore, 1899), p. 481; and Lewis L. Gould, *The Spanish-American War and President McKinley* (Lawrence, Kans., 1982), p. 438.

21. Lodge, *The War with Spain*, p. 32; L. White Busby, *Uncle Joe Cannon: The Story of a Pioneer American* (New York, 1927), p. 186; Foraker, *Notes of a Busy Life*, 2:20; Clark, *Quarter Century of American Politics*, 1:401; Cullom, *Fifty Years of Public Service*, pp. 283–84.

22. Watterson, *History of the Spanish-American War*, p. 42; Richard R. Titherington, *A History of the Spanish-American War of 1898* (New York, 1900), p. 70; Peck, *Twenty Years of the Republic*, p. 544; Williams, Current, and Freidel, *History of the United States*, p. 255; Mary S. Mander, "Public Opinion and the Spanish-Cuban/American War," in Benjamin R. Beede, ed., *The War of 1898 and U.S. Interventions, 1898–1934: An Encyclopedia*

(New York, 1994), p. 451. Variations of this view are found in Carl Russell Fish, *The Path of Empire* (New Haven, 1919), p. 108; Samuel Flagg Bemis, ed., *The American Secretaries of State and Their Diplomacy*, 11 vols. (New York, 1927–63), 9:75; and Chapman, *History of the Cuban Republic*, p. 84;

23. Kennan, *American Diplomacy*, p. 15 ("unfortunate"); James Ford Rhodes, *McKinley and Roosevelt Administrations, 1897–1909* (New York, 1922), p. 67, and Hollingsworth, *The Whirligig of Politics*, p. 136 ("unnecessary"); Akira Iriye, *From Nationalism to Internationalism* (London, 1977), p. 134 ("unnecessary and perhaps even unavoidable"); Wolfgang Drechsler, "Congress and the Spanish-Cuban/American War," in Beede, *The War of 1898*, p. 119 ("foolish and unnecessary"); Dulles, *Prelude to World Power*, p. 180 ("totally unnecessary"); Leuchtenburg, "Needless War with Spain," p. 33. Flack, *Spanish-American Diplomatic Relations*, pp. 41–82, and Allan Nevins and Henry Steele Commager, *A Short History of the United States*, 5th ed. (New York, 1966), p. 413, also argued that the war was needless.

24. Kennan, *American Diplomacy*, p. 22, and *Memoirs, 1950–1963* (New York, 1972), p. 72; Robert E. Riegel and David F. Long, *The American Story*, 2 vols. (New York, 1955), 2:122;

25. John D. Hicks, George E. Mowry, and Robert E. Burke, *The American Nation* (Boston, 1970), p. 278; Bailey, *Diplomatic History*, p. 464.

26. Leuchtenburg, "Needless War with Spain," p. 95; Randolph Greenfield Adams, *A History of the Foreign Policy of the United States* (New York, 1933), p. 274; Norman A. Graebner, "The Year of Transition: 1898," in Norman A. Graebner, ed., *An Uncertain Tradition: American Secretaries of State in the Twentieth Century* (New York, 1961), p. 16; James C. Bradford, Introduction to James C. Bradford, ed., *Crucible of Empire: The Spanish-American War and Its Aftermath* (Annapolis, 1993), p. xiii; Harold Underwood Faulkner, *American Political and Social History* (New York, 1957), p. 645. For similar views, see Thomas A. Bailey and David M. Kennedy, *American Pageant*, 2 vols. (Lexington, Mass., 1987), 2:603; Samuel Flagg Bemis, *A Diplomatic History of the United States*, 5th ed. (New York, 1965), p. 450; E. Berkeley Tompkins, *Anti-Imperialism in the United States: The Great Debate, 1890–1920* (Philadelphia, 1970), p. 92; and Henretta et al., *America's History*, p. 638.

27. *New York Herald Tribune Book Review*, February 11, 1962, p. 8; Bailey, *The Man in the Street*, pp. 7–8; Trask, *The War with Spain*, p. 59, George Brown Tindall, *America: A Narrative History*, 2 vols. (New York, 1984), 2:877.

28. Bailey and Kennedy, *American Pageant*, 2:603; Carl Russell Fish, *The Path of Empire* (New Haven, 1919), p. 169; *New York Herald Tribune Book Review*, February 11, 1962, p. 8; Drechsler, "Congress and the Spanish-Cuban/American War," pp. 119, 121.

29. Bemis, *Diplomatic History*, p. 445; James P. Warburg, *The United States in a Changing World* (New York, 1954), p. 196; Sears, *History of American Foreign Relations*, p. 439; Rhodes, *McKinley and Roosevelt Administrations*, pp. 54–55; W. E. Woodward, *A New American History* (New York, 1938), p. 684; Roger Burlingame, *The American Conscience* (New York, 1957), p. 375; Joseph E. Wisan, *The Cuban Crisis as Reflected in the New York Press, 1895–1898* (New York, 1934), p. 458; Richard W. Leopold, *The Growth of American Foreign Policy* (New York, 1962), p. 176. For a similar account, see Henretta et al., *America's History*, p. 638.

30. Morgan, *America's Road to Empire*, p. 14; Oscar Handlin, *Chance Or Destiny: Turning Points in American History* (Boston, 1955), p. 127.

31. Gould, *Spanish-American War*, p. 24; John L. Offner, *An Unwanted War: The Diplomacy of the United States and Spain over Cuba, 1895–1898* (Chapel Hill, 1992), p. 39.

32. Richard B. Olney to Grover Cleveland, September 25, 1895, Grover Cleveland Papers, Manuscript Division, Library of Congress, Washington, D.C.

33. Foraker, *Notes of a Busy Life*, 2:22.

34. James MacGregor Burns, *The Workshop of Democracy* (New York, 1985), p. 236; Gerald C. Eggert, *Richard Olney: Evolution of a Statesman* (University Park, Pa., 1974), p. 254; *Philadelphia Inquirer*, August 6, 1898, p. 6; "General Garcia and Cuban Conduct," *Literary Digest* 17 (July 30, 1890): 121–22; *Journal of Commerce*, August 10, 1898, p. 1.

35. Henretta et al., *America's History*, p. 638; John Spencer Bassett, *Expansion and Reform, 1889–1926* (New York, 1926), p. 75; Drechsler, "Congress and the Spanish-Cuban/American War," p. 119.

36. Herbert Croly, *Marcus Alonzo Hanna: His Life and Work* (New York, 1912), pp. 277–78.

37. Trask, *The War with Spain*, pp. 58–59, 474.

38. Bailey, *Diplomatic History*, p. 463; Richard E. Welch Jr., "William McKinley: Reluctant Warrior, Cautious Imperialist," in Norman A. Graebner, ed., *Traditions and Values: American Diplomacy, 1865–1945* (Lanham, Md., 1985), p. 37; Irwin Unger, *These United States* (Boston 1978), p. 603; Oscar Handlin, *The History of the United States*, 2 vols. (New York, 1968), 1:257; DeConde, *History of American Foreign Policy*, 1:315; E. Berkeley Tompkins, *Anti-Imperialism in the United States: The Great Debate, 1890–1920* (Philadelphia, 1970), p. 92; John Spencer Bassett, *Expansion and Reform, 1889–1926* (New York, 1926), p. 71; Tindall, *America: A Narrative History*, 2:877. For similar versions see Iriye, *From Nationalism to Internationalism*, p. 133; Dulles, *America's Rise to World Power*, p. 41; Bailey and Kennedy, *American Pageant*, 2:11, 603; Ronald J. Caridi, *20th Century American Foreign Policy* (Englewood Cliffs, N.J., 1974), p. 17; Hollingsworth, *The Whirligig of Politics*, pp. 135–36.

39. Leuchtenburg, "Needless War with Spain," p. 95; Leopold, *Growth of American Foreign Policy*, p. 172. See also Bemis, *Diplomatic History*, p. 447.

40. Williams, Current, and Freidel, *History of the United States*, p. 255; Wayne S. Cole, *An Interpretive History of American Foreign Relations* (Homewood, Ill., 1968), p. 271; Rhodes, *McKinley and Roosevelt Administrations*, p. 64; Frederick Merk, *Manifest Destiny and Mission in American History* (New York, 1963), p. 251; Burlingame, *American Conscience*, p. 376; Dulles, *Prelude to World Power*, p. 181.

41. Gerald F. Linderman, *The Mirror of War* (Ann Arbor, 1974), p. 31; Ruhl Bartlett, *Policy and Power: Two Centuries of American Foreign Relations* (New York, 1963), p. 126; Charles A. Beard and Mary R. Beard, *New Basic History of the United States*, 2d ed. (New York, 1960), p. 322; Samuel Eliot Morison, *The Oxford History of the American People* (New York, 1965), p. 799; Leland D. Baldwin, *The Stream of American History*, 2 vols., 2d ed. (New York, 1957), 2:331; Harold Underwood Faulkner, *Politics, Reform, and Expansion, 1890–1900* (New York, 1900), p. 232. Similar views are expressed in Samuel Eliot Morison, Henry Steele Commager, and William E. Leuchtenburg, *The Growth of the American Republic*, 2 vols., 7th ed. (New York, 1980), 2:251, and Unger, *These United States*, p. 603.

42. Flack, *Spanish-American Diplomatic Relations*, p. 45; Karp, *The Politics of War*, p. 88; Bartlett, *Policy and Power*, p. 126; D. A. Graber, *Crisis Diplomacy: A History of U.S. Intervention Policies and Practices* (Washington, D.C., 1959), p. 78; William Appleman

Williams, *Americans in a Changing World* (New York, 1978), p. 42; Horace Samuel Merrill and Marion Galbraith Merrill, *The Republican Command, 1897–1913* (Lexington, Ky., 1971), p. 52; Hollingsworth, *The Whirligig of Politics*, p. 132; Philip S. Foner, *The Spanish-Cuban-American-War and the Birth of American Imperialism*, 2 vols. (New York, 1972), 2:239; Robert C. Hildebrand, *Power and the People: Executive Management of Public Opinion in Foreign Affairs, 1897–1921* (Chapel Hill, 1981), pp. 17–18.

43. Karp, *The Politics of War*, pp. 91–92.

44. Julius W. Pratt, "McKinley and Manifest Destiny," in Earl Schenck Miers, ed., *The American Story* (Great Neck, N.Y., 1956), p. 262; Rhodes, *McKinley and Roosevelt Administrations*, pp. 63–64; Henry Bamford Parkes, *The United States of America: A History* (New York, 1963), p. 524.

45. William MacDonald, *Three Centuries of American Democracy* (New York, 1923), p. 254; Woodward, *New American History*, p. 688; Nelson M. Blake and Oscar T. Barck Jr., *The United States in Its World Relations* (New York, 1960), p. 391; Leopold, *Growth of American Foreign Policy*, p. 175; Bailey, *Diplomatic History*, p. 506; Arthur M. Schlesinger, *Political and Social Growth of the United States, 1852–1933*, rev. ed. (New York, 1935), pp. 298–99; John S. Bassett, *A Short History of the United States, 1492–1938*, 3d ed. (New York, 1939), p. 788.

46. Morison, *Oxford History of the American People*, p. 801; Adams, *Foreign Policy of the United States*, p. 274; Warburg, *The United States in a Changing World*, p. 197.

CHAPTER FOUR

1. Alvey A. Adee to William R. Day, April 7, 1898, William R. Day Papers, Manuscript Division, Library of Congress, Washington, D.C.; *New York Times*, August 5, 1898, p. 2; Domingo Méndez Capote, *Trabajos*, 3 vols. (Havana, 1929–30), 3:78; *New York Times*, December 24, 1898, p. 9; Elihu Root to Leonard Wood, January 9, 1901, Elihu Root Papers, Manuscript Division, Library of Congress, Washington, D.C.

2. Frank R. McCoy to Parents, n.d., Frank R. McCoy Papers, Manuscript Division, Library of Congress, Washington, D.C.; *New York Times*, July 23 (p. 1), August 7 (p. 2), 1898; U.S. Congress, Senate, *Report of the Commission Appointed by the President to Investigate the Conduct of the War Department in the War with Spain*, 56th Cong., 1st sess., ser. 3859–66, 8 vols. (Washington, D.C., 1900), 5:1954; General William R. Shafter to Adjutant General Henry C. Corbin, July 31, 1898, File 110293, Adjutant General's Office, Records, 1780s–1917, Record Group 94, National Archives, Washington, D.C.; Herbert H. Sargent, *The Campaign of Santiago de Cuba*, 3 vols. (Chicago, 1907), 2:43, 164–66.

3. Stephen Crane, *The War Despatches of Stephen Crane*, ed. R. W. Stallman and E. R. Hageman (New York, 1964), p. 182.

4. *New York Evening Post*, July 21, 1898, p. 2; *New York Times*, July 29, 1898, p. 2.

5. Burr MacIntosh, *The Little I Saw in Cuba* (New York, 1899), p. 74.

6. *New York Tribune*, August 7, 1898, p. 6; *New York Evening Post*, July 21, 1898, p. 2.

7. *New York Times*, July 24 (p. 2), 29 (p. 4), August 7 (p. 2), 1898.

8. H. C. Corbin to William R. Shafter, May 31, 1898, in Fitzhugh Lee, ed., *Cuba's Struggle against Spain* (New York, 1899), p. 344; John D. Miley, *In Cuba with Shafter* (New York, 1899), p. 58; Arthur L. Wagner, *Report of the Santiago Campaign, 1898* (Kansas City, Mo., 1908), p. 14; *Nation* 66 (May 12, 1898): 354.

9. U.S. field reports are filled with accounts of Cuban cooperation in reconnaissance

and intelligence operations. See Lieutenant J. D. L. Hartman to Assistant Adjutant General, June 27, 1898, and General S. B. M. Young to Adjutant General, June 29 1898, Joseph Wheeler Papers, Correspondence, June 1–30, 1898, Alabama Department of History and Archives, Montgomery. See also David F. Trask, "American Intelligence during the Spanish American War," in James C. Bradford, ed., *Crucible of Empire: The Spanish-American War and Its Aftermath* (Annapolis, 1993), pp. 23–46.

10. William R. Shafter to Adjutant General, June 23, 1898, G. Creighton Webb Papers, General Shafter's File, Manuscript Department, New-York Historical Society, New York, N.Y.

11. See O. O. Howard, "The Conduct of the Cubans in the Late War," *Forum* 26 (October 1898): 153. On June 2 U.S. army commander Nelson Miles had communicated with General García soliciting Cuban cooperation. "It would be a very great assistance," Miles explained to García, "if you could have as large a force as possible in the vicinity of the harbor of Santiago de Cuba and communicate any information . . . either to our navy or to our army on its arrival, which we hope will be before many days." Miles continued: "It would also assist us very much if you could drive in and harass any Spanish troops near or in Santiago de Cuba, threatening or attacking them at all points and preventing by every possible means any reinforcements coming to that garrison. While this is being done, and before the arrival of our army, if you can seize and hold any commanding position to the east or west of Santiago de Cuba, or both, that would be advantageous for the use of our artillery, it will be exceedingly gratifying to us." See Nelson A. Miles to Calixto García, June 2, 1898, in Nelson A. Miles, *Serving the Republic* (New York, 1911), p. 277. For a detailed account of Cuban military participation, see "La cooperación militar de los cubanos," *Maceo* 1 (October 20, 1898), pp. 15–28.

12. Ramón Blanco to José Toral, July 2, 1898, in Pascual Cervera y Topote, *The Spanish-American War: A Collection of Documents Relative to the Squadron Operations in the West Indies* (Washington, D.C., 1899), p. 120.

13. Federico Escario, "Diary of the Operations of Campaign of the Forces of the Manzanillo Division, June 22 to July 3, 1898," July 3, 1898, in José Müeller y Tejeiro, *Battles and Capitulations of Santiago de Cuba* (Washington, D.C., 1899), pp. 116–24. See also Aníbal Escalante Beatón, *Calixto García: Su campaña en el 95* (Havana, 1978), pp. 572–75.

14. Müeller y Tejeiro, *Battles and Capitulations*, p. 162; J. Rodríguez Martínez, *Los desastres y la regeneración: Relatos e impresiones* (La Coruña, 1899), p. 8.

15. G. J. A. O'Toole, *The Spanish War: An American Epic—1898* (New York, 1985), p. 342; Alfred Thayer Mahan, *Lessons of the War with Spain and Other Articles* (Boston, 1899), pp. 189–90.

16. Among the best accounts of the Cuban campaign in June and July 1898 in Oriente province are Enrique Collazo, *Los americanos en Cuba* (Havana, 1905); Cosme de la Torriente, *Calixto García cooperó con las fuerzas armadas de los EE. UU. en 1898, cumpliendo órdenes del gobierno cubano* (Havana, 1952); Escalante Beatón, *Calixto García*, pp. 465–672; Emilio Roig de Leuchsenring, *La guerra hispano-cubanoamericana fué ganada por el lugarteniente general del Ejército Libertador Calixto García Iñiguez* (Havana, 1955); and Herminio Portell Vilá, *Historia de la guerra de Cuba y los Estados Unidos contra España* (Havana, 1949).

17. George Kennan, *Campaigning in Cuba* (New York, 1899), pp. 79–80. The first two

quotations in this paragraph are from William T. Sampson, "The Atlantic Fleet in the Spanish War," *Century Magazine*, April 1899, p. 905, and Richard Goldhurst, *Pipe Clay and Drill: John J. Pershing: The Classic American Soldier* (New York, 1977), p. 72.

18. William R. Shafter, "Address of Major General William R. Shafter, U.S. Army, before the Chamber of Commerce, Los Angeles, California," in Society of Santiago de Cuba, *The Santiago Campaign: Reminiscences of the Operations for the Capture of Santiago de Cuba in the Spanish American War* (Richmond, Va., 1927), p. 248; Theodore Roosevelt, *The Rough Riders* (New York, 1920), p. 75.

19. William R. Shafter, "The Capture of Santiago de Cuba," *Century Magazine*, February 1899, p. 615, and "Address . . . before the Chamber of Commerce, Los Angeles," p. 250.

20. William Addleman Ganoe, *The History of the United States Army* (New York, 1924), p. 373; C. Joseph Bernardo and Eugene H. Bacon, *American Military Policy: Its Development since 1775* (Harrisburg, Pa., 1961), p. 279; Office of the Chief of Military History, U.S. Army, *American Military History* (Washington, D.C., 1969), pp. 324–25; W. E. Woodward, *A New American History* (New York, 1938), p. 689; Graham A. Cosmas, *An Army for Empire: The United States Army in the Spanish-American War* (Columbia, Mo., 1971), pp. 141, 165, 171, 212.

21. See Graham A. Cosmas, "Joint Operations in the Spanish-American War," in Bradford, *Crucible of Empire*, pp. 102–26.

22. Miley, *In Cuba with Shafter*, pp. 84, 87–88, 154.

23. Theodore Roosevelt to Henry Cabot Lodge, July 3 (2:317), 7 (1:322), in Henry Cabot Lodge, ed., *Selections from the Correspondence of Theodore Roosevelt and Henry Cabot Lodge*, 2 vols. (New York, 1925) (emphasis in original).

24. Russell A. Alger, *The Spanish-American War* (New York, 1901), p. 177; E. J. McClernand, "The Santiago Campaign," *Infantry Journal* 21 (September 1922): 298–99.

25. Arsenio Linares to [Spanish] Ministry of War, July 12, 1898, in Alger, *The Spanish-American War*, pp. 202–3.

26. Valeriano Weyler, *Mi mando en Cuba*, 5 vols. (Madrid, 1910–11), 5:597, 607.

27. Víctor M. Concas y Palau, *La escuadra del almirante Cervera*, 2d ed. (Madrid, n.d.), p. 127.

28. For U.S. accounts, see Thomas Winthrop Hall, *The Fun and Fighting of the Rough Riders* (New York, 1899); Theodore W. Miller, *Rough Rider: His Diary as a Soldier* (Akron, Ohio, 1899); Burr McIntosh, *The Little I Saw of Cuba* (New York, 1899); Charles Fuller, *What a New York Trooper Saw of the War* (New York, 1900); and Roosevelt, *The Rough Riders*. For Cuban accounts, see Mariano Corona Ferrer, *De la manigua (ecos de la epopeya)* (Santiago de Cuba, 1900); Rodolfo Bergés Tabares, *Cuba y Santo Domingo: Apuntes de la guerra de Cuba de mi diario de campaña, 1895–1898* (Havana, 1905); Manuel Arbelo, *Recuerdos de la última guerra por la independencia de Cuba, 1896–1898* (Havana, 1918); Luis Rodolfo Miranda, *Diario de campaña del comandante Luis Rodolfo Miranda*, ed. Manuel I. Mestre (Havana, 1954); and Luis Miranda y de la Rua, *Con Martí y con Calixto García (recuerdos de un mambí del 95)* (Havana, 1943).

29. Hall, *Fun and Fighting*, p. 114; Theodore Roosevelt, "The Fifth Corps at Santiago," in Fitzhugh Lee, ed., *Cuba's Against Spain* (New York, 1899), p. 645; William E. Horton, "The Battle of San Juan," in Society of Santiago de Cuba, *The Santiago Campaign*, pp. 413–14; George Kennan, *Campaigning in Cuba* (New York, 1899), p. 92.

30. *New York World*, July 27, 1898, p. 3.

31. John H. Parker, *History of the Gatling Gun Detachment, Fifth Army Corps, at Santiago* (Kansas City, Mo., 1898), p. 78.

32. *New York Tribune*, August 5, 1898, p. 3.

33. Roosevelt, *The Rough Riders*, p. 173; E. J. McClernand to Joseph Wheeler, July 4, 1898, in Joseph Wheeler, *The Santiago Campaign of 1898* (New York, 1898), p. 300.

34. *Washington Post*, July 6, 1898, p. 3.

35. Roosevelt, "The Fifth Army Corps at Santiago," p. 645.

36. Stephen Bonsal, *The Fight for Santiago* (New York, 1899), p. 377.

37. *New York Times*, July 28, 1898, p. 4; *Chicago Tribune*, July 13, 1898, p. 3.

38. Thomas R. Dawley Jr., "With Our Army at Tampa" (Manuscript, 1898, P. K. Yonge Collection, University of Florida Library, Gainesville), p. 146.

39. *New York World*, July 14, 1898, p. 3; Howard, "Conduct of the Cubans in the Late War," p. 155.

40. Shafter quoted in Gerald Linderman, *The Mirror of War: American Society and the Spanish-American War* (Ann Arbor, 1974), p. 142.

41. Calixto García to Pedro Pérez, August 12, 1898, in Juan J. E. Casasús, *Calixto García (el estratega)* (Havana, 1962), p. 284.

42. William R. Shafter to Adjutant General, July 23, 1898, in U.S. Congress, Senate, *Report of the Commission Appointed by the President to Investigate the Conduct of the War Department in the War with Spain*, 56th Cong., 1st sess., 8 vols. (Washington, D.C., 1900), 2:1042; Bonsal, *The Fight for Santiago*, pp. 441–42.

43. Calixto García to William R. Shafter, July 17, 1898, in Calixto García, *Palabras de tres guerras* (Havana, 1942), pp. 107–10.

44. Cuba, Ejército Libertador, *Parte oficial del lugarteniente general Calixto García al General en Jefe Máximo Gómez, 15 de julio de 1898 sobre la campaña de Santiago de Cuba* (Havana, 1953), pp. 22–23.

45. John Hay to Theodore Roosevelt, July 27, 1898, in William Roscoe Thayer, *The Life and Letters of John Hay*, 2 vols. (Boston, 1915), 2:337; Henry Cabot Lodge to John Hay, August 17, 1898, in John A. Garraty, *Henry Cabot Lodge: A Biography* (New York, 1968), p. 195; Shafter, "Address . . . before the Chamber of Commerce, Los Angeles," p. 257.

46. Louis M. Hacker and Benjamin B. K. Kendrick, *The United States since 1865*, 4th ed. (New York, 1949), p. 292; H. Addington Bruce, *The Romance of American Expansion* (New York, 1909), p. 199; Harold Underwood Faulkner, *American Political and Social History*, 7th ed. (New York, 1957), p. 647; Henry Bamford Parkes, *The United States of America: A History* (New York, 1963), p. 525; Foster Rhea Dulles, *The United States since 1865* (Ann Arbor, 1959), p. 166; James Truslow Adams, *The Epic of America* (New York, 1941), p. 338.

47. Richard J. Walton, *Beyond Diplomacy* (New York, 1970), p. 80; William A. Robinson, *Thomas B. Reed: Parliamentarian* (New York, 1930), p. 369; Charles Morris, *The War with Spain* (Philadelphia, 1899), pp. 310, 531; Harry T. Peck, *Twenty Years of the Republic, 1885–1905* (New York, 1905), pp. 617–18.

48. Walter Millis, *The Martial Spirit: A Study of Our War with Spain* (Boston, 1931), pp. 320, 361–62.

49. Richard H. Collin, *Theodore Roosevelt: Culture, Diplomacy, and Expansion* (Baton Rouge, 1985), p. 135; William Wood and Ralph Henry Gabriel, *In Defense of Liberty* (New Haven, 1928), p. 190.

50. Barbara Tuchman, *The Proud Tower* (New York, 1966), p. 156; James Truslow Adams, *The Epic of America*, p. 337.

51. Carl Russell Fish, *The Path of Empire* (New Haven, 1919), pp. 155, 166–67; Morris, *The War with Spain*, pp. 257, 266; Frederick Merk, *Manifest Destiny and Mission in American History* (New York, 1966), pp. 250–51; John R. Musick, *Cuba Libre: A Story of the Hispano-American War* (New York, 1900), p. vii; William Harding Carter, *The Life of Lieutenant General Chaffee* (Chicago, 1917), p. 156. The tendency to attribute valor as the decisive factor of U.S. success has been especially pronounced in the biographies of the U.S. officers who participated in the Santiago campaign. See, for example, the early biographies of Theodore Roosevelt, most notably William Draper Lewis, *The Life of Theodore Roosevelt* (New York, 1919), pp. 134–47; Godfrey R. Benson, *Theodore Roosevelt* (Boston, 1923), pp. 50–52; William Roscoe Thayer, *Theodore Roosevelt: An Intimate Biography* (Boston, 1919), pp. 109–30; and Joseph Bucklin Bishop, *Theodore Roosevelt and His Time*, 2 vols. (New York, 1920), 1:92–108. See also Carter, *The Life of Lieutenant General Chaffee*; Paul H. Carlson, *"Pecos Bill": A Military Biography of William R. Shafter* (College Station, Tex., 1989); and Heath Twichell, *Allen: The Biography of an Army Officer, 1859–1930* (New Brunswick, 1974).

52. Frank Freidel, *The Splendid Little War* (New York, 1958), p. 3; Allan Nevins and Henry Steele Commager, *America: The Story of a Free People* (Boston, 1943), p. 424.

53. Robert L. Beisner, *From the Old Diplomacy to the New, 1865–1900* (Arlington Heights, Ill., 1986), p. 130; Julius W. Pratt, "McKinley and Manifest Destiny," in Earl Schenck Miers, ed., *The American Story* (Great Neck, N.Y., 1956), p. 263; Pendleton Herring, *The Impact of War* (New York, 1941), pp. 41–42; T. Harry Williams, *Americans at War* (Baton Rouge, 1960), p. 95; Oscar Handlin, *The History of the United States*, 2 vols. (New York, 1968), 2:259; Walter T. K. Nugent, *Modern America* (Boston, 1973), p. 153; Woodward, *New American History*, p. 691; Charles M. Dollar, Joan R. Gunderson, Reid A. Holland, and John Hammond, *America: Changing Times: A Brief History*, 2d ed. (New York, 1984), p. 405.

54. William Miller, *A New History of the United States* (New York, 1958), p. 332; Winthrop Jordan and Leon Litwack, *The United States*, 7th ed. (Englewood Cliffs, N.J., 1991), pp. 552–54; John Morton Blum, Bruce Catton, Edmund S. Morgan, Arthur Schlesinger Jr., Kenneth M. Stamps, and C. Van Woodward, *The National Experience* (New York, 1963), p. 506; Dulles, *The United States since 1865*, p. 167; Roderick Nash, *From These Beginnings* (New York, 1973), p. 271; Edwin C. Rozwenc, *The Making of American Society*, 2 vols. (Boston, 1973), 2:125; Thomas A. Bailey, *Probing America's Past*, 2 vols. (Lexington, Mass., 1973), 2:487–88; John K. Mahon, "Santiago Campaign, Cuba (1898)," in Benjamin R. Beede, ed., *The War of 1898 and U.S. Interventions, 1898–1934* (New York, 1994), pp. 495, 497–98.

55. Freidel, *Splendid Little War*, pp. 81, 88; Hermann Hagedorn, *Leonard Wood: A Biography*, 2 vols. (New York, 1931), 1:160; Irving Werstein, *1898: The Spanish-American War* (New York, 1966), p. 70; Allan Keller, *The Spanish-American War: A Compact History* (New York, 1969), pp. 126–27; Robert Leckie, *The Wars of America*, rev. ed. (New York, 1981), p. 555; Maurice Matloff, *American Wars and Heroes* (New York, 1985), p. 215.

56. Donald Barr Chidsey, *The Spanish-American War* (New York, 1971), p. 123; George Brown Tindall, *America: A Narrative History*, 2d ed. (New York, 1988), p. 915.

57. Millis, *The Martial Spirit*, p. 266; James A. Henretta, W. Elliott Brownlee, David Brody,

and Susan Ware, *America's History*, 2d ed. (New York, 1993), p. 679; Richard Current, T. Harry Williams, and Frank Freidel, *American History: A Survey*, 3d ed. (New York, 1971), p. 524; Keith Ian Polakoff, Norman Rosenberg, Grania Bolton, Ronald Story, and Jordan Schwarz, *Generations of Americans: A History of the United States*, 2 vols. (New York, 1976), 2:496. In fact, the characterization of Spanish military operations, the historiographical persistence notwithstanding, is inconsistent with U.S. first-person accounts of the campaign. Contemporary reports of Spanish conduct often alluded to the resolve of Spanish soldiers. "The Spaniards contested every inch of ground bitterly and fought with unexpected coolness and courage," cabled the *Washington Post* after the battle of El Caney. General M. B. Stewart remembered the defense of El Caney by "the gallant Spanish force." Theodore Roosevelt reached the same conclusion. Spanish soldiers, he later wrote of San Juan Hill, "made a stiff fight," "fighting stubbornly," and showing themselves "to be brave foes, worthy of honor for their gallantry." At the time, he informed Henry Cabot Lodge: "The Spaniards fight very hard and charging these entrenchments against modern rifles is terrible." See *Washington Post*, July 4, 1898, p. 1; M. B. Stewart, "The Regulars," in Society of Santiago de Cuba, *The Santiago Campaign: Reminiscences of the Operations for the Capture of Santiago de Cuba in the Spanish American War* (Richmond, Va., 1927,), p. 50; Roosevelt, *The Rough Riders*, pp. 155–56; Roosevelt to Lodge, July 3, 1898, in Lodge, *Selections from the Correspondence of . . . Roosevelt and . . . Lodge*, 1:317. See also Joseph Edgar Chamberlain, "How the Spaniards Fought at Caney," *Scribner's Magazine*, September 1898, pp. 278–82.

58. Carlson, *"Pecos Bill,"* p. 185; Jerald A. Combs, *The History of American Foreign Policy* (New York, 1986), pp. 148–49; Jack Cameron Dierks, *A Leap to Arms: The Cuban Campaign of 1898* (Philadelphia, 1970), pp. 182–84.

59. John Scott Reed, "San Juan Hill, Cuba, Battle (1898)," in Beede, *The War of 1898*, p. 489; David Healy, *Drive to Hegemony: The United States in the Caribbean, 1898–1917* (Madison, 1988), p. 45; David F. Trask, *The War with Spain in 1898* (New York, 1981), p. 208; Thomas G. Paterson, J. Garry Clifford, and Kenneth J. Hagan, *American Foreign Relations: A History*, 2 vols., 4th ed., (Lexington, Mass., 1995), 1:227; Jules R. Benjamin, *The United States and the Origins of the Cuban Revolution* (Princeton, 1990), p. 53.

60. Alan Brinkley, Richard N. Current, T. Harry Williams, and Frank Freidel, *American History: A Survey*, 2 vols., 8th ed. (New York, 1991), write that the war ended quickly and successfully, "in part because the Cuban rebels had already greatly weakened the Spanish resistance. The American intervention, therefore, was in many respects a 'mopping up' exercise"; in fact, Spanish commanders "seemed to be paralyzed by a series of reversals at the hands of the insurgents" (2:601–2). See also John Tebbel, *America's Great Patriotic War with Spain* (Manchester Center, Vt., 1996).

CHAPTER FIVE

1. *New York Times Book Review*, October 29, 1961, p. 22.

2. *Mississippi Valley Historical Review* 49 (June 1962): 160–61.

3. *New York Herald Tribune Book Review*, February 11, 1962, p. 8.

4. Robert Endicott Osgood, *Ideals and Self-Interest in America's Foreign Relations* (Chicago, 1953), p. 43; H. H. Powers, "The War as Suggestion of Manifest Destiny," *Annals of the American Academy of Political and Social Science* 12 (September 1898): 175; Brooks Adams, *America's Economic Supremacy* (New York, 1900), p. 25; Howard Jones, *The*

Course of American Diplomacy, 2 vols., 2d ed. (Chicago, 1988), 2:255; Solomon Bulkey Griffin, *People and Politics* (Boston, 1923), p. 367.

5. William McKinley, *Speeches and Addresses of William McKinley from March 1, 1897 to May 30, 1900* (New York, 1900), p. 134.

6. Theodore Salisbury Woolsey, *America's Foreign Policy* (New York, 1898), p. vi; Charles S. Olcott, *The Life of William McKinley* (Boston, 1916), p. 380; Robert E. Riegel and David F. Long, *The American Story*, 2 vols. (New York, 1955), 2:128; Jack Cameron Dierks, *A Leap to Arms: The Cuban Campaign of 1898* (Philadelphia, 1970), p. ix; John M. Dobson, *America's Ascent: The United States Becomes a Great Power, 1880–1914* (De Kalb, Ill., 1978), p. 2.

7. William McKinley, "Instructions to the Peace Commissioners," September 16, 1898, in U.S. Department of State, *Papers Relating to the Foreign Relations of the United States, 1898* (Washington, D.C., 1901), p. 907, and *Speeches and Addresses*, pp. 186–87.

8. Ernest May, *Imperial Democracy: The Emergence of America as a Great Power* (New York, 1961), p. 159; Richard W. Leopold, *The Growth of American Foreign Policy* (New York, 1965), p. 170; Dobson, *America's Ascent*, p. 106; James A. Henretta, W. Elliott Brownlee, David Brody, and Susan Ware, *America's History*, 2d ed. (New York, 1993), p. 638; Margaret Leech, *In the Days of McKinley* (New York, 1959), p. 189; H. Wayne Morgan, *William McKinley and His America* (Syracuse, 1963), p. 374; Walter Karp, *The Politics of War: The Story of Two Wars Which Altered Forever the Political Life of the American Republic, 1890–1920* (New York, 1977), p. 4.

9. William James to Thomas Flournoy, June 17, 1898, in Ralph Barton Perry, *The Thought and Character of William James*, 2 vols. (Boston, 1935), 2:308; William E. Leuchtenburg, "The Needless War with Spain," *American Heritage*, February 1957, p. 95; G. J. A. O'Toole, *The Spanish War: An American Epic—1898* (New York, 1984), p. 17.

10. McKinley, *Speeches and Addresses*, p. 288; A. Lawrence Lowell, "The Colonial Expansion of the United States," *Atlantic Monthly*, February 1899, p. 147; Henry William Elson, *History of the United States of America* (New York, 1905), pp. 113–14; Samuel Flagg Bemis, *A Diplomatic History of the United States*, 4th ed. (New York, 1955), p. 475; Samuel Flagg Bemis, *A Short History of American Foreign Policy and Diplomacy*, rev. ed. (New York, 1964), p. 275; Henretta et al., *America's History*, p. 678; S. E. Forman, *Our Republic: A Brief History of the American People* (New York, 1929), p. 686.

11. Tony Smith, *America's Mission* (Princeton, 1994), p. 59; *New York Herald Tribune Book Review*, February 11, 1962, p. 8; O'Toole, *The Spanish War*, p. 18; John Richard Alden, *Rise of the American Republic* (New York, 1963), p. 578; Osgood, *Ideals and Self-Interest*, p. 42; Gilman M. Ostrander, *American Civilization in the First Machine Age, 1890–1940* (New York, 1970), pp. 111–12; H. W. Brands, *The Reckless Decade: America in the 1890s* (New York, 1995), p. 4.

12. Charles Conant, *The United States in the Orient* (Boston, 1900), p. 63.

13. James A. Field Jr., "American Imperialism: The 'Worst Chapter' in Almost Any Book," *American Historical Review* 83 (June 1978): 645.

14. George F. Kennan, *American Diplomacy, 1900–1950* (Chicago, 1951), p. 19; Daniel M. Smith, *The American Diplomatic Experience* (Boston, 1972), p. 210; Leopold, *Growth of American Foreign Policy*, p. 177; William H. Nelson and Frank E. Vandiver, *Fields of Glory* (New York, 1960), p. 156; Allan Keller, *The Spanish-American War: A Compact History* (New York, 1969), p. 85; Robert H. Ferrell, *American Diplomacy: A History*, rev. ed. (New York, 1969), p. 382; Riegel and Long, *The American Story*, 2:122, 125.

15. Foster Rhea Dulles, *Prelude to World Power, 1898–1954* (New York, 1954), p. 179; Harry J. Carman, Harold C. Syrett, and Bernard W. Wishy, *A History of the American People*, 2 vols., 3d ed. (New York, 1967), 2:295–96; Sidney Lens, *The Forging of the American Empire* (New York, 1971), p. 174; Robert H. Wiebe, *The Search for Order, 1877–1920* (New York, 1967), p. 241; Alex Waugh, *A Family of Islands* (Garden City, N.Y., 1964), p. 313; Thomas A. Bailey, *A Diplomatic History of the American People*, 7th ed. (New York, 1964), p. 468.

16. Joseph E. Wisan, *The Cuban Crisis as Reflected in the New York Press, 1895–1898* (New York, 1934), p. 460; O'Toole, *The Spanish War*, pp. 388, 390; Frank Thistlethwaite, *The Great Experiment* (Cambridge, Mass., 1955), p. 288; H. Wayne Morgan, *America's Road to Empire: The War with Spain and Overseas Expansion* (New York, 1965), p. 83; Thomas A. Bailey and David M. Kennedy, *The American Pageant*, 2 vols. (Lexington, Mass., 1987), 2:612; James Truslow Adams, *The Epic of America*, 2d ed. (New York, 1941), p. 337.

17. Woolsey, *America's Foreign Policy*, pp. 106–7.

18. For useful historiographical discussions of the treatment of imperialism, see Edward P. Crapol, "Coming to Terms with Empire: The Historiography of Late-Nineteenth-Century American Foreign Relations," *Diplomatic History* 16 (Fall 1992): 573–97; Joseph A. Fry, "Imperialism, American Style, 1890–1916," in Gordon Martel, ed., *American Foreign Relations Reconsidered, 1890–1993* (London, 1994), pp. 52–70; and Ernest R. May, "American Imperialism: A Reinterpretation," *Perspectives in American History* 1 (1967): 121–283.

19. Morgan, *America's Road to Empire*, pp. xii, 113; Richard H. Collin, *Theodore Roosevelt: Culture, Diplomacy, and Expansion* (Baton Rouge, 1985), pp. 107–8, 138; Leopold, *Growth of American Foreign Policy*, p. 180.

20. Dierks, *A Leap to Arms*, pp. 201–2.

21. Lloyd C. Gardner and William L. O'Neill, *Looking Backward: A Reintroduction to American History*, 2 vols. (New York, 1974), 2:264.

22. McKinley, *Speeches and Addresses*, pp. 188–89, 312, 318–19, 340.

23. Louis B. Wright et al., *The Democratic Experience: A Short American History* (New York, 1963), p. 316; Julius W. Pratt, *America's Colonial Experiment* (New York, 1950), pp. 2–3; Allan Nevins and Henry Steele Commager, *America: The Story of a Free People* (Boston, 1943), p. 425; Tony Smith, *The United States and the World Wide Struggle for Democracy in the Twentieth Century* (Princeton, 1994), p. 43; Dexter Perkins and Glyndon G. Van Deusen, *The American Democracy: Its Rise to Power* (New York, 1962), p. 405; Dexter Perkins and Glyndon G. Van Deusen, *United States of America: A History*, 2 vols. (New York, 1962), 2:261–63.

24. Talcott Williams, "Cuba and Armenia," *Century Magazine*, February 1898, p. 635; Joseph B. Foraker, "Our War with Spain: Its Justice and Necessity," *Forum* 25 (June 1898): 394.

25. *Congressional Record*, 1901, 34, app., pt. 4:357.

26. Roger Burlingame, *The American Conscience* (New York, 1957), p. 377.

27. O'Toole, *The Spanish War*, pp. 17–18; Osgood, *Ideals and Self-Interest*, pp. 29, 42.

28. Charles M. Thompson, *History of the United States*, rev. ed. (Chicago, 1922), p. 474; Collin, *Theodore Roosevelt*, p. 105; J. Rogers Hollingsworth, *The Whirligig of Politics* (Chicago, 1963), p. 156.

29. David F. Trask, *The War with Spain in 1898* (New York, 1981), p. ix; Morgan, *America's*

Road to Empire, p. ix; Benson Lossing, *History of the United States from the Aboriginal Times to the Present Day*, 8 vols. (New York, 1909), 7:1988; Irving Werstein, *1898: The Spanish-American War* (New York, 1960), p. 128; Robert D. Schulzinger, *American Diplomacy in the Twentieth Century*, 3d ed. (New York, 1994), p. 16.

30. William McKinley, "Message of the President," December 5, 1899, in U.S. Department of State, *Papers Relating to the Foreign Relations of the United States, 1899* (Washington, D.C., 1901), p. xxix.

31. Harry F. Guggenheim, *The United States and Cuba* (New York, 1934), p. 17; Sumner Welles, *Relations between the United States and Cuba* (Washington, D.C., 1934), p. 2; Harry S. Truman, "Address before a Joint Session of the Congress in Observance of the 50th Anniversary of Cuban Independence," April 19, 1948, in *Public Papers of the Presidents of the United States: Harry S. Truman, 1948* (Washington, D.C., 1964), p. 225; *Washington Post*, April 27, 1948, p. 12; Earl E. T. Smith, *The Fourth Floor* (New York, 1962), p. 23.

32. *New York Times*, July 19, 1898, p. 6.

33. *Congressional Record*, 1901, app.:357; Elihu Root to Leonard Wood, January 1, March 2, 1901, Correspondence between General Leonard Wood and Secretary of War, 1899–1902, Records of the Bureau of Insular Affairs, Record Group 350, National Archives, Washington, D.C.

34. *Congressional Record*, 1901, app.:358 (Scudder), and 34, pt. 4:3375 (Gibson); Orville H. Platt, "The Solution of the Cuban Problem," *The World's Work* 2 (May 1901): 731.

35. Roberto Fernández Retamar, "Cuba Defended: Countering Another Black Legend," *South Atlantic Quarterly* 96 (Winter 1997): 106.

36. Emilio Roig de Leuchsenring, *Cuba no debe su independencia a los Estados Unidos* (Havana, 1950), p. 153. For a general discussion of revisionist historiography, see Duvon C. Corbitt, "Cuban Revisionist Interpretations of Cuba's Struggle for Independence," *Hispanic American Historical Review* 32 (August 1963): 395–404.

37. *Revolución*, January 3, 1959, p. 4; Fidel Castro, *Pensamiento de Fidel Castro*, 2 vols. (Havana, 1983), 1:3.

38. César Leante, "El día inicial," in José Rodríguez Feo, ed., *Aquí once cubanos cuentan* (Montevideo, 1967), p. 90.

39. "24 de febrero," *Revolución*, February 23, 1959, p. 24.

40. Esteban Montejo, *The Autobiography of a Runaway Slave*, trans. Jocasta Innes (1966; New York, 1968), pp. 218–19. For interviews with other *mambises*, see Félix Contreras, "Con el centenario a cuestas," *Cuba*, October 1968, pp. 48–51.

41. Enrique Gay Calbó, "Síntesis republicana de Cuba," *Humanismo* 7 (January–April 1959), p. 108.

42. Teresa Casuso, *Cuba and Castro*, trans. Elmer Grossberg (New York, 1961), pp. 43, 49.

43. *Revolución*, January 5, 1959, p. 4.

44. *Revolución*, January 14 (p. 2), 17 (p. 14), February 20 (p. 2), 1959,

45. *Revolución*, February 25, 1959, p. 4.

46. *Revolución*, January 7, 1959, p. 5; Guillermo Cabrera Infante, "Somos actores en una historia increíble," *Revolución*, January 16, 1959, p. 15; Bernardo Díaz, "Justicia americana," *Revolución*, January 16, 1959, p. 4; "Contra el perdón," *Revolución*, January 15, 1959, p. 4; "Esta tarde la cita es en Palacio," *Revolución*, January 16, 1959, p. 1.

47. *New York Times Book Review*, October 29, 1961, p. 22; Ruby Hart Phillips, *Cuba: Island of Paradox* (New York, 1959), p. 7; *Public Papers of the Presidents of the United States: Dwight D. Eisenhower, 1959* (Washington, D.C., n.d.), p. 271.

48. Philip S. Foner titled his history *The Spanish-Cuban-American War and the Birth of American Imperialism*, 2 vols. (New York, 1972). Editor Benjamin R. Beede in his encyclopedia used "Spanish-Cuban/American War" and explained that this usage was meant to convey "the fact that the war in Cuba had been largely won by the Cuban revolutionaries before [the] U.S. intervention"; Beede, *The War of 1898 and U.S. Interventions, 1898–1934* (New York, 1994), p. xi. Thomas G. Paterson called the conflict the "Spanish-American-Cuban-Filipino War in order to represent all the major participants and to identify where the war was fought and whose interests were most at stake"; Paterson, "United States Intervention in Cuba, 1898: Interpretations of the Spanish-American-Cuban-Filipino War," *History Teacher* 29 (May 1996): 341. In recognition that the Cubans "already had the Spanish armies so hard pressed," Gilbert L. Lycan suggested that it "should not be called the 'Spanish-American War,' but the 'Cuban-Spanish-American War' "; Lycan, *Twelve Major Turning Points in American History* (Deland, Fla., 1968), p. 112. Samuel Flagg Bemis entitled his chapter on 1898 the "Cuban-Spanish-American War" and wrote in his prefatory comments: "On the fiftieth anniversary of Cuban independence occurred a symposium of Cuban historians met to commemorate the battle of Santiago, where American soldiers had assisted Cuban veterans to turn decisively the tide to victory over Spain in 1898. The war, declared the Cuban scholars, was a *Cuban*-Spanish-American War, not merely a Spanish-American War as historians in the United States and elsewhere had been calling it. The corrective is well pointed. It was in truth a Cuban-Spanish-American War, and henceforth so it should be called"; Bemis, *A Short History*, p. 275.
49. Sumner Welles, "Is America Imperialistic?" *Atlantic Monthly*, September 1924, p. 414.

BIBLIOGRAPHICAL ESSAY

The reader with an interest in 1898 has available a vast and an extraordinarily rich body of literature from which to choose, from articles to books, from sweeping surveys to narrowly focused monographic studies. This essay provides a general guide to various aspects of the literature considered useful for further reading and research. It does not intend to be comprehensive but suggestive, with a particular if selective focus on titles that deal with the United States and Cuba. An equally voluminous collection exists on perspectives derived from the experiences of Spain, the Philippine Islands, and Puerto Rico.

Perhaps the most complete bibliographical guide to the U.S. literature is found in Anne Cipriano Venzon, *The Spanish-American War: An Annotated Bibliography* (New York, 1990), a volume that contains nearly 1,200 annotated entries and a useful subject index. The single most comprehensive annotated guide to the Cuban historical literature is found in Araceli García Carranza, *Bibliografía de la guerra de independencia, 1895–1898* (Havana, 1976).

The most useful essays examining various historiographical facets of 1898 include Thomas G. Paterson, "United States Intervention in Cuba, 1898: Interpretations of the Spanish-American-Cuban-Filipino War," *History Teacher* 29 (May 1996): 341–61; Hugh DeSantis, "The Imperialist Impulse and American Innocence, 1865–1900," in Gerald K. Haines and J. Samuel Walker, eds., *American Foreign Relations: A Historiographical Review* (Westport, Conn., 1981), pp. 65–90; Edward P. Crapol, "Coming to Terms with Empire: The Historiography of Late-Nineteenth-Century American Foreign Relations," *Diplomatic History* 16 (Fall 1992): 573–97; Walter LaFeber, "That 'Splendid Little War' in Historical Perspective," *Texas Quarterly* 11 (1968): 89–98; Joseph A. Fry, "William McKinley and the Coming of the Spanish-American War: A Study of the Besmirching and Redemption of an Historical Image," *Diplomatic History* 3 (Winter 1979): 77–97; Ephraim K. Smith, "William McKinley's Enduring Legacy: The Historiographical Debate on the Taking of the Philippine Islands," in James C. Bradford, ed., *Crucible of Empire: The Spanish-American War and Its Aftermath* (Annapolis, 1993), pp. 205–49; Joseph A. Fry, "From Open Door to World Systems: Economic Interpretations of Late-Nineteenth-Century American Foreign Relations," *Pacific Historical Review* 65 (May 1996): 277–303; and Alexander DeConde, *American Diplomatic History in Transformation* (Washington, D.C., 1976). One of the better essays on the changing trends in Cuban historiography on 1898 is Duvon C. Corbitt, "Cuban Revisionist Interpretations of Cuba's Struggle for Independence," *Hispanic American Historical Review* 32 (August 1963): 395–404.

• • •

Among the most valuable sources for the study of the war are the official government documents, correspondence, and reports appearing at the time. Of particular use are the U.S. Department of State's *Papers Relating to the Foreign Relations of the United States*, especially between 1895 and 1898. The U.S. War Department published vast quantities of documentation in the years immediately following the war, the most important of which are U.S. War Department, Adjutant General's Office, *Correspondence Relating to the War with Spain* (Washington, D.C., 1898) and *Military Notes on Cuba* (Washington, D.C., 1898); and U.S. War Department, *Annual Report of the War Department, 1899* (Washington, D.C., 1899). Salient congressional documents include U.S. Congress, Senate, *Report of the Commission Appointed by the President to Investigate the Conduct of the War Department in the War with Spain*, 56th Cong., 1st sess., 8 vols. (Washington, D.C., 1900); U.S. Congress, *Report of the Committee on Foreign Relations: Affairs in Cuba*, 55th Cong., 2d sess. (Washington, D.C., 1898); and U.S. Congress, Senate, *Consular Correspondence Respecting the Condition of the Reconcentrados in Cuba, the State of the War in That Island, and the Prospects of the Projected Autonomy*, 55th Cong., 2d sess. (Washington, D.C., 1898). Other government sources of value are U.S. Navy Department, *Sampson-Schley: Official Communications* (Washington, D.C., 1899), and U.S. Treasury Department, *Report on the Commercial and Industrial Condition of Cuba* (Washington, D.C., 1899).

A significant number of documentary sources were also published in Cuba. Between 1903 and 1958 the annual *Boletín del Archivo Nacional de Cuba* provided some of the most important archival materials relating to the war for independence and the U.S. intervention. Among other sources, the most useful are Cuba, Secretaria de Gobernación, *Documentos históricos* (Havana 1912); Academia de la Historia de Cuba, *Crónicas de la guerra de Cuba* (Havana, 1957); Joaquín Llaverías y Martínez and Emeterio Santovenia, eds., *Actas de las Asambleas de Representantes y del Consejo de Gobierno durante la guerra de independencia*, 6 vols. (Havana, 1927–33); and León Primelles, ed., *La revolución del 95 según la correspondencia de la delegación cubana en Nueva York*, 5 vols. (Havana, 1932–37).

• • •

Some of the most meaningful sources for the study of 1898 are available in the form of first-person narratives. The published autobiographies, memoirs, diaries, and correspondence of prominent participants in the events of 1898, including politicians, military officers, diplomats, and journalists, constitute an extensive body of material of vital importance in the study of U.S. domestic politics and foreign policy during the final years of the nineteenth century. The first-person literature provides information and insight in ways often unobtainable from other sources. Of particular value are the general works of government officials who witnessed or participated in the formulation of policy in 1898. The most important of these are the accounts by Secretary of War Russell A. Alger, *The Spanish-American War* (New York, 1901), and Senator Henry Cabot Lodge, *The War with Spain* (Boston, 1899). Also useful is the diary of McKinley's secretary of the navy, John Davis Long, edited by L. S. Mayo, entitled *America of Yesterday as Reflected in the Journal of John David Long* (New York, 1923). Many prominent members of Congress, some of whom played important roles in the events of 1898, also provided vital information in memoirs and autobiographies. The most helpful include Shelby M. Cullom, *Fifty Years of Public Service* (Chicago, 1911); Joseph Benson Foraker, *Notes of a Busy Life*, 2 vols., 3d ed. (Cincinnati, 1917); George F. Hoar, *Autobiography of Seventy Years*, 2 vols. (New York, 1903); and Champ Clark, *My Quarter Century of American Politics*, 2 vols. (New York, 1920).

Other autobiographies provide insight into military and diplomatic aspects of the coming and conduct of the war. General James H. Wilson, who played a leading role in the development of U.S. policy in Cuba and served as governor of Matanzas province during the U.S. military occupation of the island, produced a highly informative memoir, *Under the Old Flag: Recollections of Military Operations in the War for the Union, the Spanish War, and the Boxer Rebellion*, 2 vols. (New York, 1912). Horatio Rubens, *Liberty: The Story of Cuba* (New York, 1932), a memoir written by the legal counsel of the Cuban junta in New York, offers insight into some of the most important facets of the coming of the war from the Cuban view. Theodore Roosevelt, *Autobiography* (1913; New York, 1946), is limited but informative. The autobiography of General Nelson A. Miles, the chief of the U.S. army during the war, *Serving the Republic* (New York, 1911), provides a detailed account of the campaign in Cuba and Puerto Rico. Also of value is the study by naval officer French E. Chadwick, *The Relations of the United States and Spain: The Spanish-American War*, 2 vols. (New York, 1911). The diary of Whitelaw Reid, *Making Peace with Spain: The Diary of Whitelaw Reid, September–December 1898*, ed. H. Wayne Morgan (Austin, 1965), is a valuable source for the study of treaty negotiations with Spain from the U.S. perspective. Other useful memoirs include Oliver O. Howard, *Fighting for Humanity* (New York, 1898); Frederick Funston, *Memories of Two Wars* (New York, 1914); and (Mrs.) Garrett Hobart, *Memories* (Mt. Vernon, N.Y., 1930).

The Cuban campaign, both as army operations and as naval actions, has produced a vast literature. The first-person accounts of army and naval personnel, reporters, and participants of all kinds constitute a splendid corpus of sources. In the United States the popularity of the war all but guaranteed an eager reading public for these chronicles. Among the most useful accounts written by U.S. officers and soldiers are Theodore Roosevelt, *The Rough Riders* (New York, 1920); John D. Miley, *In Cuba with Shafter* (New York, 1899); Arthur L. Wagner, *Report of the Santiago Campaign, 1898* (Kansas City, Mo., 1908); E. J. McClernand, "The Santiago Campaign," *Infantry Journal* 21 (September 1922): 280–303; Joseph Wheeler, *The Santiago Campaign of 1898* (New York, 1898); James A. Moss, *Memories of the Campaign of Santiago* (San Francisco, 1899); Burr MacIntosh, *The Little I Saw in Cuba* (New York, 1899); Thomas Winthrop Hall, *The Fun and Fighting of the Rough Riders* (New York, 1899); Theodore W. Miller, *Rough Rider: His Diary as a Soldier* (Akron, Ohio, 1899); Charles Fuller, *What a New York Trooper Saw of the War* (New York, 1900); John H. Parker, *History of the Gatling Gun Detachment, Fifth Army Corps, at Santiago* (Kansas City, Mo., 1898); Charles F. Gauvreau, *Reminiscences of the Spanish-American War in Cuba and the Philippines* (New York, 1915); and Charles J. Post, *The Little War of Private Post* (Boston, 1960). The Society of Santiago de Cuba, *The Santiago Campaign: Reminiscences of the Operations for the Capture of Santiago de Cuba in the Spanish-American War* (Richmond, Va., 1927), contains more than thirty separate first-person accounts of various aspects of U.S. military operations, including the artillery, infantry, Rough Riders, chaplaincy corps, and quartermaster's department.

Among the first-person accounts of naval operations in Santiago de Cuba are Charles E. Clark, *My Fifty Years in the Navy* (Boston, 1917); William A. M. Goode, *With Sampson through the War* (New York, 1899); Edward Stratemeyer, *Fighting in Cuban Waters; or, Under Schley on the Brooklyn* (Boston, 1899); Joseph C. Gannon, *The*

U.S.S. Oregon and the Battle of Santiago (New York, 1958); and Robley D. Evans, *An Admiral's Log* (New York, 1910).

The journalists who accompanied the U.S. army to Cuba also provide valuable insight into the Santiago campaign. These include George Kennan, *Campaigning in Cuba* (New York, 1899); Stephen Bonsal, *The Fight for Santiago* (New York, 1899); John Bigelow, *Reminiscences of the Santiago Campaign* (New York, 1899); Richard Harding Davis, *The Cuban and Porto Rican Campaigns* (New York, 1898); Irving Hancock, *What One Man Saw, Being the Personal Impressions of a War Correspondent in Cuba* (New York, 1898); and Thomas J. Vivian, *The Fall of Santiago* (New York, 1898). Also informative are the dispatches prepared by Stephen Crane, subsequently compiled and entitled *The War Despatches of Stephen Crane*, ed. R. W. Stallman and E. R. Hageman (New York, 1964). The memoir by British journalist John B. Atkins, *The War in Cuba: The Experience of an Englishman with the United States Army* (London, 1899), gives different perspectives on U.S. military operations. Charles H. Brown, *The Correspondents' War: Journalists in the Spanish-American War* (New York, 1967), is a highly informative account of the role and importance of journalists during the war.

No less valuable are the first-person reports of Cuban officers and soldiers. Some of the most informative accounts of the conduct of the war for independence, before and after the U.S. intervention, can be found in the memoirs and reminiscences of Cuban *insurrectos*. Among the best representatives of this literature are Máximo Gómez, *Diario de campaña del mayor general Máximo Gómez* (Havana, 1940); Manuel Arbelo, *Recuerdos de la última guerra por la independencia de Cuba, 1896–1898* (Havana, 1918); Luis Miranda y de la Rúa, *Con Martí y con Calixto García (recuerdos de un mambí del 95)* (Havana, 1943); Luis Rodolfo Miranda, *Diario de campaña del comandante Luis Rodolfo Miranda*, ed. Manuel I. Mestre (Havana, 1954); Mariano Corona Ferrer, *De la manigua (ecos de la epopeya)* (Santiago de Cuba, 1900); Rodolfo Bergés Tabares, *Cuba y Santo Domingo: Apuntes de la guerra de Cuba de mi diario de campaña, 1895–1898* (Havana, 1905); Manuel Piedra Martel, *Memorias de un mambí* (Havana, 1966); Bernabé Boza, *Mi diario de guerra, desde Baire hasta la intervención americana*, 2 vols. (Havana, 1900–1904); and Walfredo Ibrahim Consuegra, *Diario de campaña: Guerra de independencia, 1895–1898* (Havana, 1928).

• • •

The first histories of the war were published almost immediately after the armistice. Contemporary historical texts tend to be impressionistic, often journalistic in style, and are generally of limited value, except that they are themselves a product of the time and thereby serve as a useful insight into perceptions and perspectives of 1898. The most complete include Henry F. Keenan, *The Conflict with Spain* (Philadelphia, 1898); Henry B. Russell, *An Illustrated History of Our War with Spain: Its Causes, Incidents, and Results* (Hartford, 1898); Henry Houghton Beck, *Cuba's Fight for Freedom and the War with Spain* (Philadelphia, 1898); Trumbull White, *United States in War with Spain and the History of Cuba* (Chicago, 1898); Marrion Wilcox, *A Short History of the War with Spain* (New York, 1898); James Rankin Young, *History of Our War with Spain* (n.p., 1898); Henry Watterson, *History of the Spanish-American War, Embracing a Complete Review of Our Relations with Spain* (Boston, 1898); Oscar Phelps Austin, *Uncle Sam's Soldiers: A Story of the War with Spain* (New York, 1899); Nathan C. Green, *The War with Spain and Story of Spain and Cuba* (Baltimore, 1898); Elbridge S. Brooks, *The Story of Our War with Spain* (Boston, 1899); William A. Johnston, *History up to Date: A Concise*

Account of the War of 1898 between the United States and Spain, Its Causes and the Treaty of Paris (New York, 1899); Charles Morris, *The War with Spain: A Complete History of the War of 1898 between the United States and Spain* (Philadelphia, 1899); Richard H. Titherington, *A History of the Spanish-American War of 1898* (New York, 1900); and John R. Musick, *Cuba Libre: A Story of the Hispano-American War* (New York, 1900).

Murat Halstead, *Full Official History of the War with Spain* (Philadelphia, 1899), provides one of the earliest compilations of official U.S. communications and correspondence during the war. Along similar lines, Henry F. Keenan, *The Conflict with Spain: A History of the War with Spain Based upon Official Reports and Descriptions of Eyewitnesses* (Philadelphia, 1898), includes useful accounts of the campaign in Cuba and the Philippines.

A number of richly illustrated contemporary publications provide extraordinary photographic records of the war in both the Caribbean and the Pacific. Among the most complete are *Harper's Pictorial History of the War with Spain* (New York, 1899), and Trumbull White, *Pictorial History of Our War with Spain for Cuba's Freedom* (Chicago, 1898).

In the decades that followed, general accounts of the war with Spain appeared with almost predictable regularity. The works tend to be uneven in quality and often limited in scope, but in the aggregate they constitute the corpus of historical literature that frames the larger historiographical issues of 1898 in the United States. The earlier published works include Horace Edgar Flack, *Spanish-American Diplomatic Relations Preceding the War of 1898* (Baltimore, 1906); Walter Millis, *The Martial Spirit: A Study of Our War with Spain* (Boston, 1931); Julius W. Pratt, *The Expansionists of 1898* (Baltimore, 1936); and Irving Werstein, *1898: The Spanish-American War* (New York, 1966). Frank Freidel, *The Splendid Little War* (Boston, 1958), is a highly accessible account of the war. Allan Keller, *The Spanish-American War: A Compact History* (New York, 1969), provides a general overview of the international dimensions of the war.

Among representative titles of general histories of the war published during the last thirty years are H. Wayne Morgan, *America's Road to Empire: The War with Spain and Overseas Expansion* (New York, 1965); Jack Cameron Dierks, *A Leap to Arms: The Cuban Campaign of 1898* (Philadelphia, 1970); Donald Barr Chidsey, *The Spanish-American War* (New York, 1971); Philip S. Foner, *The Spanish-Cuban-American War and the Birth of American Imperialism*, 2 vols. (New York, 1972); David F. Trask, *The War with Spain in 1898* (New York, 1981); Lewis L. Gould, *The Spanish-American War and President McKinley* (Lawrence, Kans., 1982); and G. J. A. O'Toole, *The Spanish War: An American Epic—1898* (New York, 1984). The nine essays published in James C. Bradford, ed., *Crucible of Empire: The Spanish-American War and Its Aftermath* (Annapolis, 1993), deal variously with diplomacy, naval and military operations, and historiography. John Tebbel, *America's Great Patriotic War with Spain* (Manchester Center, Vt., 1996), gives a lively history of the war, with particular attention to the role of racism in the shaping of U.S. policy. A well-researched account of the conflict is found in John L. Offner, *An Unwanted War: The Diplomacy of the United States and Spain over Cuba, 1895–1898* (Chapel Hill, 1992). Gerald F. Linderman, *The Mirror of War: American Society and the Spanish-American War* (Ann Arbor, 1974), provides a highly informative account of the domestic facets of the war. A vast and exceedingly useful encyclopedic compendium was edited under the careful supervision of Benjamin R. Beede, *The War of 1898 and U.S. Interventions, 1898–1934* (New York, 1994).

Treatment of the war with Spain and its aftermath also forms a central part of the literature that deals generally with the rise of the United States as a world power during the final decades of the nineteenth century and the early years of the twentieth. Some of the most complete accounts of these years include Foster Rhea Dulles, *Prelude to World Power: American Diplomacy History, 1860–1900* (New York, 1965); Walter LaFeber, *The New Empire: An Interpretation of American Expansion, 1860–1898* (Ithaca, 1963); Charles S. Campbell, *The Transformation of American Foreign Relations, 1865–1900* (New York, 1976); John M. Dobson, *America's Ascent: The United States Becomes a Great Power, 1880–1914* (DeKalb, Ill., 1978); Walter Karp, *The Politics of War: The Story of Two Wars Which Altered Forever the Political Life of the American Republic, 1890–1920* (New York, 1979); Richard H. Collin, *Theodore Roosevelt: Culture, Diplomacy, and Expansion* (Baton Rouge, 1985); and Robert L. Beisner, *From the Old Diplomacy to the New, 1865–1900* (Arlington Heights, Ill., 1986).

A number of published articles merit consultation, including Alex Campbell, "The Spanish-American War," *History Today* 8 (April 1958): 239–47; Philip S. Foner, "Why the United States Went to War with Spain in 1898," *Science and Society* 32 (1968): 39–65; Nancy L. O'Connor, "The Spanish-American War: A Re-Evaluation of Its Causes," *Science and Society* 22 (1958): 129–43; and William E. Leuchtenburg, "The Needless War with Spain," *American Heritage* 8 (February 1957): 32–41, 95. Also useful is the essay by James A. Field Jr., "American Imperialism: The 'Worst Chapter' in Almost Any Book," *American Historical Review* 83 (June 1978): 644–68, published in the format of the "AHR Forum," which includes thoughtful responses from Walter LaFeber and Robert L. Beisner.

Cuban scholars have accorded the war of independence between 1895 and 1898 a place of singular prominence in the national historiography. The literature encompasses the separatist processes, often represented as a thirty-year struggle beginning in 1868 with the Ten Years War and culminating in 1898 with the U.S. intervention. The latter approach is best represented in Emilio Roig de Leuchsenring, *La guerra libertadora cubana de los treinta años, 1868–1898* (Havana 1952). Among the more useful works dealing with the period 1895–98 are Evelio Rodríguez Lendián, *La revolución de 1895* (Havana, 1926); Miguel Varona Guerrero, *La guerra de independencia de Cuba, 1895–1898*, 3 vols. (Havana, 1946); and Ramón de Armas, *La revolución pospuesta* (Havana, 1975). The U.S. intervention has been a particular theme in Cuban historiography, usually with 1898 serving as the point of departure and concluding with the end of the military occupation in 1902. The outstanding works include Herminio Portell Vilá, *Historia de la guerra de Cuba y los Estados Unidos contra España* (Havana, 1949), and the magisterial *Historia de Cuba en sus relaciones con los Estados Unidos y España*, 4 vols. (Havana, 1938–41). Emilio Roig de Leuchsenring, *Cuba no debe su independencia a los Estados Unidos* (Havana, 1950), advanced one of the earliest and most compelling cases for revisionist historiography.

Other useful general works dealing with 1898 in Cuba are Enrique Collazo, *Los americanos en Cuba* (Havana, 1905); José Navas, *Cuba y los Estados Unidos* (Havana, 1915); José Antonio Medel, *La guerra hispano-americana y sus resultados* (Havana, 1929); and Felipe Martínez Arango, *Cronología crítica de la guerra hispano-cubano-americana* (Santiago de Cuba, 1960). Also of value are Herman Reichard Esteves, "The United States, Spain, and the *Maine*, or the Diplomacy of Frustration," *Revista / Review Inter-*

americana 2 (1973): 549–58, and Rear Admiral George W. Melville, "The Destruction of the Battleship 'Maine,'" *North American Review* 193 (June 1911): 831–49.

• • •

Much of the U.S. historical literature has focused on specific facets of the coming of the war and the campaign in Cuba. The role of the press and public opinion has long constituted a subject of special interest. One of the better, if now slightly dated, analyses of the relationship between the coming of the war and the press is found in Joseph E. Wisan, *The Cuban Crisis as Reflected in the New York Press, 1895–1898* (New York, 1934). The relationship between public opinion and foreign policy is dealt with expertly in Marcus M. Wilkerson, *Public Opinion and the Spanish-American War* (Baton Rouge, 1932). Other useful treatments of the role of public opinion in 1898 are found in Thomas A. Bailey, *The Man in the Street: The Impact of American Public Opinion on Foreign Policy* (New York, 1948); Gabriel A. Almond, *The American People and Foreign Policy*, 2d ed. (New York, 1960); John E. Mueller, *War, Presidents, and Public Opinion* (New York, 1973); and Robert C. Hildebrand, *Power and the People: Executive Management of Public Opinion in Foreign Affairs, 1897–1921* (Chapel Hill, 1981).

The destruction of the *Maine* has been a staple of the 1898 literature. Charles D. Sigsbee, who was captain of the ship when it sank in Havana harbor, provided a valuable first-person account in *The "Maine": An Account of Her Destruction in Havana Harbor* (New York, 1899). A reexamination of the original court of inquiry, with far different conclusions, was provided by Admiral Hyman G. Rickover, *How the Battleship "Maine" Was Destroyed* (Washington, D.C., 1976). Other accounts of interest include Gregory Mason, *Remember the "Maine"* (New York, 1939); John Edward Weems, *The Fate of the "Maine"* (New York, 1958); and Peggy Samuels and Harold Samuels, *Remembering the "Maine"* (Washington, D.C., 1995). A useful Cuban account is found in Tiburcio P. Castañeda, *La explosión del Maine y la guerra de los Estados Unidos con España* (Havana, 1925).

Specialized studies have made important contributions to an understanding of vital aspects of the war. Graham A. Cosmas, *An Army for Empire: The United States Army and the Spanish-American War* (Columbia, Mo., 1971), provides the best single account of the U.S. army in the conflict. Perspectives on the naval campaign can be obtained in George Edward Graham, *Schley and Santiago* (Chicago, 1902). Also useful is Richard D. Challener, *Admirals, Generals, and American Foreign Policy, 1898–1914* (Princeton, 1973). Among the better works dealing with the African-American experience and the war include Willard B. Gatewood Jr., *"Smoked Yankees" and the Struggle for Empire: Letters from Negro Soldiers, 1898–1902* (Urbana, Ill., 1971), and *Black Americans and the White Man's Burden, 1898–1903* (Urbana, Ill., 1975).

Interest in U.S. military operations in Cuba—the Santiago campaign—has produced a useful body of literature. One of the most detailed accounts is found in Herbert H. Sargent, *The Campaign of Santiago de Cuba*, 3 vols. (Chicago, 1907). Other works include Anastasio C. M. Azoy, *Charge! Story of the Battle of San Juan Hill* (New York, 1961), and W. C. Dodson, *The Santiago Campaign of Major General Joseph Wheeler* (Atlanta, Ga., 1899).

The Cuban literature on the final months of the war in Oriente province is similarly helpful and should be used in conjunction with U.S. accounts. Perhaps the most detailed study is found in Aníbal Escalante Beatón, *Calixto García: Su campaña*

en el 95 (Havana, 1978). Other important Cuban studies include Cosme de la Torriente, *Calixto García cooperó con las fuerzas armadas de los EE. UU. en 1898, cumpliendo
órdenes del gobierno cubano* (Havana, 1952), and Emilio Roig de Leuchsenring, *La guerra
hispano-cubanoamericana fué ganada por el lugarteniente general del Ejército Libertador Calixto
García Íñiguez* (Havana, 1955).

• • •

That 1898 intersected at a vital juncture of U.S. history all but guaranteed that the
war would figure prominently in almost all genres of the historical literature. This
period is particularly well treated in biographies of some of the most prominent
political and military leaders of the time, many of whom were involved, in some
form, with the coming of the war, the conduct of the war, or postwar policies.
Among the more useful biographies of Grover Cleveland are Roland Hugins, *Grover
Cleveland: A Study in Political Courage* (New York, 1922); Allan Nevins, *Grover Cleveland: A Study in Courage* (New York, 1932); Rexford G. Tugwell, *Grover Cleveland*
(New York, 1968); and Richard E. Welch Jr., *The Presidencies of Grover Cleveland*
(Lawrence, Kans., 1988).

For the more informative biographies of William McKinley, see Charles H.
Grosvenor, *William McKinley: His Life and Work* (Washington, D.C., 1901); Charles S.
Olcott, *The Life of William McKinley* (Boston, 1916); Margaret Leech, *In the Days of
McKinley* (New York, 1959); H. Wayne Morgan, *William McKinley and His America*
(Syracuse, 1963); and Lewis L. Gould, *The Presidency of William McKinley* (Lawrence,
Kans., 1980).

Useful biographies of Cleveland's secretary of state, Richard Olney, include
Henry James, *Richard Olney and His Public Service* (Boston, 1923), and Gerald C.
Eggert, *Richard Olney: Evolution of a Statesman* (University Park, Pa., 1974). A usable
biography of McKinley's secretary of state, John Sherman, is found in Theodore E.
Burton, *John Sherman* (Boston, 1906).

Biographies of Theodore Roosevelt have assumed the proportions of a cottage
industry. They include William Draper Lewis, *The Life of Theodore Roosevelt* (New
York, 1919); William Roscoe Thayer, *Theodore Roosevelt: An Intimate Biography* (Boston, 1919); Joseph Bucklin Bishop, *Theodore Roosevelt and His Time*, 2 vols. (New York,
1920); Godfrey R. Benson, *Theodore Roosevelt* (Boston, 1923); Walter F. McCaleb,
Theodore Roosevelt (New York, 1931); Henry F. Pringle, *Theodore Roosevelt: A Biography*
(New York, 1931); John Morton Blum, *The Republican Roosevelt* (Cambridge, Mass.,
1954); David Henry Burton, *Theodore Roosevelt* (New York, 1972); and Nathan Miller,
Theodore Roosevelt: A Life (New York, 1992).

This was also an era of powerful senators, many of whom participated in the
multiple facets of the formulation of foreign policy. The historical literature is
replete with biographies of many senators who figured prominently in the political
transactions of 1895–98. Among the most useful are Leon Burr Richardson, *William E. Chandler: Republican* (New York, 1940); Frederick H. Gillett, *George Frisbie
Hoar* (Boston, 1934); Richard E. Welch Jr., *George F. Hoar and the Half-Breed Republicans* (Cambridge, Mass., 1971); Dorothy Ganfield Fowler, *John Coit Spooner: Defender
of Presidents* (New York, 1961); Elmer Ellis, *Henry Moore Teller: Defender of the West*
(Caldwell, Idaho, 1941); Louis A. Coolidge, *An Old-Fashioned Senator: Orville H. Platt
of Connecticut* (New York, 1910); Oscar Doane Lambert, *Stephen Benton Elkins* (Pitts-

burgh, 1955); Everett Walters, *Joseph Benson Foraker: An Uncompromising Republican* (Columbus, Ohio, 1948); Karl Schriftgiesser, *The Gentleman from Massachusetts: Henry Cabot Lodge* (Boston, 1944); John A. Garraty, *Henry Cabot Lodge: A Biography* (New York, 1953); Nathaniel Wright Stephenson, *Nelson W. Aldrich: A Leader in American Politics* (New York, 1930); Claude G. Bowers, *Beveridge and the Progressive Era* (Cambridge, Mass., 1932); and Herbert Croly, *Marcus Alonzo Hanna: His Life and Work* (New York, 1912). Biographies of House members during these years include William A. Robinson, *Thomas B. Reed: Parliamentarian* (New York, 1930); James McGurrin, *Bourke Cochran* (New York, 1948); and Sam Hanna Acheson, *Joe Bailey: The Last Democrat* (New York, 1932).

The biographies of military officers are also an important source of information. For the most relevant to 1898, see William Harding Carter, *The Life of Lieutenant General Chaffee* (Chicago, 1917); John P. Dyer, *"Fightin' Joe" Wheeler* (Baton Rouge, 1941); Edward G. Longacre, *From Union Stars to Top Hat: A Biography of General James Harrison Wilson* (New York, 1972); Virginia W. Johnson, *The Unregimented General: A Biography of Nelson A. Miles* (Boston, 1962); Paul H. Carlson, *"Pecos Bill": A Military Biography of William R. Shafter* (College Station, Tex., 1989); A. J. Bacevich, *Diplomat in Khaki: Major General Frank Ross McCoy and American Foreign Policy, 1898–1949* (Lawrence, Kans., 1989); Heath Twichell, *Allen: The Biography of an Army Officer, 1859–1930* (New Brunswick, N.J., 1974); and Hermann Hagedorn, *Leonard Wood: A Biography*, 2 vols. (New York, 1931).

• • •

Finally, of the various genres of U.S. historical scholarship, the subject of 1898 looms largest in the literature on U.S. foreign relations. From general college textbooks to specialized monographic studies, 1898 figures prominently in all discussions of late-nineteenth-century foreign policy and diplomacy. The literature is indeed voluminous, varied, and very uneven. Representative texts include Randolph Greenfield Adams, *A History of the Foreign Policy of the United States* (New York, 1933); John Holladay Latané and David W. Wainhouse, *A History of American Foreign Policy*, 2d ed. (New York, 1940); Richard W. Van Alstyne, *American Diplomacy in Action* (Stanford, 1947); Richard W. Leopold, *The Growth of American Foreign Policy* (New York, 1962); Dexter Perkins, *The Evolution of American Foreign Policy*, 2d ed. (New York, 1966); Julius W. Pratt, *A History of United States Foreign Policy*, 3d ed. (Englewood Cliffs, N.J., 1972); Wayne S. Cole, *An Interpretative History of American Foreign Relations*, rev. ed. (Homewood, Ill., 1974); Armin Rappaport, *A History of American Diplomacy* (New York, 1975); Robert H. Ferrell, *American Diplomacy: A History* (New York, 1975); Jerald A. Combs, *The History of American Foreign Policy* (New York, 1986); Howard Jones, *The Course of American Diplomacy*, 2 vols., 2d ed. (Chicago, 1988); Thomas G. Paterson, J. Garry Clifford, and Kenneth J. Hagan, *American Foreign Relations: A History*, 2 vols., 4th ed. (Lexington, Mass., 1995); Samuel Flagg Bemis, *A Diplomatic History of the United States* (New York, var. ed.); Alexander DeConde, *A History of American Foreign Policy*, 2 vols. (New York, var. ed.); and Thomas A. Bailey, *A Diplomatic History of the American People* (New York, var. ed.).

Some of the more specialized works that merit consultation include Foster Rhea Dulles, *America's Rise to World Power, 1898–1954* (New York, 1954), and *Prelude to World Power: American Diplomatic History, 1869–1900* (New York, 1965); Ernest R. May, *Impe-*

rial Democracy: The Emergence of America as a Great Power (New York, 1961); John A. S.
Grenville and George Berkeley, *Politics, Strategy, and American Diplomacy: Studies in
Foreign Policy, 1873–1917* (New Haven, 1966); David Healy, *U.S. Expansionism: The
Imperialist Urge in the 1890s* (Madison, 1970); and Walter LaFeber, *The American Age*,
2 vols., 2d ed. (New York, 1994).

INDEX

Griggs, John, 82
Guam, 3, 131
Guggenheim, Harry, 123

Hawkins, Hamilton, 92
Hay, John, 98
Hearst, William Randolph, 71, 73
Howard, O. O., 97

Imperialism, 3; in U.S. historiography, 39, 43, 59, 78, 116–19, 120
Irving, Washington, 6

Jefferson, Thomas, 5, 6, 46
Joint Resolution (1898), 30, 31, 34, 49; Cuban response to, 21; and Elihu Root, 33, 49; and Platt Amendment, 34; in U.S. historiography, 38

Lee, Fitzhugh, 10; on Cuban insurrection, 12
Linares, Arsenio, 104, 105; and defense of Santiago de Cuba, 93–95
Lodge, Henry Cabot: view of Cuban independence, 12; and defense of U.S. interests, 50; on public opinion, 69; on destruction of *Maine*, 78; on cause of war, 98
Ludlow, William, 29

Maceo, Antonio, 20, 26
McKinley, William, 8, 32, 46; opposition to Cuban independence, 12, 14, 30, 37; and de Lôme letter, 16; and armistice (1898), 17, 56; and U.S. intervention, 18, 54; message of Congress, 19, 48; and Joint Resolution, 21, 30; and Teller Amendment, 29, 48; decision for war, 41; and public opinion, 41, 74, 75–76, 77–78; in U.S. historiography, 43–44, 74–77, 112; and *Maine*, 58, 61, 75–76; relations with Congress, 76–77, 79–80; explanation of war, 111; role as wartime president, 112–14; and Philippines, 113, 118–19

Mahan, Alfred Thayer, 48; on cause of war, 50; and Santiago campaign, 88
Maine (battleship), 10, 16, 112; suspected Cuban role of, 54–55; explosion of, 58; and William McKinley, 58, 61, 75–76; explanation as cause of war, 58–64, 114–15; in U.S. historiography, 62–64, 68–69, 112, 114–15; and public opinion, 64–69, 70, 76
Marcy, William L., 4
Martí, José, 20
Masó, Bartolomé, 10; opposition to armistice, 18
Méndez Capote, Domingo, 12
Miles, Nelson A., 60
Monroe, James, 5
Moret, Segismundo, 16
Music, as expression of sympathy for Cuban independence, 24–26

Olney, Richard, 8; opposition to Cuban independence, 13; on Teller Amendment, 28; and public opinion, 73
Ostend Manifesto, 5

Philippine Islands, 3, 43, 49, 120, 131; insurrection in, 8; and battle of Manila, 21; and William McKinley, 113, 118–19
Pierce, Franklin, 5
Pi y Margall, Francisco, 10
Platt, Orville: on Teller Amendment, 28, 30–31; and Platt Amendment, 33; and Cuban constituent assembly, 124
Platt Amendment, 126, 129, 132; and U.S. policy, 33, 35; Cuban opposition to, 33–34; acceptance of, 34; Leonard Wood on, 35; and Cuban independence, 35–36, 37–38; in U.S. historiography, 38, 44; and Elihu Root, 124
Press: "yellow journalism," 16; William Randolph Hearst, 71, 73; role in pre-

cipitating war, 72–73; in U.S. historiography, 72–74
Public opinion: sympathy for Cuban
independence, 39–40; as cause of
war, 39–40, 48, 70–74; in U.S. historiography, 40–41, 44, 69–72, 73;
influence on William McKinley, 41,
74, 75–76, 77–78; and explosion of
Maine, 64–69, 77–78
Puerto Rico, 3, 21–22, 43, 49, 131

Quesada, Gonzalo de, 20

Reid, Whitlaw, 19; opposition to Teller
Amendment, 28
Roosevelt, Theodore, 48, 50, 99; on
Cuban independence, 36; and explo-
sion of *Maine*, 60, 78; participation in
Santiago campaign, 92; on Cuban
army, 95, 96
Root, Elihu, 32, 83; and Platt Amend-
ment, 33, 34, 124; on Joint Resolu-
tion (1898), 33, 49; and defense of
U.S. strategic interests, 48–49
Rubens, Horatio, 17; and U.S. interven-
tion, 20

Sampson, William T., 82–83
Sanguily, Manuel, 34
Santiago campaign, 52; and William
Shafter, 85; Cuban participation in,
86–89, 93–96, 99–101; and U.S.
operations, 91–102; in U.S. historiography, 99–107

Scudder, Townsend, 32, 120; and Platt
Amendment, 34
Shafter, William R., 82, 92; opposition
to Cuban independence, 29; relations with Cuban army, 83–84, 98;
and Santiago campaign, 86, 89–90,
104
Sherman, John, 9; on Cuban independence, 11
Smith, Earl E. T., 123

Teller Amendment, 21, 24, 32, 48, 118;
and public opinion, 28; opposition
to, 28–29; interpretation of, 30–31;
in U.S. historiography, 37; as source
of intervention, 42; and Elihu Root,
49
Toombs, Robert, 4
Truman, Harry, 123

Webster, Daniel, 5
Welles, Sumner, 132
Wheeler, Joseph, 92
Wilson, James H., 28–29
Wood, Leonard: and U.S. occupation of
Cuba, 32; and Platt Amendment, 34,
35
Woodford, Stewart, 15–16; opposition
to Cuban independence, 14; pro-
posed purchase of Cuba, 16; and
armistice (1898), 16, 17

Young, Samuel B. M., 92